Rethinking Difference in Gender, Sexuality, and Popular Music

D1743130

In studies of gender and sexuality in popular music, the concept of difference is often a crucial analytic used to detect social agency; however, the alternative analytic of ambiguity has never been systematically examined. While difference from heterosexual norms is taken to be the multivalent sign of resistance, oppression, and self-invention, it can lead to inflated claims of the degree and power of difference. This book offers critically oriented case studies that examine the theory and politics of ambiguity. Ambiguity means that there are *both* positive and negative implications in any gender and sexuality practices, *both* sameness and difference from heteronormativity, and unfixed *possibility* in the diverse nature of discourse and practice (rather than just "difference" among fixed multiplicities). Contributors present a diverse array of approaches through music, sound, psyche, body, dance, performance, race, ethnicity, power, discourse, and history. A wide variety of popular music genres are broached, including gay circuit remixes, punk rock, goth music, cross-dress performance, billboard 100 songs, global pop, and nineteenth-century minstrelsy. The authors examine the ambiguities of performance and reception, and address the vexed question of whether it is possible for genuinely new forms of gender and sexuality to emerge musically. This book makes a distinctive contribution to studies of gender and sexuality in popular music, and will be of interest to fields including Popular Music Studies, Musicology/Ethnomusicology, Cultural Studies, Queer Studies, and Media Studies.

Gavin Lee is Assistant Professor at Soochow University School of Music in China. He completed his doctoral studies at Duke University on avant-garde music in Singapore, and his core research interests include postcolonial theory, affect theory, queer theory, global modernity and modernism, and the Sinophone world. Lee's research is published in *Journal of the Royal Musical Association*, *Music Analysis* (forthcoming), and in a book funded by the Singapore National Arts Council, *Scions of the Musical West*.

Routledge Studies in Popular Music

For a full list of titles in this series, please visit www.routledge.com.

Rethinking Difference in Gender, Sexuality, and Popular Music

Theory and Politics of Ambiguity

Edited by
Gavin Lee

Routledge
Taylor & Francis Group

LONDON AND NEW YORK

First published 2018
by Routledge

2 Park Square, Milton Park, Abingdon, Oxfordshire OX14 4RN
52 Vanderbilt Avenue, New York, NY 10017

Routledge is an imprint of the Taylor & Francis Group, an informa business

First issued in paperback 2020

British Library Cataloguing-in-Publication Data
A catalogue record for this book is available from the British Library

Library of Congress Cataloging-in-Publication Data
Names: Lee, Gavin
Title: Rethinking difference in gender, sexuality, and popular music: theory and politics of ambiguity / edited by Gavin Lee.
Description: Abingdon, Oxon; New York, NY: Routledge, 2018. | Series: Routledge studies in popular music | Includes bibliographical references and index.
Identifiers: LCCN 2017048588
Subjects: LCSH: Gender identity in music. | Homosexuality in music. | Popular music—Social aspects.
Classification: LCC ML3918.P67 R49 2018 | DDC 781.6408—dc23
LC record available at https://lccn.loc.gov/2017048588

ISBN: 978-1-138-96005-3 (hbk)
ISBN: 978-0-367-59314-8 (pbk)

Typeset in Times New Roman
by codeMantra

Contents

List of figures

List of contributors

Paul Attinello is a Senior Lecturer at Newcastle University who has taught at the University of Hong Kong and UCLA. He received his PhD from UCLA and is training as a psychoanalyst at the Jung-Institut Zürich; he is published in journals and collections including *Queering the Pitch: The New Lesbian & Gay Musicology*. He has written on contemporary musics, music about AIDS, philosophical, and psychological topics.

Matthew Bannister is a musician and academic. He presently teaches at Waikato Institute of Technology (Hamilton, Aotearoa/New Zealand). His main research interests are gender, memory, creativity, and popular music, but he also enjoys playing the ukulele. He has published two books, *White Boys, White Noise: Masculinities and 1980s Indie Guitar Rock* and *Positively George Street: A Personal History of Sneaky Feelings and the Dunedin Sound* as well as original music with groups such as Sneaky Feelings, the Dribbling Darts of Love, The Weather, and the Changing Same.

Ellie M. Hisama is Professor of Music at Columbia University. Her recent publications address music by Julius Eastman and Ruth Crawford, and freestyle in hip-hop. She has served as Editor of the peer-reviewed journals *Women and Music: A Journal of Gender and Culture* and *Journal of the Society for American Music*.

Gavin Lee is Assistant Professor at Soochow University School of Music in China. He completed his doctoral studies at Duke University on avant-garde music in Singapore, and his core research interests include postcolonial theory, affect theory, queer theory, global modernity and modernism, and the Sinophone world. Lee's research is published in *Journal of the Royal Musical Association*, *Music Analysis* (forthcoming), and in a book funded by the Singapore National Arts Council, *Scions of the Musical West*.

Jared Mackley-Crump is a Lecturer in event studies in the School of Hospitality and Tourism and the Auckland University of Technology. His areas of research and teaching include contemporary issues in event management, event studies, Pacific festivals, music festivals, and queer events.

Helen L. Reddington played bass in the 1970s in a Brighton punk band. After seven years as musician, she became a lecturer at the University of Westminster and published *The Lost Women of Rock Music: Female Musicians of the Punk Era*. She now lectures at the University of East London.

Mario Rey is Associate Professor of Ethnomusicology at the East Carolina University School of Music, where he teaches world music, ethnomusicology, theory, and directs the Afro-Andean ensemble. His published works cover a variety of topics including bimusicality, gender and immigrant identities, and the traditional musics of Latin America.

Gillian M. Rodger is Associate Professor of Musicology and Ethnomusicology in the Music Department at University of Wisconsin-Milwaukee. Her ongoing research interests cluster around popular musical theater of nineteenth-century America, working-class popular culture, and questions of gender and sexuality. She has also published on the British synth-pop group Eurythmics and the Scottish singer Annie Lennox.

Carol Siegel writes on the representation of sexuality in literature, film, television, and music. Her books include *Sex Radical Cinema, Goth's Dark Empire, New Millennial Sexstyles*, and *Male Masochism,* and the collections *Forming and Reforming Identity* and *Eroticism and Containment*. She co-edits with Ellen E. Berry the online journal *Rhizomes.*

Qian Wang earned his PhD from IPM, the University of Liverpool. He is currently a lecturer at the School of Literature and Journalism, Yibin University. His research is mainly focused on Chinese popular music. He is the author of *Rock Crisis: Research on Chinese Rock Music in the 1990s.*

Kirsten Zemke is a Senior Lecturer in ethnomusicology in the department of Anthropology at the University of Auckland. Her areas of research and teaching include hip-hop, New Zealand hip-hop, gender and popular music, rock history, and Pacific Popular Music.

1 Introduction

From difference to ambiguity

Gavin Lee

I was in San Francisco when, on 26 June 2015, the United States Supreme Court released its decision in *Obergefell v. Hodges*. This decision overturned the Sixth Circuit appeals court ruling which upheld the constitutionality of state bans on same-sex marriage. Thus, *Obergefell* enabled same-sex marriage in all 50 states, forcing the last 14 states which still resisted same-sex marriage to capitulate. Of course, the Supreme Court had already decided exactly two years earlier on the same date in *United States v. Windsor* (2013) that the Defense of Marriage Act, which defines on a federal level that marriage is limited to opposite-sex couples, was unconstitutional. Browsing the web for fun activities that summer of 2015, which I spent in San Francisco, I came across an event at a bar, Oasis, which ran this description for its party, "Gay Pride [28 June] we celebrated the Freedom TO Marry. But freedom cuts both ways. So this Independence Day [4 July], join us the Morning After for the Freedom NOT to Marry."[1] This, in tandem with the rise of the discourse of the religious "freedom" to refuse to hold same-sex weddings in churches or to bake wedding cakes for said occasions,[2] might be taken as evidence that "freedom" has gone post-structural. Now that same-sex couples are free to marry, they need to be freed from being compelled to marry, and furthermore, religious persons whose beliefs are impinged upon by the Supreme Court decisions need to be freed from having to comply with these decisions.

In our contemporary moment, the discursive slippage discerned by post-structuralists has entered into mainstream American social life and media, displaying a proliferation of narratives. The Oasis event was humorously portrayed as a celebration of the freedom to fuck, paralleling the more sober academic injunction to continue to take the polymorphousness of queerness seriously, even as same-sex marriage—modeled after that august heterosexual institution—has now come to fruition.[3] To quote the classic formulation by David Halperin of queerness as something that cannot be pinned down: "Queer is... *whatever* is at odds with the normal, the legitimate, the dominant. *There is nothing in particular to which it necessarily refers*. It is an identity without an essence."[4] Halperin's pronouncement captures for us one definition of the concept of "difference," which as indicated by the recently published *Rethinking Difference in Music Scholarship*, continues to be a source of contention.[5] The crux of the matter lies perhaps in that quixotic formulation, an "identity without an essence." If essence refers to permanent characteristics of an identity that remain unchanged, an "identity without an essence" would be pure difference—pure difference from the normative and hegemonic. But how do we reconcile pure difference with group "identity," which surely has to have some degree of stability—a *core* definition that stays the *same*—in order for members of that group to identify as such? Stable identity may take the form of negative stereotypes or give rise to the impression of group homogeneity without internal variation, but doesn't the instability of pure difference create chaos—a chaos which is the nemesis of the actualization of new conventions like same-sex marriage? The anxious dialectic of identity and difference has been the focal point of debates in queer musicology. It is also this dialectic to which *Rethinking Difference in Music Scholarship* responds, under the multiple rubrics of race, postcolonialism, gender, and sexuality.

This volume is committed to a rethinking of difference using the parameters of gender and sexuality. Conceptually, there is divergence between "difference" in terms of race and postcolonialism versus gender and sexuality. Difference is especially fraught in studies in gender and sexuality because of the unresolved ethical problems of articulating versus destabilizing identities. In contrast, the notion of "strategically" essentialist identity (purported identity differences between "whites" and "people of color") for the purposes of political organization has gained traction as a necessary, albeit dangerous, fiction in critical race studies, even though such an identity may also occlude diversity of gender, sexuality, race, and class within that identity group.[6] We can observe the problematics of identity in gender and sexuality studies in the following. From one controversial perspective, male-to-female transgenderism has been viewed as the colonization of women by men.[7] This argument reinforces the binary gender identity system, failing to destabilize it through queer theorizing. The same problem is found in strands of transsexual theory that emphasize the experiences of preoperative transgenders who feel that they are in the "wrong" body, thereby supporting the notion of "right," unambiguously polarized, binary genders.[8] From these studies of gender arises a notion of difference in the sense of reified binary identities that perpetuate harmful stereotypes, *yet the subjective transgender or transsexual quest for stable gender identity demands ethical consideration.*

Other strands of queer theory have engaged the concept of identity by working against the stability of the social order itself. Lee Edelman has argued that queerness is the site where the heterosexual social order crumbles.[9] For Edelman, heterosexuality is anchored in the figure of the child, which provides the raison d'être for maintaining the heteronormative status quo—in order to preserve a future for the child. It is reproductive futurity—a defining attitude of the culture of heterosexual reproducers, if not exactly a conventional "identity"—which is disrupted by queerness. Tavia Nyong'o has modified Edelman's theory, criticizing him for retaining an identity-bias in that social crumbling is identified with queerness. Instead, she argues, the catalyst for social order and disorder can be located flexibly and dialectically; in her case study, queer subculture is utilized by punk to counter heteronormativity while at the same time becoming stereotypically portrayed.[10] From these studies in queer theory arises a notion of *difference from heteronormativity* in the form of fluid social relations and forces that *destabilize* identities and stereotypes.

What emerges from this overview of the terrain of gender and sexuality studies is a tension around the stability and destabilization of gender and sexual identities. Some contributors to the foundational volumes *Musicology and Difference* and *Queering the Pitch*, published in the early to mid-90s, arguably employ some form of identity essentialism.[11] In later edited volumes, the post-structural bent of queer theory can be felt in chapters which emphasize nonnormative, destabilized gender, in *Sexing the Groove, Queering the Popular Pitch*, and *Oh Boy! Masculinities and Popular Music*.[12] Some approaches in the same vein focus in particular on vocality and hermeneutic reading. For Freya Jarman-Ivens, voices are queer when they are critically flawed, e.g. Maria Callas had audible breaks that accentuate the difference between gendered vocal registers associated with the "masculine" chest and "feminine" head.[13] Judith Peraino's *Listening to the Sirens* embarks on hermeneutical assays, e.g. the heroic Odysseus is cast as a queen tied to a mast in order that he may enjoy the song of the sirens.[14] Yet a dialectical turn away from the "destabilization" strategy can be discerned in essays within *Queering the Popular Pitch* that advocate for a stabilization of gender and sexual identity, in accordance with the musical-cultural participants' subjective sense of self and group belonging.[15] In a similar vein, Jodie Taylor's monograph *Playing It Queer* focuses on substantive queer subculture and world-making rather than radical queer deconstruction. She examines how a "queer," gender fluid, and women-friendly clubbing scene in Brisbane differentiates itself from a male-centric "gay" clubbing culture, through eclectic musical selections that counter what is perceived to be the commercialized house music of beauty-obsessed gay men.[16] In Taylor's study, there is the subtle confluence of gender fluidity which defines a stable queer subject position.

The crux of the tension around identity as (un)stable may be expressed as a politics of difference. Of particular salience here is the manner in which difference seems to alternately oppress and emancipate. Identity allows for both the cultivation of subcultural group support as well as the formation of stereotypical, binary gender and sexual identities. Destabilized identities allow for the avoidance of stereotype and yet are viewed with dismay by those who are unable to discern in them the potential for galvanized political action, which in equal rights struggle is critically dependent on the articulation of a recognizable identity. This ambiguous conceptual terrain is in a way not unexpected, given the post-structuralist bent of queer theory. In fact, queer theory, including the work by Edelman and Nyong'o, has long since moved pointedly away from the dialectics of difference and identity alone, towards consideration of social formations with alignments *between* different oppressed social groups. Edelman, for instance, theorizes that the common ground between the Republican objection to abortion and to homosexuality is the threat that both are considered to pose to reproduction.[17] The contributors to this volume aim to *rethink* difference using the analytic of *ambiguity*. Ambiguity is not the invention of this volume, and difference and identity will necessarily be part of our discourse. What we can offer here is focused attention on the ambiguity of three aspects related to musical performance and gender/sexuality politics—action, reception, and ontology—explicating each of them through multiple lenses. Ambiguity means that political *action* through gender performance has effects that cannot be comprehended through the calculus of identity/difference alone—rather, the additional consideration of intention and pleasure helps us to grasp the full effects of political action. Ambiguity also refers to the *reception* and dissemination of gender performance across different constituencies, different historical periods, and in re-creations (covers, biopics). Finally, ambiguity refers to the uncertain *ontology* and nature of proliferating categories, material possibilities, and desires.

Action. In the performative theory of gender, the everyday becomes a spectrum of repetitive, performative acts that veer between confirming and destabilizing essentialized gender identities.[18] However, there is still utility in separating "onstage" performance and recorded playback from "offstage" reception or re-creation. Although the agency of performers and audiences can be mutually impacting, the diffraction of musical performance through time, social groups, and re-creations means that multiple social and historical scenes will inevitably emerge. The three chapters in this section feature *stage performers* who are of key theoretical concern in dealing with issues of transgenderism and power, even as audiences are also taken into account to various degrees.

Ambiguity of gender, as read through Judith Butler's articulation, is expressed in the failure of performative gender practices to match up to feminine and masculine ideals. There are many ways to critique Butler's work, including her own clarification that gender is not something that can be chosen in the same way that drag queens adopt a (hyper)feminine identity on stage. Jay Prosser has described Butler's work as transgender "troping"—using the figure of the transgender, a person whose gender identity is at odds with their anatomy, to advance what he calls "queer feminism."[19] This brand of feminism, Prosser argues, privileges gender over sex. In queer feminism, even sex is really gender: essentially, psychoanalysis is the means by which biological anatomy is enculturated as *gender*.[20] The result of the privileging of gender is that a whole new register of transgender troping becomes available. Since masculinity and femininity are no longer tied exclusively to anatomy, anyone can combine binary genders as they wish. Queer feminism, Prosser asserts, is thus at odds with the experience of transgenders who wish to obtain a stable, authentic coherence between gender identity and anatomy. Critiquing Prosser, Judith Halberstam argues that a range of transgenders exist, ranging from those with none to partial to full sex reassignment surgery, and this spectrum challenges the binary genders and associated biases expressed in the discourse of gender authenticity.[21] The ambiguity of transgender performance is examined in Mario Rey's chapter on Thomas Neuwirth's stage persona of Conchita Wurst. Winner of the song competition Eurovision 2014, Conchita presents the marked *juxtaposition* of feminine and masculine visual signifiers that indicate a deviation from the exaggerated femininity of drag performance.

The second and third chapters examine the dynamics between dominant culture and subcultures. Carol Siegel explicates the politics of eroticized S/M power play in the lyrics and music videos of songs by goth bands. While S/M dynamics can seem to reproduce pain-inflicting women as a figment of male imagination, women can be invested with agency if they too are read as pleasure-experiencing agents. Helen L. Reddington appraises the female punk bands of the 70s to discern whether a feminist politics was successfully articulated through the eclectic combination of aggressive male punk band music, reggae style (in spite of its sexist lyrics), and nonnormative gender and sexuality. These chapters can be read against theories of power relations between social groups. José Esteban Muñoz's concept of "disidentification" addresses the means by which subcultural groups engage dominant culture through involuntary alignment as well as subversive disalignment.[22] As explicated by Stuart Hall, "articulation" is a term that addresses the relation between dominant culture and subcultures in terms of both difference between them and the contingent "unities" that sometimes occur when the two spheres present the same cultural phenomena.[23] All three chapters in this section work to destabilize reified identities and assumed power relations (the masculine appropriation of femininity by the drag queen, the S/M female who merely enacts male fantasy, the sexist reggae musician) by examining how political action creates contextual specificities.

Reception. Reception studies in popular music is a powerful means for examining how the ambiguity of gender and sexuality proliferates once we leave the performer's stage (or video) and follow the dissemination of the performance through its audience. The study of reception provides us with an additional angle with which to parse popular music, which historical nature is increasingly accentuated with each passing decade of the twenty-first century. This kind of historical work is critical because it provides an opportunity for us to examine how audiences appropriate performances, above and beyond the performers' own actions and politics, such that reception might be better termed as *performance* in its own right. Qian Wang's chapter examines how Li Yugang, the Peking opera performer who also sings popular songs, moves across mediatized social spaces. Li, who has inspired drag queens, maintains a gender and sexual ambiguity that allows him to cross between straight and queer, and governmental and commercial spaces. Gillian M. Rodger explores how cross-dressing on the variety stage in the nineteenth-century took on a different valence from our contemporary moment, which privileges transgender troping. While male impersonators were able to find a degree of acceptance in variety circles, their performances served to consolidate male working-class identity by making fun of "middle-class" traits rather than challenge the binary gender system. Matthew Bannister examines re-creation in the male rock star biopic, which reverses the masculine ideology of rock music by placing the female viewer in the empowered position of gazing at the eroticized male star.

Ontology. By ontological ambiguity, I refer to the fundamental ambiguity of identity labels, desire, and materiality that is explored in the three chapters in this section. While they draw on different philosophical threads, the authors articulate an ambiguity within musical performance, action, and reception that creates the potential for redirection away from reified structures of power. We can think of identity as fluidly changing, giving rise to a proliferation of identity labels. We can think of desire as roaming over different objects, giving rise to new kinds of social relationships. We can also think of the materiality of sound, image, and movement as the basis of a politics of gender and sexual ambiguity.

Jared Mackley-Crump and Kirsten Zemke's chapter examines the proliferation of nonnormative categories of gender and sexuality used by gay male rappers in New York City and New Jersey. Identity is not constructed by legal or medical experts as part of a heteronormative process of self-validation (as with the "homosexual" in late nineteenth-century), but, rather, is articulated by subjects in agential acts.[24] Gavin Lee's chapter examines how the obsession of gay men with Britney Spears offers an opportunity to theorize how homonormative desire (gay desire for men) can be queered into a desire centered on Britney Spears aesthetics of mesmerizing surfaces and airy voice. Desire is not locked onto a fixed sexual object such that identity and social relationships are predetermined, but is free to roam over aesthetics, sound, and image.[25]

The final chapter in this section by Ellie Hisama examines how women of color actors insert a register of ambiguity into white patriarchal or other male narratives that are destabilized in Isaac Julien's huge multi-screen art installations, the three-screen *True North* and the 18-screen *Ten Thousand Waves*, in which sound and folk song or music are weaved indeterminately with visuals, as the spectator walks into the space of the installation. The dissonance of placing women in stereotypically male spaces, and people of color in stereotypically white spaces, creates a productive ambiguity that aligns with the inherent multiplicity of experiences enabled by the multiple screens in interaction with sound and music.

Of critical importance in many of the studies in this volume is the intersectional analysis of gender, sexuality, race, and transnationalism. Studies by Bannister, Reddington, Rey, Wang, and Zemke & Mackley-Crump recognize the ways in which race and transnationalism on the one hand, and gender and sexuality on the other, are critically entangled. These studies acknowledge the multiple ways in which racial and transnational issues are inextricably bound with embodied gender and sexual life practices; the confluence of multiple social pressures results in alignments and disalignments, giving rise to opportunities for both positive and negative political action (alliance formation between oppressed groups, marginalization on multiple fronts).[26] The variety of global contexts and musical genres covered in this volume presents a concerted effort to expand the purview of popular music studies beyond Anglo-American contexts and beyond mainstream pop rock genres: Chinese pop, the Eurovision song contest, nineteenth-century minstrelsy, goth bands, female punk bands, gay male rappers, and Inuit song.

Through case studies, each chapter reflects on the ethical conundrums posed by the concept of difference and puts forward ambiguity as an analytic. At stake is the reconceptualization of the politics of gender and sexuality, of which our understanding has evolved to a point of sophistication beyond what "difference" can encompass—the limitations of difference are evidenced in the contradictory implications drawn from the term. Ambiguity means that there are *both* positive and negative implications in any gender and sexuality practices, *both* sameness and difference from heteronormativity, and unfixed *possibility* in the diverse nature of discourse and practice (rather than just "difference" among fixed multiplicities). Ambiguity cuts across political action and reception, and into the very heart of musical performance, identity, desire, and labor. Ambiguity crystalizes and gives a name to an insight already present in much scholarship that provides finessed conceptualization of contradictions and multiplicities, in ways that shed light on issues of gender and sexuality in popular music and beyond.

Notes

1 "Morning After: Celebrating the Freedom NOT to Marry." http://sanfrancisco. gaycities.com/events/538579-morning-after-celebrating-the-freedom-not-to-marry (retrieved on 17 August 2015).
2 On 26 March 2015, the widely decried "Religious Freedom Restoration Act" became the law in Indiana. Critics maintain that this law was passed to allow for discrimination against LGBTQ persons. https://iga.in.gov/legislative/2015/bills/senate/568 (retrieved on 17 August 2015).
3 Judith Butler discusses how same-sex marriage can occlude non-heterosexual forms of kinship and sexual practice. Judith Butler, "Is Kinship Always Already Heterosexual?" *Differences* 13 (2002), 17.
4 David M. Halperin, *Saint Foucault: Towards a Gay Hagiography* (Oxford: Oxford University Press, 1995), 62 (emphasis original).
5 Olivia Bloechl, Melanie Lowe, and Jeffrey Kallberg eds., *Rethinking Difference in Music Scholarship* (Cambridge: Cambridge University Press, 2015).
6 Gayatri Chakravorty Spivak, *Outside in the Teaching Machine* (New York: Routledge, 1993), 3.

7 Sheila Jeffreys is critical of the "entryism" of male-to-female transgender persons into the category "woman." Sheila Jeffreys, *Gender Hurts: A Feminist Analysis of the Politics of Transgenderism* (New York: Routledge, 2014), 3. Feminists such as Jeffreys are referred to in online media as TERF, or trans-exclusionary radical feminist. www.huffingtonpost.com/kelsie-brynn-jones/transexclusionary-radical-terf_b_5632332.html.

8 Judith Halberstam critiques female-to-male transsexuals who reinforce binary genders through their avowal of masculine identity. Judith Halberstam, *Female Masculinity* (Durham, NC: Duke University Press, 1998), 154.

9 Lee Edelman calls this figure of queerness "sinthomosexuality," a combination of "homosexuality" and "sinthome," the archaic spelling of the Lacanian psychoanalytic symptom, which is the key to disrupting the heteronormative psyche. Lee Edelman, *No Future: Queer Theory and the Death Drive* (Durham, NC: Duke University Press, 2004), 33.

10 Tavia Nyong'o examines how symbols of queer subculture such as fashion were employed in punk to create distance from normative social embodiment. Tavia Nyong'o, "Do You Want Queer Theory (or Do You Want the Truth)? Intersections of Punk and Queer in the 1970s," *Radical History Review* 100 (2008), 114.

11 Ruth A. Solie ed., *Musicology and Difference: Gender and Sexuality in Music Scholarship* (Berkeley: University of California Press, 1993); see chapters by Susan McClary and Lawrence Kramer, and also, Mary Ann Smart book review in *Journal of the American Musicological Society* 47 (1994), 547. Philip Brett, Elizabeth Wood, and Gary C. Thomas eds., *Queering the Pitch: The New Gay and Lesbian Musicology* (New York: Routledge, 1994); see the chapter by Jennifer Rycenga, and also, Ruth A. Solie's book review in *Journal of the American Musicological Society* 48 (1995), 313.

12 Sheila Whiteley ed., *Sexing the Groove: Popular Music and Gender* (New York: Routledge, 1997); Sheila Whiteley and Jennifer Rycenga eds., *Queering the Popular Pitch* (New York: Routledge, 2006); Freya Jarman-Ivens ed., *Oh Boy! Masculinities and Popular Music* (New York: Routledge, 2007).

13 Freya Jarman-Ivens, *Queer Voices: Technologies, Vocalities, and the Musical Flaw* (New York: Palgrave Macmillan, 2011), 23.

14 Judith A. Peraino, *Listening to the Sirens: Musical Technologies of Queer Identity from Homer to Hedwig* (Berkeley: University of California Press, 2006), 18.

15 See chapters by Stephen Amico, Stan Hawkins, Mario Rey, and Vanessa Knights in Whiteley and Rycenga eds., *Queering the Popular Pitch*, and also, Dana Baitz's book review in *Women & Music* 13 (2009), 110.

16 Jodie Taylor, *Playing It Queer: Popular Music, Identity and Queer World-Making* (New York: Peter Lang, 2012), 184.

17 Edelman, *No Future*, 15.

18 Judith Butler, *Bodies That Matter: On the Discursive Limits of "Sex"* (New York: Routledge, 1993), 233.

19 Jay Prosser, *Second Skins: The Body Narratives of Transsexuality* (New York: Columbia University Press, 1998), 21.

20 Butler's argument is that the heterosexual psychic prohibition or "loss" of same-sex choice of partners is compensated by one's own literal sex. Judith Butler, *Gender Trouble: Feminism and the Subversion of Identity* (New York: Routledge, 1999), 96.

21 Halberstam, *Female Masculinity*, 163.

22 José Esteban Muñoz, *Disidentifications: Queers of Color and the Performance of Politics* (Minneapolis: University of Minnesota Press, 1999), 11–12.

23 Articulation is "the form of the connection that can make a unity of two different elements, under certain conditions. It is a linkage which is not necessary, determined, absolute and essential for all time." Stuart Hall, "On Postmodernism and

Articulation: An Interview with Stuart Hall," in David Morley and Kuan-Hsing Chen eds., *Stuart Hall: Critical Dialogues* (Routledge, London, 1996), 141.
24 Susan Gustafson argues that the agency of the subject in Foucault's work shifted from volumes one to three of the *History of Sexuality*, and then to the "Technologies of the Self" seminar. Whereas in *The Will to Knowledge* (volume 1), the homosexual subject was constructed by legal and medical authorities, in "Technologies of the Self," a new kind of self gestured towards self-expression and agency. Susan E. Gustafson, *Men Desiring Men: The Poetry of Same-Sex Identity and Desire in German Classicism* (Detroit, MI: Wayne State University Press, 2002), 31.
25 On the queering of fixated forms of desire, see Tim Dean, *Beyond Sexuality* (Chicago, IL: University of Chicago Press, 2000), 216.
26 See chapters 5–7 in Donald E. Hall and Annamarie Jagose, with Andrea Bebell and Susan Potter eds., *The Routledge Queer Studies Reader* (New York: Routledge, 2013); Cathy J. Cohen, "Punks, Bulldaggers, and Welfare Queens: The Radical Potential of Queer Politics," 74–95; E. Patrick Johnson, "'Quare' Studies, Or '(Almost) Everything About Queer Studies I Learnt From My Grandmother," 96–118; Roderick A. Ferguson, "Introduction: Queer of Color Critique, Historical Materialism, and Canonical Sociology," 119–133.

Bibliography

Amico, Stephen. "*Su Casa Es Mi Casa*: Latin House, Sexuality, Place." In *Queering the Popular Pitch*, edited by Sheila Whiteley and Jennifer Rycenga, 131–154. New York: Routledge, 2006.

Baitz, Dana. "Review of Sheila Whiteley and Jennifer Rycenga eds., *Queering the Popular Pitch*," *Women & Music* 13 (2009), 109–112.

Bloechl, Olivia, Melanie Lowe, and Jeffrey Kallberg, eds. *Rethinking Difference in Music Scholarship*. Cambridge: Cambridge University Press, 2015.

Bloechl, Olivia, and Melanie Lowe, "Introduction: Rethinking Difference." In *Rethinking Difference in Music Scholarship*, edited by idem. and Jeffrey Kallberg, 10. Cambridge: Cambridge University Press, 2014.

Brett, Philip, Elizabeth Wood, and Gary C. Thomas, eds. *Queering the Pitch: The New Gay and Lesbian Musicology*. New York: Routledge, 1994.

Butler, Judith. *Bodies That Matter: On the Discursive Limits of "Sex."* New York: Routledge, 1993.

———. *Gender Trouble: Feminism and the Subversion of Identity*. New York: Routledge, 1999.

———. "Is Kinship Always Already Heterosexual?" *Differences* 13.1 (2002): 14–44.

Cohen, Cathy J. "Punks, Bulldaggers, and Welfare Queens: The Radical Potential of Queer Politics." In *The Routledge Queer Studies Reader*, edited by Donald E. Hall and Annamarie Jagose, with Andrea Bebell and Susan Potter, 74–95. New York: Routledge, 2012.

Dean, Tim. *Beyond Sexuality*, 216. Chicago, IL: University of Chicago Press, 2000.

Edelman, Lee. *No Future: Queer Theory and the Death Drive*. Durham, NC: Duke University Press, 2004.

Ferguson, Roderick A. "Introduction: Queer of Color Critique, Historical Materialism, and Canonical Sociology." In *The Routledge Queer Studies Reader*, edited by Donald E. Hall and Annamarie Jagose, with Andrea Bebell and Susan Potter, 119–133. New York: Routledge, 2012.

Grosz, Elizabeth. "Experimental Desire: Rethinking Queer Subjectivity." In *Supposing the Subject*, edited by Joan Copjec, 133–157. New York: Verso, 1994.

Gustafson, Susan E. *Men Desiring Men: The Poetry of Same-Sex Identity and Desire in German Classicism*, 31. Detroit, MI: Wayne State University Press, 2002.

Halberstam, Judith. *Female Masculinity*. Durham, NC: Duke University Press, 1998.

Hall, Donald E. and Annamarie Jagose, with Andrea Bebell and Susan Potter, eds. *The Routledge Queer Studies Reader*. New York: Routledge, 2013.

Hall, Stuart. "On Postmodernism and Articulation: Critical Dialogues in Cultural Studies." In *Stuart Hall: Critical Dialogues*, edited by David Morley and Kuan-Hsing Chen, 131–150. New York: Routledge, 1996.

Halperin, David M. *Saint Foucault: Towards a Gay Hagiography*. Oxford: Oxford University Press, 1995.

———. *How to Do the History of Homosexuality*. Chicago, IL: University of Chicago Press, 2002.

Hawkins, Stan. "On Male Queering in Mainstream Pop." In *Queering the Popular Pitch*, edited by Sheila Whiteley and Jennifer Rycenga, 279–294. New York: Routledge, 2006.

Jarman-Ivens, Freya, ed. *Oh Boy! Masculinities and Popular Music*. New York: Routledge, 2007.

Jarman-Ivens, Freya. *Queer Voices: Technologies, Vocalities, and the Musical Flaw*. New York: Palgrave Macmillan, 2011.

Jeffreys, Sheila. *Gender Hurts: A Feminist Analysis of the Politics of Transgenderism*. New York: Routledge, 2014.

Johnson, E. Patrick. "'Quare' Studies, Or '(Almost) Everything About Queer Studies I Learnt From My Grandmother." In *The Routledge Queer Studies Reader*, Donald E. Hall and Annamarie Jagose, with Andrea Bebell and Susan Potter, 96–118. New York: Routledge, 2012.

Knights, Vanessa. "Tears and Screams: Performances of Pleasure and Pain in the Belero." In *Queering the Popular Pitch*, edited by Whiteley and Rycenga, 83–100.

Kramer, Lawrence. "*Carnaval*, Cross-Dressing, and the Woman in the Mirror." In *Musicology and Difference*, edited by Ruth A. Solie, 305–325. Berkeley: University of California Press, 1993.

McClary, Susan. "Narrative Agendas in 'Absolute Music': Identity and Difference in Brahms's Third Symphony." In *Musicology and Difference*, edited by Solie, Ruth A., 326–344.

Moreno, Jairo. "Difference Unthought." In *Rethinking Difference in Music Scholarship*, edited by Olivia Bloecl, Melanie Lowe, and Jeffrey Kallberg, 382–421. Cambridge: Cambridge University Press, 2014.

Muñoz, José Esteban. *Disidentifications: Queers of Color and the Performance of Politics*. Minneapolis: University of Minnesota Press, 1999.

Nyong'o, Tavia. "Do You Want Queer Theory (or Do You Want the Truth)? Intersections of Punk and Queer in the 1970s." *Radical History Review* 100 (2008): 103–119.

Peraino, Judith A. *Listening to the Sirens: Musical Technologies of Queer Identity from Homer to Hedwig*. Berkeley: University of California Press, 2006.

Prosser, Jay. *Second Skins: The Body Narratives of Transsexuality*. New York: Columbia University Press, 1998.

Rey, Mario. "Albita Rodríguez: Sexuality, Imaging, and Gender Construction in the Music of Exile." In *Queering the Popular Pitch*, edited by Sheila Whiteley and Jennifer Rycenga, 115–130. New York, Routledge, 2006.

Rycenga, Jennifer. "Lesbian Compositional Process: One Lover-Composer's Perspective." In *Queering the Pitch*, edited by Philip Brett, Elizabeth Wood, and Gary C. Thomas, 275–296. New York, Routledge, 2006.

Smart, Mary Ann. "Review of Ruth A. Solie ed. Musicology and Difference: Gender and Sexuality in Music Scholarship." *Journal of the American Musicological Society* 47 (1994): 541–549.

Solie, Ruth A., ed. *Musicology and Difference: Gender and Sexuality in Music Scholarship.* Berkeley: University of California Press, 1993.

Solie, Ruth A. "Review of Philip Brett, Elizabeth Wood, and Gary C. Thomas eds., *Queering the Pitch: The New Gay and Lesbian Musicology.*" *Journal of the American Musicological Society* 48.2 (1995): 311–323.

Spivak, Gayatri Chakravorty. *Outside in the Teaching Machine.* New York: Routledge, 1993.

Taylor, Jodie. *Playing It Queer: Popular Music, Identity and Queer World-Making.* New York: Peter Lang, 2012.

Tomlinson, Gary. "Beneath Difference, Or, Human Evolutionism." In *Rethinking Difference in Music Scholarship*, edited by Olivia Bloecl, Melanie Lowe, and Jeffrey Kallberg, 366–381. Cambridge: Cambridge University Press, 2014.

Whiteley, Sheila, ed. *Sexing the Groove: Popular Music and Gender.* New York: Routledge, 1997.

Whiteley, Sheila and Jennifer Rycenga, eds. *Queering the Popular Pitch.* New York: Routledge, 2006.

Part I
Ambiguity of action

2 When the bearded lady sings

Ambiguity aesthetics, queer identity, and the gendering of the presentational voice

Mario Rey

"We are unity and we are unstoppable!" declares the first-place winner of the 2014 Eurovision Song Contest (ESC), the world's largest international popular song festival, thrusting the trophy up into the air like a fist. Representing Austria, the victor is a startling sight, donning a sequined fishtail gown, pumps, heavy makeup with dramatic eyelashes, and a full beard. Challenging any sense of congruity, the perceived incoherence is stupefying. The image cannot be read as depicting man, woman, or any socially recognized category, catapulting the viewer's state of mind—saddled by the parallel processing of graphic and sonic information—into an interpretive crisis. Within the multiple identities being articulated, who exactly is the entity referred to by the pronoun "we"?[1]

Austrian contender Thomas Neuwirth (b. 6 November 1988) ignited controversy on a global scale by performing the winning song "Rise like a Phoenix" in the guise of a stage persona named Conchita Wurst. The immensely popular ESC, a media cultural landmark, is characterized by campy production numbers featuring dancers, elaborate lighting effects, and sanitized suggestive costumes operating as extra-musical variables to influence televoting. Austria's entry required no pyrotechnics. Dispensing with the choreography and bloated theatrics that exemplifies the style of the show, "Rise like a Phoenix" was presented with a lone performer onstage, suggesting that the image imparted by Conchita Wurst provided spectacle enough. Austria's win constituted not only a national victory, but also an artistic triumph riddled with political significance and embodied dissidence. Neuwirth's iconoclastic performance and soaring vocals galvanized the live telecast of the ESC Grand Prix, and gave the spectator much to contemplate, most significantly, the precise nature of the impression that he means to impart with his stage persona. There is little doubt that the impression is a queer one.

In the viewer's flow of perception, there is a sense of both the familiar and the uncanny, a complex visual reconfiguration indicating that the sound-object is advancing along very oblique lines. While the bodily image presents a point of view towards the world, it cannot be described by conventional notions of gender and sexuality. There is heightened femininity attended by a recontextualized marker of hypermasculinity. Conflicting with the normalcy of feminine codes, the facial hair is a salient cue obscuring any intelligibility as to sexual category, and shattering the promise of pretense, the result of which is more gender collision than illusion.

In keeping with the media entertainment industry's penchant to serve up the female body as spectacle for the gaze, there is ostensibly an attempt at sexualization, but the bodily presentation is not truly manufactured to elicit sexual desire. Although the waist is cinched, her unpadded curves and pelvic shape are not erotically accentuated, her bosom not amplified, thus mitigating the secondary feminine features while emphasizing the tertiary traits. Neuwirth undoubtedly makes full use of the traditional codes of feminine enticement—luster, sparkle, and glamorous excess—but the viewer hesitates at the sight of a full beard, an indication that all other characteristics are unreliable markers of feminine construction. The interweaving of feminine and masculine attributes inhibits discernment of conventional gender polarity. The resultant display of denaturalized femininity is, at once, both excessive and insufficient. The androgyny disrupts any structure of desire based on the normative binarisms of sex and sexual category. However, the androgyny exhibited is characterized not by the erasure of visual gender signifiers, but by their accentuation and mixture in a single performing body (Figure 2.1).

Neuwirth's performance aesthetics proffers a disorienting aggregate of cues and affectations that highlights the arbitrary quality of gender norms, flooding our simplistic binary framework with puzzling variance. It creates a queer impression in every sense of the word. Forsaking a conventionally discernible identity conveys an incomplete gender crossing, a partial transformation into the other sex. If bodies narrativize, the story reads "not one or the other." His unflinching self-representation, imprinted in a "divaesque" sensibility, has generated image descriptions remarkably varied across the media: "gender-bending," "indeterminate," "unique," "vulgar." The visual interpenetration of opposites at the heart of the enactment flirts with the imagination, and then—shifting the focus from the gaze to the ear—there is the voice. As a secondary sex characteristic, vocal pitch is an elevated gender marker, and his tenorial voice sonorously contributes to the visible excess of indeterminacy, evincing that the ambiguity aesthetics can be realized through sound alone.

In due course, the audience ponders whether such performative complexity, not entirely unfamiliar in gay club culture but rarely deployed in the international stage, is an artistic pursuit, an act of defiance, or a far more radical physical presentation camouflaging as gender critique. A multivalent performance that, like the androgyny it conceptually surpasses, transmits more than one message concerning the nature of identity. Neuwirth's winning interpretation articulates the complex politics of nonnormative sexual subjectivity via the self-invented theatrical persona. His creation offers up an intricate encoding of multiple discourses that defies simple deconstruction.

Figure 2.1 Conchita Wurst.

A cleverly constructed display of indeterminacy, Neuwirth's performances provoke the gaze, and subvert not only the illusion of female, but also the expectation of drag. Equal measures of absurdity and sincerity, the net effect is not so much a curious parody of female impersonation or even an appropriation of "bear" or "skag" drag, as it is the claiming of a transgressive, transgendered space, positing the centrality of the body in the representation of identity.

Crafting an experience that merges the sonic and the visual with the political on the international music stage, Conchita tenders a unique case study of a social agent constructing a performative persona and marketing it as an individual identity, attesting to the volitional aspects of gender appropriation. This chapter examines the manner in which Neuwirth models dissent through performative ambiguity, challenging the social construction of gender, sexuality, corporeality, and the trope of drag queening to assert individual agency and narrative authority. Directing our attention toward the musical substance, he entrusts the audience with the task of untangling the song's narrator from the stage persona and the performer's subjectivity. His navigation of the masculine and the feminine at the intersection of popular music discourse problematizes binarism. I argue that the appearance of comically unconvincing drag is, in fact, a powerful form of contestation grounded in emancipatory ideology, destabilizing the fiction of a gender-based classification of sexuality. Narratological analysis of the song texts provides insights into the listener's negotiation of the various "voices" implicated, and the effects that the ambiguous gendering has on the lyrics' interpretation. These multivocal tactics support the aesthetics that Neuwirth enunciates at the outset through the artifices of dress, gesture, and vocal style. Offering a dissident construction that undermines the very idea of gender and sexuality as keystones of identity, his rendering of Conchita Wurst has important implications for queer narrative and the poetics of transgression.

A beard and a wig: the construction of a diva

Born in Gmunden, Austria, pop music artist Thomas Neuwirth was raised in a small conservative village in the mountainous Styrian countryside. His musical career began at the age of 18 as a contestant in the Austrian television talent show *Starmania* (2002–2009). In 2007, he founded the short-lived boyband *Jetzt Anders!* ("Now Different!"), but subsequently opted for a solo career. Earlier interests in fashion and drag allowed him to craft the theatrical stage persona Conchita Wurst, known mononymously as "Conchita," complete with biographical backstory and a beard, thus launching the musical *act* epithetically dubbed by the media as "The Bearded Lady."

Disentangling the incongruous fragments of visual and sonic facts, the spectator fails to make sense of the composite. Deciphering the queer conundrum that is Conchita necessitates ascertaining whether Neuwirth is cross-gendered, transgender, transvestite, female impersonator, or drag queen as king. Conchita may be regarded as a cross-gendered performance rather than transgender,[2] despite contemporary usage favoring the latter as a catchall term subsuming any variety of gender outlaw (e.g. transvestite, transsexual, androgyne, intersexual, drag queen/king). Neuwirth has asserted that his particular style of gender play should not be misconstrued as transgenderism.[3] Citing a personal practice of fluidity regulated by the fluctuating exigencies of public and private life, he demarcates the boundaries between being and performing. These distinctions, however, are blurred in view of the fact that Conchita is not confined to the stage, since Neuwirth strolls her out on the streets as a fully functioning identity. Such self-marketing enactments of "non-performance," seemingly conflated with expressive gender variance, undermine the discernment between the performative and the authentic.

The fiction of Conchita depicts a particular brand of gender obfuscation that combines dominant masculine and theatrical feminine qualities of self-representation, subverting the decoding process of drag logic.[4] Dismissing such contraventions as mere flamboyant stage folly fails to consider the clever deployment of queer performance aesthetics in the theatrics of sexual subjectivity. Articulating a radical notion of embodiment committed to social differentiation, Conchita not only transcends the conceptual boundaries of gender through the dialectical opposites of secondary and tertiary characteristics, but also revises the parameters for the ontological dualities of sex and sexuality. Neuwirth's creative expression of bodily ambiguity, which challenges the current mainstreaming of gay and lesbian culture, constitutes an anti-assimilationist model of male gender queering as alterity. As such, he asserts a Foucauldian privileging of the body as object for his own artistic self-creation and performative agency.[5] Bearing in mind, however, that he doesn't so much perform gender as he theatricalizes it via aesthetic contextualization and fictional narrativity.

Theatrical gender impersonation is hardly uncommon in Euro-American culture, and cross-dressing has a long and complex history in the West.[6] The theatricality of such representational practices on the professional stage fostered the exploration of various related issues, such as sexual identity—the complex figuration of desires, conceptualization, and behaviors that have been historically dichotomized into homosexual and heterosexual. Theatrical cross-dressing, in varying degrees of artful illusion, also provided titillation, an opportunity to gaze at the taboo of sexual ambiguity.

Emerging from American minstrelsy, the "fairy impersonator" and "comic *travesti*" are well documented in vaudeville and burlesque. Male impersonators—females singing popular ditties in male character—were active in the English musical halls and American variety theater from the mid-nineteenth to early twentieth century. While such acts both celebrated and denigrated various gender constructions, audiences thrilled at the spectacle of inversion. Despite the challenges of concealing their physical attributes, most performers were successful at "passing" convincingly onstage, but the voice generally undermined the realism. Despite the appeal of gender play as theatrical entertainment, the emerging visibility of sexual minorities contributed to the public opprobrium and subsequent demise of the form. It is unsurprising that the sharp decline in popularity of theatrical cross-dressing, irrespective of parodic intent, approximately coincides with the advent of psychoanalytical and medical discourses of sexual pathologies, which triggered the stigmatization of the taxonomies of erotic activity and variance. Thus, cross-dressed performances were increasingly associated with sexual perversion in the public imagination, and subsequently disparaged as unnatural.

Linked to the historic practice of theatrical cross-dressing is drag, commonly accomplished through dress and mannerism, or as Judith Halberstam states, "performing theatrically in a recognizable, gendered costume."[7] In the mainstream, drag queening is largely understood as a matter of "outrageous artificiality" for the performance of femininities as entertainment.[8] In Conchita's guise, the practice also contextualizes the narrative voice. However, the multiple incongruities of performance suggest that Conchita is not conventional drag. Arguably, Neuwirth does not appropriate the female form as object of erotic desire, although his embodiment of a specific imagination of the feminine draws on aestheticizations. Abandoning standard hypersexualizing through garish, provocative costuming that burlesques femininity, and the posturing associated with traditional drag queening, he imbues Conchita with a vagueness of meaning and illegibility that is however wrapped in the ostentation of elegant *couture*.[9] It is not the unintended ambiguity that often cloaks transgendered personhood, but rather, one that deliberately straddles the binary oppositions of homo- and heterosexuality, male and female, masculine and feminine. Undoubtedly, the enactment of Conchita elevates explicit gender ambiguity not only as a form of dissent but also as an art form.

Despite Neuwirth's slender frame, heightened femininity, and thoroughly ambiguous voice—aptly suited for compellingly female impersonation from every angle—he nonetheless serves up Conchita as not quite *femme réal*. The intent is not imitation or burlesque, but something altogether different, more subversive. For the spectator, the real act is the perceived inadequacy of Neuwirth's femininity as a convincing act. However, this presumed failure does not frame Conchita as a lampooning of female impersonation, or a parodic deconstruction, much less an abortive attempt as cisgendered illusion. Examining the performative expression of self as text to be interpreted, the nonbinary image does not evoke a "wrong body" narrative, but rather, a "subverted passing narrative," that in its very ambivalence reveals greater truths.[10]

The "Bearded Transvestite" as a social act

The manner in which Neuwirth strategically models dissent through ambiguity of musical performance, subverting what is expected and accepted, and recontextualizing identity markers linked to both femininity and masculinity poses a unique form of contestation. The time-worn artifices of dress, gesture, and singing style undermine gender orthodoxies, and dismantle the standards set by social convention. Transforming into something distinctly divergent, Conchita has taken the shape of her history. The musical performance, which is collapsed with hyperbolic modes of signification, underlines the very instability of gender-based identity, and at the midst of such visual incongruence, the gaze converges on the beard.

While drag queening with a beard may not be an unfamiliar trope in gay club culture and drag bars, it has essentially no visibility in the mainstream.[11]

In Neuwirth's naturally smooth, boyish face, the appropriation of the hyper-masculine is another artifice, a fragment of masculine construction material as masquerade. This renders Conchita as a double-disguise, amplifying and fusing dual sex characteristics, but nonetheless decoded as male-bodied through the engagement of drag discourses, as well as public acknowledge-ment of embodied realness. Contextualized within the performative per-sona, the bearing of the beard enacts a symbolic act of subversion. Its focal role in the visual representation of Conchita hints at a larger purpose. It marks the point of deviation.[12]

A secondary sexual characteristic, the beard, in its various configurations, has served across history and cultures as a nonverbal communicatory de-vice broadcasting an array of male aspirations such as dominance, wisdom, virility, and strength, as well as any number of masculine scripts of behav-ior. Correlated with indices of intersexual attraction,[13] facial hair is also historically associated with the concepts of disguise, revelation, and trans-formation. Subject to cross-cultural variation, the beard possesses many linguistically driven and socially determined symbolic meanings articulated through narrative and visual media. It is a key attribute of maleness,[14] and almost universally renders the ideal image of dominant masculinity.[15] Its onset marks the attainment of manhood and sexual maturity. Conversely, many cultures interpret a shaven face as manhood deferred,[16] if not a sign of outright effeminacy or physical weakness.[17] In a female subject, the beard may be construed as androgen excess, hypertrichosis (abnormal formations of hair growth), or a genetic disorder. Social stigmatization compels its removal. Bearded ladies in carnivalesque lore are relegated to circus side-shows as entertainment anomalies. In the context of Conchita, the artifice is simultaneously celebrated and denigrated.

In spite of Neuwirth's repeated pronouncements regarding the meaning of the beard as merely an artistic statement, it is, nonetheless, the source of narrative tension. The invectives launched against groomed hair surround-ing pink, glossy lips lead to the speculation of whether the criticism would have been as hostile had Neuwirth offered a conventional drag queen rather than a bearded man singing in a dress. Artistic intent notwithstanding, the beard is at the center of ambiguity,[18] and conceivably, it is the very recontex-tualization of such a powerful symbol of maleness that is most transgressive. In its enunciation of antinormativity, the beard functions as a micropolitical act in the Foucauldian sense,[19] responding to hegemonic power, and signal-ing the embodied quality of difference.

Neuwirth's multiple defections from orthodoxy belie a very conscious choice to provoke, to strike at the core of sexual intolerance, and expose any hesitation to accept voluntary deviation from the norm. This objective situ-ates the performance of Conchita squarely as sociopolitical action, marked by bearing "the sign of difference,"—the attributes by which a dominant group identifies the subordinate.[20] The act is also defined by the appro-priation of the property of instability through explicit indeterminateness for the social contestation of power asymmetries. As a self-described gay male performer that identifies with configurations of feminine practice, his performative mode conceivably stems from the imperative of sexual alterity.

Critiquing the authenticity of gender, which, as Judith Butler states, "can be neither true or false, but are only produced as the truth effects of a discourse of primary and stable identity,"[21] is concomitantly an attempt to drive nonconventional sexual subjectivities out of marginal existence, as well as any construction of personhood not authenticated by the hetero/homosexual binary. That Neuwirth targeted the ESC as the forum in which to articulate his gender project is unsurprising, given that precarious subject formations are systematically performed and problematized in urban popular music. Without doubt, the pop repertoire is a focal site for social transformation and ideological contestation in expressive culture.

Although the venerable ESC is packaged as prime time, family-friendly, mainstream entertainment for the promotion of national popular musical identity, attracting nearly 200 million viewers annually,[22] its kitsch quotient and history of openly LGBT contenders invites queer consumption and enfranchisement. As a platform of symbolic agency for the voices of European difference, the contest has attracted a strong gay following, and serves as an alternative media space for queer congregation. This is also a site of increasing "homonationalism," the linking of sexual minorities with cultural identities in national self-representation, as demonstrated in 1998 with the first-place win of Israel's contestant Dana International (née Yaron Cohen, b. 1972)—a self-identified male-to-female transsexual, and in 2007 with Serbian contender Marija Šerifović's lesbian coded performance, nuanced in butch sensibility.

Recognizing that the ESC provided a discursive stage for the construction of a new progressive European identity, social conservatives condemned Conchita's participation as a legitimization of unorthodox sexualities, heralding "the collapse of the EU's moral values" and "the end of Europe."[23] Unsure of what to make of Neuwirth's gender queerness, the detractors were reluctant to tolerate such a complete dislocation from heteronormativity, much less grant global center to a gay presence in the representation of European culture texts. Triggering outrage in certain geographies, and discourses of moral panic centered on the perceived threat of "homosocialization," Neuwirth's ESC participation foregrounded the East-West cultural wars and geopolitical divide concerning sexual epistemologies, counternormative practices, and transphobia. That Conchita would polarize the worldwide media, and elicit such vituperative responses from countries where gay issues are rarely addressed in official rhetoric, signals the volatile manner in which gender variance and nationalistic performance intersect, and play out on the international music scene. It was also during the *Sturm und Drang* of the ESC controversy that the pejoratively intended moniker "Bearded Transvestite" was coined. Conchita summarily became a double metaphor. In cultures where antinormative deviations are pathologized, Conchita was symbol of "ethno-fascism" from the "decadent West," and a metaphor for feeble, effeminate Western governments.[24]

While the ESC is ostensibly about a pan-European narrative expressed through popular music, with guidelines that explicitly forbid political lyrics, the undeniable envoicement of "soft" politics as subtext often results in voting blocs that reflect intercultural biases. In the case of Austria's entry, detractors endeavored to strip the performance of any aesthetic value, so as to undermine the social recognition of queerness and nationalism occupying the same stage. Ironically, attempts at whitewashing the homosexual presence from the national imagination also unwittingly spotlights sexuality as central to identity formation. In the final analysis, the 2014 ESC prompted a fear that the Austrian victory would reinforce new cultural norms and promote a gay agenda—a fear not entirely unfounded given Conchita's subsequent impact on European popular culture and queer iconicity. Neuwirth's gender queerness broadcasted a narrative of aesthetic self-invention, and wherever interstitial sexualities are suppressed, such assertions of autonomous self-determination destabilize not only the regulation of normativity, but also the maintenance of social, political, cultural, and sexual constructs of power.

A Voce En Travesti or Vocal Drag

Conchita is an arresting visual spectacle, without doubt. Behind the sparkle, however, Neuwirth unveils a voice of commensurate ambiguity and technical skill. Even the most cursory listening informs that the voice is roundly implicated in the masquerade. If gender is understood as performative and constructed, there is interpretive value in examining the manner in which the audible supports that structure. The listener is directed to the "voice" as the stable, authentic bearer of identity. Neuwirth's defiance of category gains him the latitude to effectively engage his unusual voice, potentially consigned to a feminine subject position through the adoption of "divaesque" vocal aesthetics. Any apparent intention to secure access to "Divadom" can be conveyed purely through the sonic material. The vocalizations channel Dame Shirley Bassey (b. 1937), 1988 ESC winner Céline Dion (b. 1968), and Cher (née Cherilyn Sarkisian, b. 1946), however unconventional the construction of such idealized femaleness may be.

Neuwirth's music enunciates a complex site where genre and voice intersect with gender and sexuality. His sexual dissidence, accorded by lived experience (antithetical to the simulacrum of difference proffered by sexual-variant poseurs such as David Bowie [née David Robert Jones, 1947–2016] and Sinéad O'Connor [b. 1966]), grants him the narrative authority to carve out an artistic space within popular culture for identity hopping and gender crossing. The multivocality of his music subverts fixed categories of sexual identity while navigating multiple binarisms (e.g. male femininity/female masculinity, black/white cultural production, dominant/subjugated, authentic/imitation).

The performative multivocality raises the question of who the listener "reads" as the narrative voice given the spectrum of agencies presented, such as the performer's subjectivity (i.e. Neuwirth), the vocal persona (i.e. Conchita), or a character in the text. Neuwirth's ambiguously tenor voice not only endows him with the versatility to occupy multiple roles, but also facilitates gender mobility across his repertoire, opening up various interpretive possibilities in the narratological imagination. Textual analysis of the musical materials (penned by various songwriters including Charlie Mason, Joacim Persson, and Sebastian Arman) reveals narrative support for multiple gendered subject positions, while an examination of the vocal production elucidates his articulation of the array of subjectivities that putatively inhabit his songs.

Neuwirth possesses a high voice for a man and cites the influence of female vocalists (and drag icons) that include Cher, Bassey, Dion, and Tina Turner (née Anna Mae Bullock, b. 1939). Male musical artists such as Prince (née Prince Rogers Nelson, 1958–2016), Justin Timberlake (b. 1981), Jeff Buckley (1966–1997), and Frankie Valli (née Francesco Stephen Castelluccio, b. 1934) have similarly courted vocal ambiguity. While these transgressions of normative masculinity may have been risky encroachments from a commercial marketing perspective, as an effeminate voice may be conflated with homosexuality, their subjectivity remained securely situated in heteronormativity. Nonetheless, queerness is legible in the voice, but ascertaining whether Neuwirth is deliberately attempting to cultivate a female voice is unknowable.[25] While not propounding the ventriloquizing of Conchita, the listener may construe an appropriation of a "queer voice" by iconoclastic emulation. That is to say, Neuwirth may be drawing from the vocal stylizations of his pantheon of divas. Alternately, the Conchita persona may serve as the embodiment of the vocal qualities produced in the pursuit of a particular aesthetic. This would, to some extent, refute the assumption of vocal drag or "cross-singing"[26] as a calculated queering strategy.

The gendering of music is a historically constructed mechanism of power asymmetries. Sonic gestures are gender codified, as is any instrument, timbre, song, genre, melodic turn, or compositional style. In effect, any musical utterance transmitted to the listener can be engaged as a gendered operator and subject to queer cultural influence. In relation to voice production, various mechanisms may be deployed to suggest maleness/femaleness, such as adjustments of the vocal fold, tongue posture in the vowels, or the tendency to "air out" on the lower register (characteristic of female pop vocalists). Such vocal manipulations produce a gender-bending sound that connects him with his icons. Enhanced with dress and physical gestures, his vocalizations render a specific category of ideal woman—the Diva. But not content to be a male diva, his construction of the ideal female is queered and positioned in a transgendered space. Most significantly, the voice is the defining element that allows the listener to discern tribute from parody, to dispel the suggestion of camp, to recognize authenticity rather than imitation.

While Neuwirth is undoubtedly conversant with stylistic conventions, there is no mimetic representation, manneristic excess, or wholesale appropriation of the divas he references. Trading a vocal style shaped by multiple musico-cultural influences, he nonetheless inhabits a powerful voice capable of original self-expression. His vocal manipulations not only convey the performance ideals, but also announce a sonic presence remarkably accomplished at sexually ambiguous musical interpretation. Informed by the particular codes governing the attribution of authenticity—a relative construct—and the cultural narratives that mediate legitimacy, the listener recognizes the veracity in the voice.

Neuwirth's vocal register tips the scale of gender. His identification with women, coupled with a vocal range that sustains a variety of gendered personae, facilitated the ambiguous vocality that informs his signature sound. It is expressive singing, but not the vulnerable voice of the stereotypical female, nor does it relinquish "male control."[27] Mostly tapping into chest voice production, he produces a healthy pop-rock belt in tenor range.[28] However, it is most emphatically with the use of falsetto, or as Joon Lee suggests, in the "joys of castration,"[29] that his voice summons a dissident masculinity, if not feminine identification. It is the sound of becoming the "other," of transcending bodily and textual constraints. In the rapturous femininity of falsetto, the voice is emancipated from the anatomical truths, and there can be little doubt that feminine and masculine currents course through his music.

Mirrors and masks: ambiguity in love song

Neuwirth's musical output lies squarely within the province of pop—a pivotal site for the representation and validation of various classes of identity. The role of sexual behavior in the negotiation of identity, a prominent theme in popular music, establishes a strong relation to gay cultural practices. Pop music's authority to revise modern sexual politics and reconfigure asymmetrical constructs of power drives the idiom to serve as a vehicle for contestation and a rallying call for social action. Although these commercial genres are chiefly marketed for sexualized consumption, the discourses surrounding pop music support Neuwirth's ideological framework and fundamental grappling with sexual subjecthood and pluralized identities. While there are no overt articulations of same-sex desire in any of Neuwirth's songs, the question arises as to whether the assumptions underlying the listener's narratological understanding of the texts facilitate the disentanglement of the performer's subjectivity from the narrative voice-subject. It is interpretively elucidating to gauge the extent to which the interplay of voice and text suggests alternate meanings, presumably demanding different semiotic strategies or "double readings." That is, does Neuwirth queer the pop?

Neuwirth's performance makes full use of Conchita's vocality (engaging the term as the intersection of sound and identity). However, variances in the perception of the voice-subject is regulated by the mode of transmission (i.e. audio versus video recording, or live performance). The restrictive medium of audio recording, deprived of visual cues, inhibits the conflation of protagonist, narrator, and performing subject. Arguably, Neuwirth can convey images and identity by sonic means, deploying vocal tactics that shape the aural representation of gender and sexuality, thereby queering the song through voice alone. As an embodied instrument, inextricable from the subjectivity and burdened by identity, the voice's authority in all matters narratological is irrefutable.

Inasmuch as vocal practices reconfigure gendered entities, Neuwirth's strategic treatment of the voice can occasionally fashion an aural experience approximating "vocal drag." Various techniques, including high registral placement, can suggest a feminized narrator. Like his self-representation, the notion of illusion—the suggestion that things are not always as they appear—gains thematic thrust throughout his debut album *Conchita* (2015). Interestingly, his output is unique from a narratological perspective in that all references to gender are excised from the lyrics. These omissions are especially destabilizing in the love songs. Despite the sexually indeterminate subject positioning, there is scarcely anything to provoke the (homo) erotic imagination. Virtually all of the numbers are characterized by lyric indeterminacy, stripping any sexual specificity that marks central aspects of identity. Moreover, the texts are invariably articulated in the confessional tone of the first-person voice, an autodiegetic narrator of unspecified sex directly addressing the love-object. Such textual indeterminateness requires listeners to fill in the gaps, granting them the license to conjure alternate meanings.

Reading the songs as literary texts reveals the central themes of obscured identities, personal autonomy, and the transformation of self. Recurring motifs that infuse the texts with symbolic meaning include mirrors, reflections, masks, charades, and the bodily (e.g. voice, skin, eyes, gazing). For example, the dominant motif of the "eye" casts doubt on the accuracy of perception. It is interesting to note that Neuwirth's expressive language is surprisingly devoid of irony, as well as the worn-out homosexual narrative of suffering and evocations of unfulfilled desire. Of particular thematic significance is the mutability of identity; lyrics such as "Peering in the window, no, that isn't me/Stranger getting nearer, who can this person be?" ("Rise like a Phoenix"), and "I'm walking past a window, reflections of someone like me/But I don't recognize what I see" ("Pure"), suggest the experience of incongruence or anatomical dysphoria described by many transgendered persons.

The textual analyses of the songs also suggest that there are no secure indications as to the narrator's biological sex, no explicit physical descriptions or (pro)nominal expressions, no signifiers in the text that would operate in the manner of a visual cue in the presentational image (such as dress, makeup, bodily gestures, etc.); there are only implicit suggestions in a handful of songs. Moreover, the gazing into the reflection, as depicted in several texts (e.g. "Rise like a Phoenix," "That's What I Am"), offers no physical descriptions. Whatever the intent of attaching an ambiguously gendered identity to the narrative voice, it emancipates the listeners' imagination and prompts the mapping out of connections among a song's character, narrator, voice-subject (Conchita), and performer (Neuwirth).

The unmarked sexuality of the narrator is particularly provocative in the more erotically charged songs where the biological sex of the love-object is similarly undetermined. Such sexual obscurity subverts the listener's expectations of defining the precise nature of the love that is being rendered. Even the impulse to mark Conchita as the voice-subject, compounded by the listener's interpretive tendencies set to heteronormative default, fails to unequivocally support any assumptions of conventional sexualities. So how does the depiction of love and desire fulfill the promise of romantic arousal when disassociated from the sexual characteristics of both the voice-subject and the love-object? Such indeterminacy, when coupled with descriptions of "skin on skin" ("Firestorm"), reads particularly evasive. The singing voice percolates with indeterminate sexual desire, propositioning the eroticized object for sensual abandonment with promises of either cross-gendered or same-sex intimacy. Such utterances of the erotic, abstracted from the concepts of gender or biological sex, depict a sexuality that is not framed in terms of man/woman, masculine/feminine, hetero/homosexual. Rather, the indeterminacy articulates a form of desire unbound by the specificity of sexual category and orientation, or anatomical constraints, thus rendering a human experience that transcends corporeal boundaries, particularly when vocal ambiguity is actuated.

Certainly, the textual ambiguity can be deployed to emancipate desire from embodiment, saddling the listener with the burden of interpretation. Heterosexuality will not be taken for granted, as constructions of queer identity are made extratextually through circulating public knowledge concerning Neuwirth's sexuality (male and gay), which may frame the narrative persona. Alternately, the feminized voice of the performative persona (Conchita) may recontextualize the relationship heteronormatively. Thus, the textual indeterminacy can comparably suggest either homosexual or heterosexual desire. This reading of an alternate discourse is akin to homoerotic rewriting, the interpretive revising that gay men and lesbians engage in when consuming music or viewing heteronormative media scenes—a mechanism that Nikki Sullivan refers to as the "gay gaze."[30]

Neuwirth's language of intimacy and the double-voicedness of the desires tendered conceivably invite a queer reading. However, reading homoeroticism as subtext should not be construed as sublimated expression, or much less a concession to mass commercial consumption. In all likelihood, decoding the nature of the sexual dynamic misses the point entirely, as it may be precisely these interpretive impulses that Neuwirth aims to dispense with as he moves beyond difference.

While Neuwirth may not unambiguously announce identity, texts can occasionally suggest a female subject position. The single instance of an implicit gender marker used in a song occurs in "Heroes,"[31] as the voice-subject sings "I dreamt I was a queen in a crimson robe." However, this implicit marker would not indubitably identify the narrator as female—a blunt assumption stemming from heteronormative conditioning—since the statement may situate the narrative voice in a female-identified subject position.

In the context of the stage persona, the text is continuously reinterpreted and subverted. Conchita amplifies the lyrics and proposes multiple levels of meaning. In "That's What I Am," for example, the statement that "You can't take your eyes off me/'Cause I'm different and my mind is free" suggests difference attributable to visual nonconformity rather than physical desirability. The line is punctuated by Neuwirth's continuous falsetto, further queering the text. His request to "come a little closer, it's just me" followed by the observation "You follow someone else's rules that are for shallow fools" invites a hesitant listener/object for similar emancipation. His vocal treatment involves resonance changes and a breathiness generally associated with youthful female pop voices. There is the glottal onset of sound uncharacteristic of male singers. He also uses his head voice to produce a sound that is clear, full, and supported, seemingly with the intent of brightening the tone. As he climbs into the extreme top of the range, there is reinforced falsetto, a vocal choice that contributes to the perceived feminization of the narrator.

In the case of the power ballad "Rise like a Phoenix," the transformative themes articulated by the voice-subject encapsulate double meaning. While the song's lyrics suggest a narrator surmounting a detrimental intimate relationship, challenges such as "You wouldn't know me today/You have got to see to believe" contain multiple significations. Covert meaning is underlined in the refrain by the adverbial clauses, "Once I'm transformed, once I'm reborn," using a reinforced male falsetto. Through the narrative voice of Conchita and the deployment of a vocal aesthetic culturally perceived as "feminine," the words hint at corporeal transformation.

Other instances alluding to transfigurations of the self or bodily transitioning are revealed in the song "Out of Body Experience." The descriptions regarding the landscape of lovemaking are punctuated with stylistic appropriations of exoticism derived from Near-Eastern musical practice and instrumentation, signifying Orientalized Otherness. The narrator's continuous incantations of "Your body"/"My body," without anatomical details or biological sex of either body epitomizes nongendered narrativity. Such textual ambiguity of the rhetorical voice is commonplace in his catalogue of love songs.

"Pure" and "Other Side of Me," undoubtedly his most confessional songs, grapple with issues of identity. Oblique desires and difference are suggested with such disclosures as "I'm moving in a different way" ("Other Side of Me"), and "The note that was wrong in their song sang of me, mine, and I/And I carried it deep inside" ("Pure") suggests the burden of subordinate mas-culinities. Both of these songs employ implicit gender markers to suggest the biological sex of the protagonists. For example, implicit genderization is articulated with the declaration "Before I was told to walk tall, to be strong/ To believe in the truth" ("Pure"), as tallness and strength are traits ascribed to traditional masculinity.[32]

The most gendered song in the track list is "Where have all the Good Men Gone?" The narrative voice is not directed at the love-object, and there is no vocative expression indicating the entity being addressed, save for the requests: "Ladies, help me sing this song," imbuing the song with self-reflexivity. The narrator's direct address is established at the onset with the statement "Remember what your daddy use to tell you about the so-called nice boys that keep on coming 'round?" The anaphoric structure of the refrain, formed by the reiterative use of the titular rhetorical question, proposes two levels of reading. While the sex of the narrator is undisclosed in the lyrics, textual information (irrespective of vocal treatment), at the very least, positions the voice-subject as female-identified.

In these examples, the listener's perception of gender and sexuality is continuously challenged by a narrative persona that nimbly shifts subject positions. Given the undercurrents of meaning that course through his cat-alogue of songs, none of which contain any revelations as to the character's biological sex, Conchita's multivocality invokes the ambiguity or implicit gender of the assumed narrator. In the love songs, the affirmation of the voice-subject and love-object dynamic is given unusual treatment, emanci-pated from gender constraints and sexual specificity. Here, Conchita articu-lates a language of intimacy stripped of sexual characteristics and biological essentialism. Such indeterminacy, however, places a few interpretative con-straints. For instance, in the less erotic songs, the narrator may be address-ing another form of self, an alter ego, or the image in the mirror. Even so, gay listeners may engage a queer reading of the musical material, whether or not there is confirmation of a homo subject position or any transmission of "insider" language. Nevertheless, the narratological possibilities support Neuwirth's multivocality, which richly informs the ambiguity aesthetics governing the performances and the rhetorical voice, thus inviting multiple readings of a song.

Conclusion

Attesting to the mutability of identity, Thomas Neuwirth has crafted a stage persona that fulfills the promise of queer performativity. Renouncing gender essentialism, he eschews the normative practice of attaching fixed sexual identities to the subjectivities and dismantles the social constructs circumscribing one's biological sex. Neuwirth distils the set of dichotomous oppositions into a composite that reflects the complexity of personhood. Exercising the narratological imperative of self-definition, he configures a plural subjectivity and allows the multiple identities to complementarily inhabit one body, transforming the object of music-making into an artistically articulated sexuality, as well as cultural artifact.

The construction of Conchita Wurst, like any problematic of self, is an adaptive strategy not only for a contemporary social world, but also for the marketing exigencies of the music entertainment industry. Showcasing the interplay of the feminine and the masculine through both corporeal and vocal performance, he contests hegemonic narratives of bodily inscription and engendering in the media. The transgressive embodiment gains Neuwirth access to the discourse of sexuality in the pluralistic constitution of identity. Claiming the authority to manufacture his own mediatized image, he deploys Conchita to problematize normative gendered embodiment and subordinate masculinities in relation to social identity, and through such aesthetic self-fashioning define queer autonomous agency.

The theatricality of subversion in popular music facilitated Neuwirth's choice to thrust himself as a gender-variant entrant in the public entertainment arena where "Image is Everything." From his position, the ESC provided an idealized stage for the recognition of marginalized subjectivities as much as pop singing. Appropriating the trope of the "Eurovision diva," his representation of transgressive Otherness through visual, aural, and textual ambiguity granted him considerable social visibility. However, such creative acts of political queering and determinate individuation found opposition from ultra-orthodox elements. The mixed public response to Conchita underscored the stark differences among diverse cultural systems and their corresponding attitudes regarding alternate sexualities.

Through Conchita, Neuwirth illustrates how the interconnectedness of gender, sexuality, and social identity is continuously renegotiated and reinterpreted in the popular music scene. Synthesizing different gendered visual and vocal qualities for commercial consumption, he embraces a constructivist approach to personhood privileged by postmodernism. In this regard, Conchita Wurst realizes a postmodern act of self-narration, of treating the body as text, and constructing queer self-images for mainstream consumption. Uncoupling from the established tropes of gay suffering, his public representation of alterity reflects resistance rather than subjugation, and revelation rather than deception. Queering the song through vocal treatment and textual indeterminacy, Neuwirth places narratological demands on the listener, who must disentangle the stage persona from the performer's subjectivity, and discern the multiple "voices" articulated by the sound-object. Ultimately, he lends audibility to suppressed voices, thereby advocating the politics of inclusion and belonging that have so profoundly informed his post-Eurovision career. By exposing the complexity of sexual lives and imagination through such convergences of nonbinary gender play and popular music, he illuminates the ways in which consumers comprehend their own identities and engage in the critical interrogation of nonnormative sexualities.

Notes

1 The remark, while ostensibly celebrating a unified collective, was in response to Russian President Vladimir Putin's LGBT Propaganda Law (30 June 2013), declaring the distribution of gay propaganda to minors a criminal offense.

2 The categories distinguish subjects who occasionally switch genders versus those seeking long-term hormonal treatment or sex reassignment surgery such as transsexuals.

3 Neuwirth uses second-person female pronouns only when referring to Conchita. See William Lee Adams, "Conchita Wurst: I am not a transgender woman!" *Wiwibloggs*, April 6, 2014, http://wiwibloggs.com/2014/04/06/conchita-wurst-transgender/45930/.

4 "Drag logic" are the discourses that support the observer's interpretations of bodily reality. See Meredith Heller, "Is She He? Drag Discourse and Drag Logic in Online Media Reports of Gender Variance," *Feminist Media Studies* 16, no. 3 (2015). doi: 10.1080/14680777.2015.1114004.

5 Michel Foucault, *The History of Sexuality, vol. 3: The Care of the Self,* trans., Robert Hurley (New York: Pantheon Books, 1986).

6 For example, the theatrical cross-casting of women in male "breeches roles" during the Restoration in England. See Vern Bullough and Bonnie Bullough, *Cross Dressing, Sex, and Gender* (Philadelphia: University of Pennsylvania Press, 1993).

7 Judith Halberstam, *Female Masculinities* (Durham, NC: Duke University Press, 1998), 232.

8 Ibid., 258–259.

9 The name Conchita Wurst articulates ambivalence in parodizing dual synecdoches loaded with gender significance. "Conchita" is diminutive for the Spanish female forename Concepción, but also a Cuban slang term for the vagina, while the surname "Wurst" denotes German sausage (in Austria, "wurst" is also used in the expression "es ist mir wurst" ["it's all the same"]).

10 See Erika Renée Williams, "Subverted Passing: Racial and Transgendered Identities in Linda Villarosa's Passing for Black," *Studies in American Fiction* 40, no. 2 (2013): 285–307.

11 The conceit of female drag with a beard may be traced to George E. Harris (1949–1982), director of the gay liberation theater troupe "The Cockettes." However, his unique style of drag is more associated with countercultural discourses and psychedelia.

12 See Michael Pickering, *Stereotyping: The Politics of Representation* (Basingstoke: Palgrave Macmillan, 2001), 48.

13 See Uta Skamel, "Beauty and Sex Appeal: Sexual Selection of Aesthetic Preferences," in *Evolutionary Aesthetics,* eds. Eckart Voland and Karl Grammer (New York: Springer, 2003), 173–200.

14 For example, the beard is a defining physical feature of the "bear" gay subculture fetishizing dominant masculinity.

15 See Nick Neave and Kerry Shields, "The Effects of Facial Hair manipulation on Female Perceptions of Attractiveness, Masculinity, and Dominance in Male Faces," *Personality and Individual Differences* 45 (2003), 373–377.

16 Some psychoanalytic interpretations regard the removal of facial hair as an act of auto-castration. See Allan Peterkin, *One Thousand Beards: A Cultural History of Facial Hair* (Vancouver: Arsenal Pulp Press, 2001), 61.

17 Ibid., 77–78.

18 Regarding public perception and criticism of his image, Neuwirth has identified the beard as the "problem." See Masha Charnay "Austria's Bearded Lady: 11 Questions for Cross-Dressing Diva Conchita Wurst," *Vocativ,* January 14,

2014, www.vocativ.com/culture/lgbt/austrias-bearded-lady-11-questions-cross-dressing-diva-conchita-wurst/.

19 Michel Foucault, "The Subject and Power," *Critical Inquiry* 8, no. 4 (1982), 777–795.

20 Michael Pickering, *Stereotyping: The Politics of Representation*, op. cit., 48.

21 Judith Butler, *Gender Trouble: Feminism and Subversion of Identity* (New York: Routledge, 1990), 174.

22 Alex Ritman, "Eurovision Song Contest Draws Almost 200 Million Viewers," *Hollywood Reporter*, June 3, 2015, www.hollywoodreporter.com/news/eurovision-song-contest-viewership-rises-799794.

23 See Nick Duffy "Russia Considers Pulling out of Eurovision, Making 'Straight' Rival Show," *Pink News*, May 14, 2014, www.pinknews.co.uk/2014/05/14/russia-considers-pulling-out-of-eurovision-making-straight-rival-show/.

24 See Madeline Chambers "Putin Ally Lambasts Western Values Embodied by Conchita Wurst," *Rueters,* May 15, 2014, www.reuters.com/article/us-germany-russia-idUSKBN0DV0YB20140515.

25 Neuwirth has stated that "Conchita" sings differently from "Tom." See Masha Charnay' "Austria's Bearded Lady: 11 Questions for Cross-Dressing Diva Conchita Wurst," *Vocativ,* op. cit.

26 See Anno Mungen, "'Anders Als Die Anderen,' Or Queering the Song: Construction and Representation of Homosexuality in German Cabaret Song Recordings before 1993," in *Queering the Popular Pitch*, eds. Sheila Whiteley and Jennifer Rycenga (New York: Routledge, 2006).

27 For an analysis of the various ways in which masculine voices perform issues of control, see Suzanne G. Cusicks, "On Musical Performances of Gender and Sex" in *Audible Traces: Gender, Identity and Music*, eds. Elaine Barkin and Lydia Hamessley (Zurich: Carciofoli Verlagshaus, 1999), 25–49.

28 Thanks to Dr. Jami Rhodes for her analysis of Thomas Neuwirth's vocal techniques.

29 See Joon Lee, "The Joy of the Castrated Boy," in *What's Queer About Queer Studies Now?,* eds. David Eng, Judith Halberstam, and Jose Muñoz, 23, no. 3–4 (2005), 35–56.

30 Nikki Sullivan, *A Critical Introduction to Queer Theory* (New York: New York University Press, 2003), 9.

31 Implicit denotes gender information derived from assumption and descriptions given in the text, for example, "handsome" and "trousers" versus "pretty" and "slacks" to imply maleness and femaleness, respectively.

32 Contextually variable masculine traits and norms are described in Ronald F. Levant, *Masculinity Reconstructed: Changing the Rules of Manhood at Work, in Relationships, and in Family Life* (New York: Dutton, 1995).

Bibliography

Adams, William Lee. "Conchita Wurst: I Am Not a Transgender Woman!" *Wiwibloggs*, April 6, 2014. http://wiwibloggs.com/2014/04/06/conchita-wurst-transgender/45930/.

Bullough, Vern, and Bonnie Bullough, *Cross Dressing, Sex, and Gender.* Philadelphia: University of Pennsylvania Press, 1993.

Butler, Judith. *Gender Trouble: Feminism and Subversion of Identity.* New York: Routledge, 1990.

Chambers, Maeline. "Putin Ally Lambasts Western Values Embodied by Conchita Wurst," *Rueters,* May 15, 2014. www.reuters.com/article/us-germany-russia-idUSKBN0DV0YB20140515.

Charnay, Masha. "Austria's Bearded Lady: 11 Questions for Cross-Dressing Diva Conchita Wurst," *Vocativ,* January 14, 2014. www.vocativ.com/culture/lgbt/austrias-bearded-lady-11-questions-cross-dressing-diva-conchita-wurst/.

Cusicks, Suzanne G., "On Musical Performances of Gender and Sex," In *Audible Traces: Gender, Identity and Music*, edited by Elaine Barkin and Lydia Hamessley, 25–49. Zurich: Carciofoli Verlagshaus, 1999.

Duffy, Nick. "Russia Considers Pulling out of Eurovision, Making 'Straight' Rival Show," *Pink News*, May 14, 2014. www.pinknews.co.uk/2014/05/14/russia-considers-pulling-out-of-eurovision-making-straight-rival-show/.

Foucault, Michel, "The Subject and Power," *Critical Inquiry* 8, no. 4 (1982), 777–795.

Foucault, Michel. *The History of Sexuality, vol. 3: The Care of the Self,* translated by Robert Hurley. New York: Pantheon Books, 1986.

Halberstam, Judith. *Female Masculinities*. Durham, NC: Duke University Press, 1998.

Heller, Meredith, "Is She He? Drag Discourse and Drag Logic in Online Media Reports of Gender Variance," In *Feminist Media Studies* 16, no. 3 (2015), 445–459. doi: 10.1080/14680777.2015.1114004.

Lee, Joon, "The Joy of the Castrated Boy," *What's Queer about Queer Studies Now?,* edited by David Eng, Judith Halberstam, and Jose Muñoz, 23, no. 3–4 (2005): 35–56.

Levant, Ronald F. *Masculinity Reconstructed: Changing the Rules of Manhood at Work, in Relationships, and in Family Life*. New York: Dutton, 1995.

Mungen, Anno, "'Anders Als Die Anderen,' Or Queering the Song: Construction and Representation of Homosexuality in German Cabaret Song Recordings before 1993," In *Queering the Popular Pitch*, edited by Sheila Whiteley and Jennifer Rycenga, 67–82. New York: Routledge, 2006.

Neave, Nick, and Kerry Shields, "The Effects of Facial Hair manipulation on Female Perceptions of Attractiveness, Masculinity, and Dominance in Male Faces," *Personality and Individual Differences* 45 (2003): 373–377.

Peterkin, Allan, *One Thousand Beards: A Cultural History of Facial Hair.* Vancouver: Arsenal Pulp Press, 2001.

Pickering, Michael. *Stereotyping: The Politics of Representation*. Basingstoke: Palgrave Macmillan, 2001.

Ritman, Alex. "Eurovision Song Contest Draws Almost 200 Million Viewers," *Hollywood Reporter*, June 3, 2015. www.hollywoodreporter.com/news/eurovision-song-contest-viewership-rises-799794.

Skamel, Uta, "Beauty and Sex Appeal: Sexual Selection of Aesthetic Preferences," In *Evolutionary Aesthetics,* edited by Eckart Voland and Karl Grammer, 173–200. New York: Springer, 2003.

Sullivan, Nikki. *A Critical Introduction to Queer Theory*. New York: New York University Press, 2003.

Williams, Erika Renée, "Subverted Passing: Racial and Transgendered Identities in Linda Villarosa's Passing for Black," *Studies in American Fiction* 40, no. 2 (2013): 285–307.

3 Détournement and female punk bands of the 1970s

Helen L. Reddington

In this chapter, I will reexamine the punk moment in Britain in the 1970s from the perspective of gender resistance and difference, informing my discussion with original research material and interviews from women band members undertaken between 2001 and 2010. I will revisit the response by the music press to the female-focused punk bands, discussing their activities and music in the context of more recent writing on queerness and subcultures, and explore the détournement they undertook within the already subversive punk subculture. Détournement is the questioning of what can appear to be the "natural order" of culture and politics through using "normal" objects or behavior in apparently radically different ways. In the words of the Situationist writer Guy Debord, "The device of détournement restores all their subversive qualities to past critical judgements that have congealed into respectable truths…"[1]

As a former punk, my own subjectivity positions me within a hierarchy that is fluid and constantly revised; the methodologies that we use to discuss (what becomes) myth are constantly shifting, and biased according to the context of the commentator.[2] Yet, though I concluded that the women musicians in punk, rather than the men, were undertaking a much more effective, questioning version of punk from their position at the *margins of the margins* of youth subculture, British punk of the 1970s is still to this day largely identified as male, because it was the male groups that sold most records and more men have documented its history. Kurt Cobain revived interest in The Raincoats and The Slits before his suicide in 1994, the riot grrrl movement was rooted in a similar joy in defiant amateurism, and Pussy Riot's seriously disruptive acts were punk acts: as a blueprint for female subversive activity, punk still has validity.

A redefinition of girlhood and womanhood was articulated by punk's female musicians and was (and is) an important commentary not only on women and girl's engagement with subcultures,[3] but also more broadly on gender definitions during the late 1970s. The general "noise" created by punk's "moral panic" effects obscured the questioning of what it meant to be female, and the undercurrent of gender dissent that was stirred up. There was a parallel specifically *women's* music making scene based around women's centers during this time period,[4] but here I shall be concentrating on those women band members who specifically aligned themselves with punk in collaboration with, or in contrast to, male punks.

Challenges to hegemonic culture and political authority were familiar in postwar Britain; the Teddy Boys in the 1950s[5] and the Mods in the 1960s[6] had instigated moral panic. Bikers and hippies in the 1960s[7] had also caused social concern; UK hippies had looked to the US for inspiration and had closely tied cultural production to their ethos in order to create their own underground.[8] By the time punk surfaced as a subculture, hippie culture had been visibly recuperated (reabsorbed into society, largely through commercialization) and no longer had countercultural agency. During the British recession in the 1970s, it became apparent that it was the younger generation who were going to suffer most as a consequence; Hansard reported a 42% increase in unemployment for people leaving school by the end of 1976.[9] Their parents generally had conservative values; their aspirations for their children were fixed and unimaginative. The older generation had experienced full employment, were filled with gratitude for the stability that postwar Britain had provided for them, and were not prepared for the collapse of the country's industrial base that challenged "the capacity of unilateral control implied through male conceptualizations of people decontextualized from social relations…"[10] If both young men and young women are excluded from work in a society where gender roles are articulated along the binary of "men work/women make homes after giving up work and marrying," this disruption challenges hegemonic assumptions about gender roles.

The cultural revolution of the 1960s had encouraged both women and men to redefine themselves. However, as Germaine Greer and others noted, this benefited men more than women; men's interpretation of women's liberation tended to favor the availability of young attractive women for sex, and the mediation of the underground was exclusively controlled by men.[11] Given a boost of confidence by the UK 1975 Sex Discrimination Act, women leaving schools and colleges in the mid-1970s for nonexistent jobs had high expectations of themselves as autonomous individuals, although they soon became disappointed; it is not surprising that the enabling ethos of punk drew many of them into the subculture. Punk's acts of détournement were being played out parallel to a hegemonic music scene that was determined to recoup its marketable aspects (notably the ironically sexualized personae of more mainstream female rock artists).

Musically, punk introduced fresh approaches to instrumentation and gender. There was time to learn: boredom could be alleviated by rehearsals and writing, and there were small and unusual places to perform in as soon as the basic rudiments of a band and songs had been pieced together. The anti-professionalism and anti-industry stance of punk (which was soon abandoned by The Sex Pistols and The Clash as they engaged with major record labels) facilitated the flow of female musicians into bands and onto stages, forcing audiences to rethink attitudes to skill, rock music roles, and aesthetics. As John Savage noted, these female groups had worked out "…how to translate an often obnoxious but proud attitude into a new form of music. No woman had made these noises before."[12] Public hostility relegated them to the edges of society where safety could only be found in the underground, or the underworld, and unemployment was trapping them in a state of perpetual childhood or adolescence. In this respect, the punk moment in the 1970s had much in common with Judith Halberstam's "queer temporality" with "stretched-out adolescences"[13] that often transcended age barriers. For example, Vi Subversa, lead singer and guitarist with the band Poison Girls, was 40 years old. There was no reason to "grow up" because the normal straight rites of passage of school-job-family had ceased to be available for many women. Indeed, Vi carried on playing right up to the end of her life, playing her last gig in Brighton in 2015 at the age of 80.[14]

Appearance: "Camp is a woman walking around in a dress made of three million feathers"[15]

Since the 1960s, young women had mostly been represented in pop and rock music in supporting roles to men. They were often sung about as whores, temptresses, or angels waiting to be defiled; in their own songs they defined themselves in binary relation to "him" and were rarely heard to voice anything other than romantic dreams and disappointments. There were some exceptions: progressive rock singer Sonja Kristina of Curved Air charted in 1971 with a song about a prostitute, *Back Street Luv*. In pop, the guitar-playing black artist Joan Armatrading defied categorization by refusing to align herself with feminism, or gender and race politics. In the mid-70s, a TV series called Rock Follies[16] told a fictitious story about three female rock and roll singers as protagonists, with their own musical careers. Generally though, British female artists in 1970s popular music conformed to stereotyped gentle and unchallenging "potential girlfriends," reflecting Judith Butler's definition of "…an identity tenuously constituted in time—an identity instituted through a *stylized repetition of acts*".[17]

This reassuring presentation of "normal" gender delineations in popular culture was first interrupted in the early 1970s by glam rock; artists such as David Bowie and Marc Bolan introduced pop music audiences to cross-dressing and the blurring of gender boundaries. Yet glam rock demonstrated that: "Gender, it seems, is reversible only in one direction, and this must surely be to do with the immense social power that accumulates around masculinity".[18] It was the *men* in 1970s pop and rock that explored the boundaries of gender, and this was often through co-opting (and sometimes parodying) either femininity-as-clothes-and-makeup, or even apparently in the case of the band The Sweet, transvestism itself.[19] Glam "became progressively disengaged from the mundane concerns of everyday life and adolescence"[20] and emphasized subversive physical appearance over political activism in its engagement with gender definition.

Historically, the British public had been quite comfortable with cross-dressing on theatre and variety stages. Even in Victorian music hall, performers such as Vesta Tilley could address social problems such as male drunkenness and womanizing safely from the stage in character as a male.[21] Using her observational skills and "magical translation"[22] of the habits of the male characters she inhabited, she became immensely popular with British working-class women. Traditional pantomimes featured female leads in "serious" male parts and male leads in comic female parts, and there were "breeches roles" for women in formal opera and theatre. Then, from 1958 onwards, the popular *Carry On* films, humorous and smutty British films, featured camp, gay actors Kenneth Williams and Charles Hawtrey. However, androgyny and cross-dressing were only tolerated in controlled and mediated environments, and not on the street. To cite Butler again:

> On the street or in the bus, the act becomes dangerous... precisely because there are no theatrical conventions to delimit the purely imaginary character of the act, indeed, on the street or on the bus, there is no presumption that the act is distinct from reality; the disquieting effect of the act is that there are no conventions that facilitate making this separation.[23]

Punk was a street subculture; punks congregated in gay and lesbian bars in metropolitan areas (such as Louise's in Soho where Siouxsie Sue and many of the "first wave" punks hung out), and Dickens in Salford (which provided a safe haven for musician and artist Linder Sterling), community centers where anarchist organizations met, shebeens (illegal late-night drinking dens), and street corners in rundown urban areas. Most punk scenes overlapped with other behaviors deemed to be socially deviant: male and female prostitution,[24] delinquency, anarchy, and homosexuality. Détournement was articulated through clothing that was often influenced by ironic references to S&M (sadomasochism) and taboo political symbolism, in particular Nazism. Inspiration came from a sequence of deviant or apocalyptic films such as Joseph Losey's *The Servant* (1963) and Stanley Kubrick's *A Clockwork Orange* (1971). Bob Fosse's film version of *Cabaret* (1972) was an obvious influence as was the Berlin cabaret music of Kurt Weill and Bertolt Brecht. Jim Sharman's 1975 film *The Rocky Horror Picture Show* featured the actor Little Nell, who had been an aficionado of McClaren and Westwood's shop *Sex* before it was rechristened *Seditionaries* in 1976. The polymorphous perversity of the artists and musicians of Andy Warhol's Factory traveled to Britain via his films and additionally, the music of The Velvet Underground featured Nico and Mo Tucker as female role models; another woman artist from New York's underground nightclub CBGBs, Patti Smith, brought distinctly unfeminine anger in her music and physical androgyny through the Mapplethorpe photograph on the cover of her 1975 album *Horses*.

Dave Laing notes that punk women's clothing varied from the male rock uniform (as worn by Gaye Back of The Adverts and Chrissie Hynde of The Pretenders), through "determinedly asexual" clothing (as worn by Fay Fife of The Rezillos and Poly Styrene), to confrontational clothing (as worn by Siouxsie and Ari Up). He compares the "glamorous" with the "forbidden," the former worn in pre-punk days by rock chicks and "accepted into a public discourse of showbusiness sexuality"[25] and the latter "...thwarting the fetishistic gaze [that] seem[s] to rest on the displacement of the fetishized garment from its customary relationship with the body."[26] For example, Siouxsie's appropriation of dog collars and the wearing of plastic macs over fetishistic underwear and, more humorously, Ari's wearing of knickers over her trousers, more reminiscent of the *St Trinian's* films than *A Clockwork Orange*. Siouxsie (alongside Jordan and Soo Catwoman) forefronted taboo elements of Britain in the standard punk style described by Dick Hebdige as "dramatizing what had come to be called "Britain's decline" by constructing a language which was, in contrast to the prevailing rhetoric of the Rock Establishment, unmistakably relevant and down to earth."[27] The separation between active and passive appearance was key to the provocative nature of punk. As Susan Sontag writes: "The difference... between "style" and "stylization" might be analogous to the difference between will and willfulness."[28] There was *force* in Siouxsie's sexualized attire; it actively served to deliver her and her band's messages of discontent and subversion. This street-camp was often misread simply because members of the public could not, or refused to, read its ironic message.

Straight pornography itself was disrupted by the artists/musician Linder Sterling, whose decoupage style became part of the Manchester record label New Hormones' identity.[29] Linder describes taking her completed images, culled from a combination of soft porn magazines (such as Playboy and Fiesta), and home-ware catalogues, to Xerox to be photocopied, only to have the staff refuse because they did not approve; yet on their wall, they were displaying photographs of topless women from *The Sun* newspaper. Even left wing printers objected to her work.[30] Later, when Manchester's Hacienda Club opened in 1982, Linder was disturbed by "too many nights... with its repetitive reels of pornography presiding over the dance floor. Pornography can never be casual and without consequence, at least not in my world."[31] Using thrown away meat from restaurants, she sewed chicken pieces on to black net to make a dress,[32] with a chicken-claw hairdo and a black dildo under her skirt. As she sang with her band Ludus, two friends, Liz Naylor and Cath Carroll, distributed "chicken innards wrapped in pornography" to the audience. This was an overt disruption to the masculine "cool" of the Hacienda and was deeply objected to by the owner of the club, Tony Wilson; it was the last performance that Ludus did there. Liz herself had formed a punk band with two other women and describes the ethos of the scene: "It was just an experience and we were *there*... Our band was there to annoy people, which is why we called ourselves The Gay Animals and were overtly lesbian, or queer."[33]

The desire to "annoy people" was typical of the oppositional nature of punk; many were against monetization of their subculture and felt betrayed when The Sex Pistols and The Clash signed to major labels. At the time, the sense of having "no future" was palpable; the collapse of apparently simple everyday services like refuse collection, ambulance provision, and other frameworks of civilized life, combined with accelerating inflation, meant that they were driven by a sense of desperation and a need to occupy their waking hours with constant subversive activity. Even the weather seemed to reflect the sense of impending doom that the backwards-running clock at punk shop *Seditionaries* and the Sex Pistols' "No Future" slogan, appeared to herald. In 1976, there was a summer heat wave that lasted for months, bringing severe drought to the UK. An "end-times" mentality contributed to punks' disengagement from the established rules of the mainstream music industry, whose more escapist product spoke an entirely different, escapist language.

To summarize, in contrast to the superficially subversive approach of glam rock, punk rock appeared more active, with disruptive content that provided meaning and agency to its participants. Yet glam, while not representing women as creative protagonists, *had* encouraged the questioning of the status quo by young women of that generation. The femininity of male rock stars like Marc Bolan and David Bowie was cited by Viv Albertine as a turning point, because, as she said,

> I, like very many young girls, [was] drawn to very female-ish boys; you don't get drawn to hairy he-men. You want control. Your sexuality is halfway between boy/girl anyway... I realized they were all girly boys. Marc Bolan wore girl's shoes, Bowie was feminine... It was quite exciting really; you could almost be kissing a girl. I used to kiss the posters. But there were no girls that turned me on until Patti Smith.[34]

Gender redefinition in the music of punk: "I never felt that I was going to turn into a lady"[35]

Punk music itself avoided lyrical cliché and he/she lyrics,[36] preferring to critique advertising (X-Ray Spex, *My Mind Is Like a Plastic Bag*), dramatize mundane locations (The Raincoats, *Fairytale in the Supermarket*) or describe the everyday minor criminal activities that were part of survival (The Slits, *Shoplifting*). It was neither essential nor desirable to relegate oneself lyrically to the role of "she" in binary opposition to the heroic "he". For women performers, this in itself was a liberation from gender tyranny. Even romantic feelings could be disconnected from an imagined recipient of love, for instance, in The Raincoats' song *In Love*, which "never discusses an object of desire."[37] This refusal of normal gendered dialogue in songs was another manifestation of détournement in punk, supported by the fact that vocal delivery was also reinvented. Different female vocal styles developed under the umbrella of punk, none of them "singerly." Often, the singing style was declamatory (Poly, Siouxsie), rejecting overt sexuality and femininity, preferring to deliver the message (usually angry), rather than being aesthetically pleasing. The closest precedents were female rockers like Janis Joplin. John Shepherd had found Joplin's "stridency" and "total closure" uncomfortable to listen to, and there is a similarity to be found in the declamatory style of women punks.[38] He compares Joplin to early blues singers such as Memphis Minnie, who were empowered by the fact that in large urban areas in the US, it was they, rather than their male counterparts, who were likely to be able to find work. Shepherd links this comparative power to their use of their "hard vocal tones."[39] Ironically, this tallies with the equality conferred by equal unemployment for women and men in the 1970s. Without traditional roles in the workplace, there was a shift in perception of traditional roles *outside* it.

Not all vocal tones were strident and hard; some singers sounded boyish rather than bratty or declamatory, and these boy-voices added to the disruption of gender perception, resisting both the post-adolescent sexualized tones of many chart acts at the time and the rock-male-identifying stridency of artists such as Suzy Quatro (who we will return to later). The Slits, The Raincoats and The Mo-Dettes used these more androgynous, pre-adolescent styles of singing in order to prioritize the lyrical message, disrupting established aesthetic values that would encourage them to be categorized and thus recuperated. The effect of the vocal style of The Slits' song *Typical Girls* is of being "sung at" (rather than "sung to") by stroppy teenagers in a deliberately amateur and unpretentious style.[40]

The simultaneous withdrawal of overt sexualization from both lyrics and vocal timbres and the creation of alternative ways of sounding pulled the women performers into gender neutral territory, which was an entirely new female aesthetic zone that had not previously been explored by British popular music. As Angela McRobbie observed, the UK music industry habitually disempowered its female performers by turning them into "family entertainers" and "charming hostesses."[41] Siouxsie had set the tone for resistance to this hegemonic channeling of femininity when she appeared alongside the Sex Pistols on Bill Grundy's ITV show in 1976, and the sheer antagonism of the women punk bands shut them out of mainstream culture even when they later tried to engage with it. The Slits wanted to appear on a children's TV show called *Tiswas* which was supposedly subversive and anarchic, but they were blocked from mainstream TV and radio by fearful male gatekeepers. It was only DJ John Peel who would give them an outlet in the UK.[42]

"Nursery rhyme gothic"[43]: finding a noise

Opposition by women from within the opposition that was already being played out in punk meant that for women musicians looking at mainstream rock from the outside, "oedipal frisson"[44] in lyrics and bodily presentation was of no relevance. Detached from familial constraints, they were reinventing themselves using a palette of different moods, attitudes, subversions, and noises. Often, despite the use of rock instruments, the music was not typically rock in style. Their "not-rock" experimented with the sounds of their instruments in a song format that bypassed simple binary opposition to rock. Even those who successfully made music that *could* be read as part of the general flow of punk rock music (for instance Siouxsie and The Banshees and The Au Pairs) had a critical approach to the canon. The Au Pairs, more overtly political than The Banshees, expressed concern with the retrogressive names of the male punk bands, deliberately resisting gender assumptions in their own choice of nomenclature. Guitarist and singer Lesley commented:

> The Stranglers, the Sex Pistols... that's menacing! Where did these names come from? It's still steeped in Hell's Angels male pathology. In a sense it's a political statement in itself. Just choosing a name like [the Au Pairs]... if it has any connotations it has very neutral connotations that are completely neutral from a gender, sexuality, color, or nationality [point of view].[45]

The female punk musicians that I interviewed cited many different role models, including men, and it was difficult to find a common thread between them. Some cited bass-playing Suzi Quatro as an influence. She had charted in the mid-1970s, although she did not write her own songs. Quatro wore a black leather jacket, normally associated with male rockers, on the BBC's *Top of the Pops*, played a bass guitar, hollered at the top of her voice, and had a defiant persona. She was unusual for her time because many female musicians on the show were either acoustic-guitar-toting Joni Mitchell sound-alikes, or piano-playing, and obviously classically trained, chanteuses. Many of her performances involved what Philip Auslander describes as "dual signification" where she sang cover versions previously delivered by a male to a female, without changing the gender of the lyrics.[46]

Issues raised by Quatro's "paradoxical position"[47] of being a *female* cock rocker were later echoed in Patti Smith's cover of the song *Gloria* in 1975, and The Raincoats' cover version of *Lola* in 1979. The Raincoats' music and vocals were more "grown up" than that of The Slits, though definitely not sonically "maternal":[48] they still embraced untrained-sounding singing and shared lead vocals, so that the tradition of having a diva-like front person was also disrupted. Caroline O'Meara compares the "vocal instability" of Ana Da Silva's singing style in the Raincoats' song *Fairytale in the Supermarket* to Johnny Rotten's phrase endings and accentuation of "important words" but she "diffuses [the technique], making it the primary mode of signification... Da Silva's punchy slides and her inexpert vocal technique fractures the musical surface, drawing the listener in without providing an opportunity for identification."[49]

Lola was originally written by Ray Davies and released by his band The Kinks in 1970. The act of covering it was effectively a double détournement. The woman described by the narrator in the song, who "talked like a woman and walked like a man" is a transgender woman encountered by a straight man. The Raincoats' version, performed by a female band that deliberately resisted gender categorization, reiterated the disruptive nature of the song that had led to the original being banned by some mainstream radio stations, with an additional layer of subversion.[50] As Gina Birch, founder member of the band, says:

> Ana [co-singer, co-guitarist] was interested in the idea of gender being confused, and not being labeled specifically but everything kind of being back to front and upside down and not necessarily what it seems. It seemed interesting for a female to do a song about a male being female, just the whole thing of subverting the subversion, turning it all upside down and shaking it up.[51]

This is a perfect example of punk's recuperation of mainstream culture. By pulling what had been a chart hit in 1970 into the détournement of punk, The Kinks' gently risqué song was redefined and redirected. This was a different type of commentary on mainstream pop music than Siouxsie's camp dramatization. The Raincoats were adopting a similar attitude to Patti Smith, who was "distancing the feminine through an assumed persona that denaturalized sexual difference."[52] *Lola* was a case of the rock establishment being parodied through its *own* language, and the song actually dramatized The Raincoats' opposition to the assumptions of rock music that had previously spoken to adolescent males, creating male-defined territory that was set against women and girls. As Gina remembers, "I think one of the things I hated about being a teenager were these self-assured, arrogant boys. I found the kind of boy culture thing, the rock bands, so hideous, so alienating."[53] In addition, by "'dragging' the song, performing words originally intended for the opposite sex, thus indicating a sexual identity as *anders* (other) or gay [and] using certain vocal mannerisms such as feminization of expression, shifting the emphasis from straight to gay," The Raincoats are participating in a European tradition of "Queering the Song" that has a history rooted in German cabaret in the 1930s.[54]

Auslander applied Simon Reynolds and Joy Press' phrase, "female machismo,"[55] to Quatro's persona, yet not all punk women were "one of the boys." They just weren't "Typical Girls" (the title of the Slits' song was a common insult targeted at girls in the 1970s). They were not competing against male punks in an attempt to "beat them at their own game" in the way that Quatro competed with male rockers,[56] but were *joining* them in their game, parodying the music industry definition of femininity and the female, thus foregrounding a gender element in punk's subversion. The cover of *Lola* has had no "sex change operation"[57] but instead is de-gendered by the lack of acting, by the authenticity of The Raincoats' decidedly natural and non-showbiz personae.

Reggae

Reggae was one of the most potentially surprising influences on all-female, or predominantly female, punk bands. This was an interesting phenomenon, because roots reggae in particular was music affiliated with Rastafarianism, a belief system that discouraged female freedom and autonomy. This stylistic influence could be interpreted as an act of active cultural appropriation, though at the time reggae was "in the air," in particular in west London where many of the bands lived and played. DJs such as Don Letts, and BBC Radio 1's John Peel also positively promoted reggae.[58]

Gina Birch, Tessa Pollitt, and Jane Woodgate (from The Mo-dettes) had all learned to play the bass, facilitated by listening to dub reggae's clarity of production, and The Slits' album *Cut* was produced by reggae musician Dennis Bovell. The all-female ska-punk band The Bodysnatchers played covers in their live set to augment their own compositions. Journalist Adrian Thrills addressed the misogynistic lyrics of the genre with the band in an interview. Their response is interesting:

> Stella: "The links we do have with ska music are through the things in it that we can use to our advantage. It's the music that we are using, not the lyrics. I mean stuff like Prince Buster's 'Ten Commandments' is so ridiculously sexist that it's hysterical. It must be tongue-in cheek."

Lead singer Rhoda Dakar goes on to dispute the latter remark, probably correctly.[59] The Bodysnatchers tried to recuperate ska by selectively ignoring the sexism of the lyrics. The recuperation of misogyny, however, is a much larger project than punk (or any of its offshoots) could take on. Although white female punk and ska musicians felt "an affinity," as Tessa Pollitt told me, with the oppression of black reggae artists, this affinity was only very occasionally reciprocated;[60] working within existing male-coded music genres started a musical conversation with the overarching gender politics within those genres, but this was a complex and ultimately unresolved communication.

Reactions

It was the violent and spectacular features of punk that were focused on by the British tabloid press, though the thriving fanzine culture of the moment took a more measured approach. In the mainstream music press, the punk generation of male rock journalists rarely knew how to write about the determined individualism of female punk musicians. Every musician "played themselves" differently, transcending the categorizations that pre-punk music had depended upon. Lora Logic, the original saxophone player with X-Ray Spex, explained: "I felt to be a woman on stage without neces-sarily having a sexual stance definitely felt different, and it *was* different, and it was a conscious image projection."[61] The BBC DJ John Peel, who boosted the careers of many of the punk bands through his late night Radio 1 show, described his feelings on meeting The Slits:

> They were quite frightening because… I was going to say they were like blokes, but obviously they weren't like blokes, but they weren't like women either, at least not women as I'd understood them up to that moment. They were just so kind of *direct*, and not flirtatious, not play-ing up to being feminine, they were just themselves…[62]

Projecting the state of *being* was an integral part of the performance of these women; this is what all of the female punk bands had in common, however their gender was (or was not) articulated. The Mo-Dettes,[63] while denying the label "women in rock" and embracing femininity, felt that being fem-inine was their right; their guitarist Kate Korris said: "When we started people used to say, 'You're too feminine, you ought to be more butch, then people won't accuse you of being girly.' But as far as I'm concerned, if I have to do that to get past the fact that I'm a girl then there's no point." In hav-ing the potentiality to opt out of typical womanhood, and by making this opt-out knowing and deliberate, they were "doing" their bodies[64] in a very different way.

Generally, women journalists understood what was happening, but writ-ing by male journalists at the time was often crude and misogynistic, demon-strating unease that these female performers were not performing *for them* and their male readers, or trying to impress them. The more sympathetic US critic Greil Marcus wrote of the collective nature of The Raincoats: "There's something wonderfully anonymous about these women and their music: as four women appearing as nothing but themselves, they demystify each other";[65] they are

> …not exactly singing "as themselves," not in the way rock'n'roll has led us to understand the idea. They are not, as would Joni Mitchell or John Lennon, singing to refine an individual sensibility or to project a per-sonality or a persona onto the world. Rather, they are singing as factors in the situations they are trying to construct.[66]

As O'Meara notes, male band members in The Raincoats were the ones written out of history, in a reversal of the norm,[67] yet "… the presence of male musicians in The Raincoats may have seemed that much more 'nor-mal' to the almost exclusively male writers" of the rock press. This possibly insulated them against some of the anger directed at other bands, particularly The Slits, until they too included men in their line-up.

The women musicians' differences *from each other* were highlighted in 1980 Deanne Pearson's *New Musical Express* article "Women in Rock," where members of The Raincoats, The Passions and The Au Pairs were gathered to talk about themselves and their relationship to feminism (Viv Albertine and The Mo-Dettes were interviewed separately). Again, the rejection of categorization is brought to the forefront, with only Barbara Grogan from The Passions defining herself as a feminist. Shepherding all the groups together under the banner of feminism must have seemed like an effective press strategy for bringing the situation back under their control, but it was the co-option of reggae that the white, male rock critics found hardest to comprehend. Some of the reviews of The Slits were merciless in their contempt. Ian Penman in particular refers to "flickety flak guitars and servant's bass... Ari's vintage whine... bullshitting, imitating West Indian religions and patois, and generally being a precious, artsy fartsy pain in the pants."[68]

The end

According to Debord, "*Détournement...* occurs within a type of communication aware of its inability to enshrine any inherent and definitive certainty."[69] For women artists, musicians, and subculturalists in punk, the act of détournement encouraged and articulated resistance through appearance, lyrical approach and sound, not only to the mainstream but also sometimes to each other, for as Butler says:

> ...one ought to consider the futility of a political program which seeks radically to transform the social situation of women without first determining whether the category of woman is socially constructed in such a way that to be a woman is, be definition, to be in an oppressed situation.[70]

Butler's observation explains why so many of the female punk bands rejected the pressure into being co-opted by second-wave feminism and its apparent essentialism, while simultaneously rejecting the cock rock stance of male punk music. In the refusal of constructed gender, both feminism and punk became fragile, yet to acknowledge being "the weaker sex" in need of the political community offered by feminism, would not have supported their feelings of individual empowerment and freedom.

After 40 years, the memories of the meaning of punk to women are colored by nostalgia and contemporary readings that ignore some of the most vital social issues that the punk women struggled with. To return to Butler, "performing one's gender wrong initiates a set of punishments both obvious and indirect, and performing it well provides the reassurance that there is an essentialism of gender identity after all."[71] The punishments meted out to the women in my original study were severe. In addition to other routine violence, I later found out about five rapes that had not been reported at the time of the interviews. Even though "[p]opular music performances are always double-coded with respect to gender identity and sexuality since they refer both to general social codes and to genre-specific codes that signify within particular musical and cultural categories,"[72] Auslander is skeptical of popular culture's ability to "undermine deep-seated social norms" and this brutality is testament to that.

The major recuperation of punk's message of individual autonomy for women by Madonna, who reintroduced sexuality-as-power to the world of popular music in the 1980s,[73] had a negative impact on the ability of women's punk bands to develop and survive. Gender fluidity once more became the prerogative of male pop stars as New Romanticism foregrounded male femininity in artists such as Boy George, who became a queer role model for the next generation, with the lone female androgynous figure of Annie Lennox appearing in a suit in 1983 for the video of the Eurhythmics' song *Sweet Dreams Are Made of This*. Ironically, it was the female punk bands that had provided the bridge between glam rock and New Romanticism; Boy George's dreadlocks echoed Ari's, and the reggae influence on Culture Club is unmistakable, yet more pleasing to the "mainstream ear" in the longer term than any music made by the bands discussed in this chapter.

The feminist writer Catherine MacKinnon had, after the 1970s,

> imagined that feminists would retheorize life in the concrete rather than spend the next three decades on metatheory, talking *about* theory, rehashing over and over in this disconnected way how theory should be done, leaving women's lives twisting in the wind.[74]

Yet as well as inspiring behaviors and affirming différance, the cultural legacy of punk has created iconic figures. Withers cites Rachael House's *Feminist Disco* installation, created in 2011 as a series of "islands" inhabited by statuettes of The Slits, Jayne County, and Poly Styrene.[75] This installation illustrates what should not be forgotten about punk, and female punk in particular: it's humor. And for queer women, punk music provides a rich source of affirmation, in spite of and because of its marginal nature; from the turbulent challenging of gender roles in the 1970s onwards when it demonstrated

> the importance of queering to the politics of popular music and the particular "pull" it exerts on both the individual and collective imagination. This has largely depended on the queer audience being able to discern sympathetic attributes in periods when homosexuality remained for the most part legally and socially proscribed...[76]

Notes

1 From Guy Debord, The Society of the Spectacle (New York: Zone Books, 1995), 144–145. The Situationist International was a group of anti-capitalist artists, writers and political activists. The movement was active between 1957 and 1972, and critiqued accepted political doctrines and social practices, often by parodying the acceptance of existing social, political, and cultural structures.

2 See for instance, Roland Barthes, *Image, Music, Text* (London: Fontana, 1977), 165–169, and Michel Foucault, *Archaeology of Knowledge* (London and New York: Routledge, 1989).

3 This had previously been acted out and chronicled as and alternative bedroom culture subservient to the activities of their male counterparts, see Angela McRobbie, *Feminism and Youth Culture* (Basingstoke: MacMillan, 1991, 2000).

4 An archive of this music can be found at http://womensliberationmusicarchive. co.uk.

5 See Dick Hebdige, *Subculture: The Meaning of Style* (London and New York: Routledge, 1979).

6 See Stan Cohen, *Folk Devils and Moral Panics: The Creation of the Mods and Rockers* (Oxford: Martin Robertson, 1993).

7 See Paul Willis, *Profane Culture* (London and Boston: Routledge and Keegan Paul, 1978).

8 See Sheila Whiteley, *The Space Between the Notes* (London and New York: Routledge, 1992).

9 http://hansard.millbanksystems.com/commons/1976/jul/20/unemployment.

10 John Shepherd, *Music As Social Text* (London: Polity, 1991), 157.

11 See Lucy O'Brien, "The Woman Punk Made Me," in *Punk Rock: So What? The Cultural Legacy of Punk*, ed. Roger Sabin (London and New York: Routledge, 1999), 186–189.

12 Jon Savage, *England's Dreaming: Sex Pistols and Punk Rock* (London: Faber and Faber, 1991), 418.

13 Judith Halberstam, "What's That Smell? Queer Temporalities and Subcultural Lives," in *Queering the Popular Pitch*, eds. Sheila Whiteley and Jennifer Rycenga (New York and Abingdon: Routledge 2006), 3.

14 Vi died in January 2016.

15 Susan Sontag, *A Susan Sontag Reader* (Harmondsworth: Penguin Books, 1982), 112.

16 ITV, first broadcast February 1976.

17 Judith Butler, "Performative Acts and Gender Constitution: An Essay in Phenomenology and Feminist Theory," *Theatre Journal* 40, no. 4 (December 1985), 519–531, 519.

18 Op.cit. Halberstam, 269.

19 Hebdige describes androgynous Bowie clones in Coventry in the early 1970s. According to Simon Frith, these young people were called "Bowie Boys" and even had their own fanzine. The author came across similar young people in a bar in Wakefield, although several of the "boys" were in fact young women dressed in drag who wore trousers and braces (suspenders); all had the distinctive shock of red spiky hair that Bowie sported at the time.

   The author visited a pub in 1975 in a small Yorkshire town far from large metropolitan influences and came upon a room full of young men and women dressed as David Bowie circa 1975. Hebdige Dick "Subculture: The Meaning of Style" (London and New York: Routledge, 1979), 60.

20 Ibid., 11.

21 Sarah Maitland, *Vesta Tilley* (London: Virago, 1986), 111–114.

22 Ibid., 121

23 Op. cit. Butler, 527.
24 See Stephen Colegrave and Chris Sullivan, *Punk: A Life Apart* (London: Cassell, 2001).
25 Dave Laing, *One Chord Wonders: Power and Meaning in Punk Rock* (Oakland: PM Press, 2015), 116.
26 Ibid., 117.
27 Op. cit. Hebdige, 87.
28 Op. cit. Sontag, 153.
29 See for instance the sleeve of the Buzzcocks' 1977 single *Orgasm Addict*, which featured a naked woman's body with smiling mouths replacing her nipples, and an iron replacing her head.
30 Talk at The Zabludowicz Collection, London, 7th February 2016.
31 By email, from interview for Tate Magazine and Uncut, 1/05/2002.
32 This was probably an influence on Lady Gaga's meat dress, 2010.
33 Interview with author 7/9/2000.
34 Interview with author, 26/3/2010. Both Patti Smith and the budding guitarist Chrissie Hynde of The Pretenders were also inspirational figures for Viv, who although she admired Suzi Quatro, was fully aware that she was under the song-writing and production control of Chinn and Chapman.
35 Interview with author 23/6/2000.
36 Op. cit. Laing, 87–92.
37 Caroline O'Meara (2003) "The Raincoats: Breaking down Punk Rock's Masculinities," in *Popular Music*, 22, no. 3 (Cambridge University Press, 2003), 299–313, 309.
38 He applies Frith and McRobbie's description of this type of singing style as "one of the boys," from Simon Frith and Angela McRobbie, (1979) "Rock and Sexuality" in *Screen Education*, no.29: 3–19: 9, in op. cit. Shepherd, 171.
39 Citing Paul Oliver, *The Story of the Blues* (London: Barrie and Jenkins, 1979), 9.
40 Op. cit., Shepherd.
41 Angela McRobbie, *Feminism and Youth Culture* (Basingstoke: MacMillan, 2000), 143.
42 Helen L. Reddington, The Lost Women of Rock Music: Female Musicians of the Punk Era (Sheffield: Equinox, 2012), 180.
43 Title of a review by Paul Morley of *Cut* by The Slits and *Join Hands* by Siouxsie and the Banshees, NME, 1/09/97, 27.
44 Richard Middleton, "Mum's the Word: Men's Singing and Maternal Law," in *Oh Boy! Masculinities and Popular Music*, ed. Freya Jarman-Ivens (New York and Abingdon: Routledge, 2007), 111.
45 Interview with author 30/7/2010.
46 Philip Auslander, "I Wanna Be Your Man: Suzi Quatro's Musical Androgyny," *Popular Music* 23 no. 1 (Cambridge University Press, 2004), 1–16, www.jstor.org/stable/3877622, 11.
47 Ibid., 7.
48 Ibid.
49 Op.cit. O'Meara 308.
50 According to Gina Birch, Davies later remarked that the band had taken a hit and made it into an album track, rather than taking an album track and making it into a hit; he was not impressed by their cover version (personal communication, 18/02/2016).
51 Interview with author 23/6/2000.
52 Op. cit. Whiteley, 2006, 256.
53 Interview with author 23/6/2000.
54 Whiteley and Rycenga citing Anno Mungen ""Anders als die Anderen," or Queering the Song: construction and representation of homosexuality in German

cabaret song recordings before 1933" in *Queering the Popular Pitch*, eds. Sheila Whiteley and Jennifer Rycenga (New York and Abingdon: Routledge, 2006). Mungen extracts a line from one of the songs: "*Wir sind nun einmal anders als die anderen* (We are in fact other than the others" (ibid.).
55 Simon Reynolds and Joy Press, *The Sex Revolts* (London: Serpent's Tail, 1995).
56 Op. cit. Auslander, 9.
57 Ibid., 10.
58 Peel was allowed to play any music so long as it was not commercial; he was the justification for the BBC's radio license, which forbade commercialization of any kind. His blend of punk, reggae, experimental and folk music earned him a large, loyal national following, and introduced both artists and their audiences to marginal music forms that they might not otherwise have heard.
59 Adrian "Rude Girls and Dirty Phone Calls," interview with Adrian Thrills in the NME, 26/01/1980 19.
60 Interview with author, 30/1/2006.
61 Interview with author 18/10/2001.
62 Interview with author, 20/10/2001.
63 The Mo-Dettes played traditional rock instruments apart from their singer, Ramona, and stressed their musicianship in interviews.
64 Op. cit. Butler, 521.
65 Greil Marcus, *Ranters and Crowd Pleasers: Punk in Pop Music 1977–92* (New York and London: Doubleday, 1993), 113.
66 Op. cit. Marcus, 178.
67 Op. cit. O'Meara, 306.
68 Ian Penman, Review of The Slits: *In the Beginning there was rhythm*/The Pop Group *Where There's a Will There's a Way* (Rough Trade) in The New Muscal Express, 15th March 1980, 21.
69 Guy Debord, *The Society of the Spectacle* (New York: Zone Books, 1994), 146.
70 Op. cit. Butler, 523.
71 Ibid., 528.
72 Op. cit. Auslander, 6.
73 Madonna had been at The Slits gigs in New York, but has never acknowledged their influence on her style and attitude.
74 Catherine MacKinnon.
75 Op. cit Withers, 80.
76 Op. cit. Whiteley and Rycenga, xiv.

Bibliography

Albertine, Viv. *Clothes, Music, Boys.* London: Faber, 2014.
Auslander, Philip. 2004. "I Wanna Be Your Man: Suzi Quatro's Musical Androgyny," *Popular Music* 23 (2000): 1–16. www.jstor.org/stable/3877622. Accessed March 03, 2016.
Barthes, Roland. *Image Music Text.* London: Fontana, 1977.
Butler, Judith. "Performative Acts and Gender Constitution: An Essay in Phenomenology and Feminist Theory," *Theatre Journal* 40, no. 4 (December 1985): 519–531.
Colegrave, Stephen, and Chris Sullivan. *Punk: A Life Apart.* London: Cassell, 2001.
Cohen, Stanley. *Folk Devils and Moral Panics: The Creation of the Mods and Rockers.* Oxford: Martin Robertson, 1993.
Debord, Guy. *The Society of the Spectacle.* New York: Zone Books, 1995.
Frith, Simon, and Angela McRobbie. "Rock and Sexuality," *Screen Education* 29 (1979): 3–19.

Halberstam, Judith. *Female Masculinity.* Durham, NC and London: Duke University Press, 1998.

Halberstam, Judith. "What's That Smell? Queer Temporalities and Subcultural Lives." In *Queering the Popular Pitch,* edited by Sheila Whiteley and Jennifer Rycenga, 3–25. New York and Abingdon: Routledge, 2006.

Heath, Joseph and Andrew Potter, *The Rebel Sell. How the Counterculture Became Consumer Culture.* Chichester, West Sussex: Capstone, 2005.

Hebdige, Dick. *Subculture: The Meaning of Style.* London and New York: Routledge, 1979.

Jarman-Ivens, Freya. *Oh Boy! Masculinities and Popular Music.* New York and Abingdon: Routledge, 2007.

Laing, Dave. *One Chord Wonders: Power and Meaning in Punk Rock.* Oakland: PM Press, 2015.

Mackinnon, Catherine A. *Points against Postmodernism,* 75 Chi.-Kent. L. Rev. 687 (2000). Available at: http://scholarship.kentlaw.iit.edu/cklawreview/vol75/iss3/5, Accessed March 03, 2016.

Maitland, Sarah. *Vesta Tilley.* London: Virago, 1986.

Marcus, Greil. *Ranters and Crowd Pleasers: Punk in Pop Music 1977–92.* New York and London: Doubleday, 1993.

McRobbie, Angela. *Feminism and Youth Culture.* Basingstoke: MacMillan, 2000.

Middleton, Richard (2007) "Mum's the Word: Men's Singing and Maternal Law." In *Oh Boy! Masculinities and Popular Music,* edited by Freya Jarman-Ivens. New York and Abingdon: Routledge, 2007.

Mungen, Anno (2006) ""Anders als die Anderen," or Queering the Song: Construction and Representation of Homosexuality in German Cabaret Song Recordings before 1933." In *Queering the Popular Pitch,* edited by Sheila Whiteley and Jennifer Rycenga, 67–80. New York and Abingdon: Routledge, 2006.

O'Brien, Lucy. "The Woman Punk Made Me." In *Punk Rock: So What? The Cultural Legacy of Punk,* edited by Roger Sabin, 186–198. London and New York: Routledge, 1999.

O'Meara, Caroline. "The Raincoats: Breaking down Punk Rock's Masculinities," *Popular Music,* 22, no. 3 (2003): 299–313.

Oliiver, Paul. *The Story of the Blues.* London: Barrie and Jenkins, 1979.

Pearson, Deanne. "Women in Rock," *New Musical Express,* 29th March 1980, pp. 27–31.

Reddington, Helen. *The Lost Women of Rock Music: Female Musicians of the Punk Era.* Sheffield: Equinox, 2012.

Reynolds, Simon, and Joy Press. *The Sex Revolts.* London: Serpent's Tail, 1985.

Robinson, Emily. "Touching the Void: Affective History and the Impossible," *Rethinking History* 14, no. 4 (2010): 503–520.

Sabin, Roger. ed. *Punk Rock: So What? The Cultural Legacy of Punk.* London and New York: Routledge, 1999.

Savage, Jon. *England's Dreaming: Sex Pistols and Punk Rock.* London: Faber and Faber, 1991.

Shepherd, John. *Music as Social Text.* London: Polity, 1991.

Susan Sontag. *A Susan Sontag Reader.* Harmondsworth: Penguin Books, 1982.

Thornton, Sara. *Club Cultures: Music, Media and Subcultural Capital.* London: Polity, 1995.

Whiteley, Sheila. *The Space between the Notes.* London and Boston: Routledge, 1992.

Whiteley, Sheila. "Popular Music and the Dynamics of Desire." In *Queering the Popular Pitch*, edited by Sheila Whiteley and Jennifer Rycenga, 249–262. New York and Abingdon: Routledge, 2006.

Whiteley, Sheila, and Jennifer Rycenga eds. *Queering the Popular Pitch.* New York and Abingdon: Routledge, 2006.

Willis, Paul. *Profane Culture.* London and Boston: Routledge and Keegan Paul, 1978.

Withers, Deborah. *Feminism, Digital Culture and the Politics of Transmission: Theory, Practice and Cultural Heritage.* London and New York: Rowman and Littlefield, 2015.

Internet

http://womensliberationmusicarchive.co.uk, Accessed March 22, 2016.

http://hansard.millbanksystems.com/commons/1976/jul/20/unemployment, Accessed March 22, 2016.

4 Ambiguities of S/M and goth cultures' sex/gender identity politics

Carol Siegel

Gender ambiguity is one of the most important features of goth style, as types of acceptable dress, makeup, and hair style can be, and usually are, the same for both male and female goths. Both typically wear makeup, often including black eyeliner and nail polish, frequently wear skirts and lacy blouses, and often wear fishnet hose and possibly high-heeled boots. Hairstyles are usually similar, loosely arranged teased locks, dreads, and side shaving are popular, with black or platinum dyes favored. Moreover, in goth's insistence on the sorts of emotionality culturally associated with femininity regardless of the performers' biological sex, goth music exemplifies ambiguous representation of gender identity. Often an observer, even one within the goth community, cannot distinguish between male and female participants in the culture, as virtually all the academic participant observers involved with goth note. Clearly such ambiguity, in relation to a mainstream culture which continues to maintain hard boundaries between masculinity and femininity, is subversive. But as many have remarked, goth's very preference for femininity, while possibly supportive of feminist efforts to revalue the female in a world that overvalues the male, nonetheless to some extent inevitably reinscribes binary gender difference. Consequently, the ambiguities of goth gender identity politics have received so much scholarly attention that one might well ask, what more is there to say about ambiguities of sex/gender politics in goth? As the title of this essay reflects, the sex side of the sex/gender dyad is what is left to talk about, and when sadomasochism (S/M) is included in the discussion, that talk becomes especially pertinent to understanding goth's deliberate and inadvertent resistance to gender norms.

My own introduction to goth came via my work as a graduate teaching assistant and my personal adventures as a live music enthusiast in San Francisco in the late 1970s and early 1980s. Initially, like many San Franciscans who supported The City's public sex culture, I was annoyed by the appropriation by punks and goths of objects that functioned as S/M preference signifiers. Our annoyance stemmed from the way these appropriations undercut the efforts of members of a sexual minority that was despised and often suppressed to recognize each other without the need for taking the risk of coming out verbally. For instance, a person wearing a long chain on the right side of his body would be seen as sexually submissive in S/M play, while one with the chain on the left would be known to be dominant. I recall seeing an undergraduate in one of my classes wearing a bracelet understood by local S/M communities to convey interest in taking a dominant role in fisting and then learning that she had no idea what her wrist was telling sex culture San Franciscans.

As she and many others told me, this was just a fashion, as was goth, to her. To my mindset, formed in the crucible of battles for sexual freedom, this apolitical position on the issue that meant the most to me was consonant with Malcolm McLaren's appropriation and depoliticization of S/M fetish clothing in his promotion of The Sex Pistols. It meant that while I might enjoy the music, I must consider the culture that surrounded it as just another meaningless fashion show. So I listened to Joy Division, Sisters of Mercy, The Cure, Bauhaus, and other bands associated with goth, without taking much interest in their possible connections to gender or sexual politics.

I became seriously interested in the goth subculture as a route to sex/gender identity formation in 1987 when I began my first tenure line academic job at Loyola, New Orleans. A number of my students there identified as goths, and I liked their music and their fashions, but more I liked their politics, their involvement in feminism and advocacy for gay and transsexual rights, and most of all I liked that they saw sexual practices as inherently political. I will never forget arguing the department chair into letting me offer a class on feminist theory and, after he predicted no one would sign up, being astounded to walk in the first day and see more than three times as many students as the room could seat standing in the classroom in hopes of being admitted to the already over-enrolled class. Many were goth.

I attribute the higher consciousness of sex/gender issues in second wave goths, like these students, partially to a general cultural shift as feminist critiques of patriarchal ways of thinking were increasingly popularized, but largely to the changes in attitudes about sexuality brought about by the AIDS pandemic. As conservatives fought to suppress sexual revolutionary freedoms and insisted that abstinence before marriage and strict chastity after were the only ways to avoid a horrible death, their sex radical opposition invited the young to explore alternative sexual practices that cannot spread STDs (sexually transmitted diseases), such as BDSM (amalgam of B/D [bondage and discipline], D/S [dominance and submission], S/M [sadism and masochism]), which can, but need not include penetration or exchange of bodily fluids. The young second wave goths I knew were enthusiastic about trying these practices and saw their sexual experimentations as a form of political resistance to the Southern religious conservative world around them. So I continued to enjoy goth music, and the closely related Industrial music which characteristically drew on S/M imagery even more, but now with an eye to their oppositional sexual politics.

In the early 1990s when I moved to Portland, Oregon and was combining pleasure and scholarship by attending music performances every week in clubs and having informal interview conversations with dozens of self-identified members of music cultures as part of researching my book *New Millennial Sexstyles*, goths were the group that stood out the most to me. Goth-Industrial subcultures became one of the foci of my study of how emergent youth cultures organized around musical tastes reflected and contributed to changes in more general American cultural understandings of gender, sexuality, and feminism. *New Millennial Sexstyles* celebrates these subcultures for their disruption of traditional gender scripts.

Goths stood out to me because the specific ways their music culture used S/M seemed to me especially resistant of mainstream gender scripts. As I and many others have argued for decades now, S/M troubles traditional heterosexual gender categories not only because it stresses the constructed and performative aspects of sexual dominance and submission, traditionally seen as having a biologically predetermined correspondence respectively to maleness and femaleness, but because it calls into question what submissiveness actually means, since most who have any experience of consensual S/M practice (active or observational) agree that the masochist controls the scene. Moreover, as Foucault pointed out, physically pleasurable new forms of sexual expression represent effective bodily resistance to the political management of sexuality, and S/M due to its reliance on gadgets and toys and inventiveness with respect to modes of sensation seeking, launches many new sexual expressions. As the ascendance of abstinence culture caused other Americans to debate whether unmarried young people should have sex lives at all, and focus shifted in popular culture from celebration of sexual experimentalism to praise of virginity, goths and S/M practitioners looked different from and therefore resistant towards the new norm.

It was certainly that way for many after the Columbine tragedy that occurred on April 20, 1999. The actions of the shooters were immediately blamed on the school's goth clique, although numerous subsequent reports established that the shooters not only did not belong to the clique, they disliked and were disliked by its members. However, American secondary schools and law enforcement agencies continued, for several years, to treat goths with great suspicion, as potential mass murderers. Under siege from school authorities who prohibited them from wearing their fashions to school and, often, subjected them to hostile scrutiny, numerous young goths I knew appealed to me to defend them.

And when a goth attending a public reading from *New Millennial Sexstyles* begged me to write a book defending goths, I took up the challenge and wrote *Goth's Dark Empire*. I anticipated being criticized for writing from outside the goth culture, since I enjoyed the music, literature, and fashions most of my interview subjects deemed goth but did not myself identify as a goth. And while I was annoyed by negative online reviews in which goths attacked the book for not upholding the hierarchical distinctions that some cultural insiders made between bands, I was not surprised. After all most adolescents are outraged to hear some adult go on about the music they consider their own without recognizing how very much superior musician X is to musician Y, who is only pop and thus not to be taken seriously. Lauren M. E. Goodlad and Michael Bibby make a convincing argument that, at least if we take "countless examples" on the internet as evidence, goths seem particularly invested in establishing "what gothic is and is not."[1]

What did surprise me was the vehemence with which not only nonacademic goths but some goth academics argued against my contention that goth had anything at all to do with sexuality, or if they were willing to consider that sex played some role in goth cultures, that the role it played was in any way resistant to or disruptive of conventional sex/gender roles. Because the concept of subcultures as resistant to the mainstream is often academically debated, it makes sense that some readers of the book would dislike my agreement with Dick Hebdige's controversial view that subcultures inevitably create "semantic disorder: a temporary blockage in the system of representation."[2] Yet the disagreements with my analysis of the cultural work of goth did not center on my view that many goths deliberately disrupted mainstream ideologies generally; they focused on my contention that goth styles—whether deliberately adopted for that reason or not—opposed mainstream cultural constructions of sexuality. After years of being mystified by the vehemence of those who rejected this seemingly not very radical view, I have gradually come to the conclusion that goth's relationship to S/M is indeed the center of the problem, but not exactly in the way the book's detractors—or I—originally thought.

Rethinking the relationship between goth music culture and S/M has brought me to a new understanding of how we might productively reconceptualize resistance to sex/gender norms, not as the creation and performance of difference but as the embracing of ambiguity. In this essay, I will begin by discussing the negative responses to my claims about goth's relation to S/M in *Goth's Dark Empire*. I will elucidate the problematic nature of declaring S/M inevitably resistant by discussing its inherent ambiguousness, exploring how it plays with existent concepts of difference and sameness while at the same time insisting on taxonomies that would seem to work against fluidity of identification. I will then go on to show how goth identities, even when they are not recognizably referencing S/M, on the one hand reinforce traditional views of sex/gender, and on the other so flood them with ambiguities that they become paradoxically legible as resistance.

Given that it was written in defense of goths, the reception of *Goth's Dark Empire* by some goths was not what I expected. I was not surprised to be contacted by goths all over the world who liked the book and felt it well represented their culture. After all, it was informed by notes from my conversations with over a hundred goths and by my participation in many goth events, including musical performances. And I was assisted in my research by Don Anderson, a friend and member of the internationally prominent Black Metal band, Agalloch. Although not a goth himself, Don was very familiar with the goth music scene and contributed a discography to the book. The surprise was the negative response the book received from some Amazon reviewers in the United States and Britain, apparently due to its thesis that the primary reason for the moral panic about goth in America was that goths' tolerance for diverse expressions of sexuality, including homosexuality, bisexuality, and S/M, which directly challenged the abstinence-only education movement that then dominated our schools.

A typical responder has this to say,

> Sometimes goth bands get a little carried away. I am the first one to admit that; I've been in a few in my life. However, this author thinks that she can prove that every major, not-so-major, and obscure goth band in the goth trend does sado-masochism in secret. Everyone. Her list really blew me away.

Interestingly there is no such list in the book, and I never make any such claim anywhere in the book. In fact, the book includes assertions that I have no idea what any band member's private practices are. What then caused such an intense and strange reaction? Looking at the less articulate and more overwrought Amazon UK reviews of the book yields some insight. The angriest response includes these statements, "This book is nothing but a pack of lies and clearly the author knows absolute NOTHING about the goth subculture. I agree with every other reviewer that this woman has never spoken to a real goth in her life." The writer goes on to express the hope that I will be beaten with baseball bats by those she considers the true goths. A number of other reviews reiterate that the book is filled with lies and misrepresentation and attribute this to my not having spoken to "real" goths. Misrepresentation of their culture is the dominant theme in these critiques which often imply or state that the goths I know, and the ones I spoke with at goth events or as a result of their being referred to me by other goths, are not representative or even authentic goths, nor are the people I quote who identify themselves as goths on websites devoted to their culture.

Debates over authenticity are typical of music cultures. One might consider, for comparison, the arguments within hip-hop over whether or not specific artists are or ever were gang members, and thus whether or not their music is a true and authentic representation of the gangster world. Still my book's central claim, that goth culture (not every single goth) is more tolerant of sexual desires and practices demonized by the moralistic than most mainstream Americans seem to be, would not initially appear to be so controversial as to warrant these furious responses. So I set out to try to work out why a book, which I introduce as being meant to defend goths from being blamed for school violence, is so harshly criticized by people who say they are goths. My first conclusion was that these informal reviewers apparently take any suggestion that they might belong to a group that tolerates others' nonmainstream sexuality as an attack on them or at the very least as stigmatizing them by imputing to them nonnormative sexual desires. But on reflection I realized that the specific connection I drew between consensual S/M practice and goth was the source of the problem, as the first review I quote above suggests. Support for that interpretation was also given by Dunja Brill's wrathful characterization of me as "[o]ne of the worst culprits in the uncritical raving about supposed gender subversion in subculture" in *Goth's Dark Empire*.[3] Determined to set the record straight, she proclaims that "What is typically represented in... Goth music acts and magazines reflects a normative Gothic ideal rather than the identities of average Goths."[4] At least here the construction of "real" goths as opposed to the faux goths presumed to have informed my study is replaced with an opposition between "average Goths" and the goths I encountered, who must be considered by Brill extraordinary. But the song remains the same, S/M is sexism "thinly veiled by a rhetoric of subversion and transgression" and—thank heavens!—not anything that the average goth wants to engage in.[5] This absolutist position seems rather strange in that goth and S/M are so frequently linked by their participants in performances, publications, and fashion trends. But it becomes comprehensible when one considers the especially ambiguous relationship of goth to sex/gender identity politics.

Unlike their punk precursors, whose DIY (do-it-yourself) ethic placed them in obvious opposition to consumer capitalism and whose allusions to S/M practice were explicitly linked by many punks to their refusal to accept enslavement to bourgeois or corporate cultures, goths have always been problematic to place on a continuum of resistance to dominant political structures, especially sex/gender systems, as numerous studies reflect. By frequently enacting the entrepreneurial spirit of the age and treating S/M as a source of fashion inspiration, goths are often read as trying to find acceptance within the mainstream rather than intentionally disrupting it, as bringing to ordinary life the sort of minor difference that reenergizes markets and spices up otherwise conventional domestic arrangements without truly changing anything. Where, for example, punks might attempt to subvert economic systems by dressing entirely in clothing gathered from dumpsters, goths produced, sold, and bought carefully created fashions, sometimes starting their own garment businesses. And where punks often contemptuously rejected long term committed relationships, goths welcomed them while also treating male cross-dressing as an attractive addition to courtship. Goodlad and Bibby sum it up thus: "goth is unabashedly consumerist and commodity-oriented," while at the same time goth resists "gender and sexual norms that have upheld capitalism since the eighteenth century" and so presents an ambiguous challenge to consumer capitalism.[6] I will argue here that goth identifications, as articulated through personal stylings, reflect a desire to fit into existing identity categories both inside and outside what is accepted as traditional. But that, just like the S/M practitioners with whom they sometimes overlap and whose public spaces they have sometimes shared, goths cannot avoid causing gender trouble because of the ambiguity of their relation to standard categories of sexual and gender identity.

In the late 1970s, when goth emerged as a subcategory of punk, the relationship between sex and gender in Britain and the US was shifting dramatically, largely due to the development of increasingly better technologies of birth control and the legalization of early term abortion in 1967 in Britain (with the caveat that continuation of the pregnancy would have harmful effects for the physical or mental health of the mother and/or her children) and in 1973 in the US where early term abortion was legalized without legal restriction. Previously, exercising sexual freedom had been primarily the province of men, and only those men who subscribed to the virgin-whore ideology, which justified the abandonment of impregnated women to whom one was not married as a strategy to escape marital entrapment to a bad woman. After the changes in technologies for managing reproduction, acting without restraint to satisfy one's sexual appetites was ungendered. Women who enjoyed casual sex could seek it without having to take the risk of their lives being altered by the birth of an unwanted child or ended by an unsafe illegal abortion. But as numerous feminist theorists have written, many women felt the sexual revolution failed them, as they experienced it as demanding of them that they have sex they did not want under circumstances they could not enjoy—that is, without the emotional attachment and trust in a committed partner that they felt were necessary to pleasure.

This sort of negative response to the new sexual freedom was reflected within punk most notably by X-Ray Specs' notorious song, "Oh, Bondage, Up Yours," which equates the corporate management of consumerism ("chain store") and the chains of S/M play with the nonconsensual slavery of the "chain gang." The Sex Pistols' John Lydon's frequent public pronouncements that sex was boring and overrated, also provocatively questioned the role of sexuality in what we might now call the biopolitics of conformity to consumerist capitalism. Like many other things punks identified as tricks meant to cause young people to submit to the dominant culture's norms, such as consumerism, giving in to the desire for sex was often rejected as something that inevitably led to conformity to others' rules. Drugs were preferable sources of pleasure because their consumption separated one from the conformist masses. The punk adoption of S/M artifacts and styles was meant by many as a mocking exposure of how sex functioned as the approved drug of these masses, something that enslaved people further to capitalism.[7] But goths responded differently. Many of these "positive punks," as they were originally called,[8] amplified the new disconnection between sex and gender by embracing S/M styles, and in many cases S/M practices, as counter to the mainstream culture of commercialized romance and monetization of allure, and most of all as a way to dissolve the stable gender categories that undergird mainstream concepts of sexual propriety.

However, from the beginning goth's relation to S/M was much more ambiguous than punk's. Goth scholar and participant-observer Paul Hodkinson, often cited as one of the world's foremost authorities on goth, notes the admiration goths showed for femininity in males as well as females and remarks that "The emphasis, for both males and females, on a feminine appearance was also linked with general acceptance and, sometimes, even veneration of sexual ambiguity."[9] He praises, as one of his favorite aspects of goth culture, "the partial transgression of boundaries of gender and sexuality."[10] It is, however, important to note that so far as he is concerned, goth transgressiveness was always predominantly "partial." In discussing goth fashions that derive from S/M fetish attire, he claims that "all but the most extreme examples of such attire were often valued more in terms of their subcultural aesthetic qualities than for their sexual connotations."[11] He also points out that some (although not the majority) of goth respondents to his questionnaire distributed at the 1997 Whitby Festival "seemed to dislike having to purchase clothes from retailers associated with the sex industry" because it might cause others to think they were interested in socially sanctioned sexual practices.[12] In *The Goth Bible*, Nancy Kilpatrick quotes an informant's complaint that his "look," which includes painted "long pointed fingernails" misleads some people into thinking he is "gay or into kinky sex" and as a result he has "to contend with more sexual harassment."[13] Fascinatingly, none of her many informants express recognition that not only the fashions and the iconography of goth (such as the photograph of a beautiful boy in manacles suspended by chains with his back marked with welts that opens her chapter on goth love affairs), but the participation of goths in public sex cultures might also encourage others to see goths as sexual nonconformists. Kilpatrick discusses her observations of goths over a five-year period as they indulge in "fetish play" with whips and chains during monthly special events for them and S/M practitioners at a local club.[14] In her view, while a "fetish purist" will be very rigid about roles in S/M and will not combine S/M activities with intercourse, Goths switch roles freely and "like their fetish play mixed with sex."[15]

Micah L. Issitt, author of *Goths: A Guide to an American Subculture*, provides a more circumspect perspective, saying

> While goth culture has always been less overtly sexual than fetish culture, the two often come into contact, sharing both the same basic hours of operation (late nights) and the same spaces, primarily clubs that are open-minded enough to welcome both groups.[16]

He strives to reassure readers that goths are not necessarily sexually transgressive, quoting at length from Tara Daynes's essay "Kinky Sex Please—We're Goths" which asks whether goth involvement with S/M comes from "genuine kinkiness" or "is just for effect," and asserts that for most it is the latter.[17]

These visions of goth's relation to S/M are contested by another authoritative participant-observer, Jeffrey Andrew Weinstock who responds directly to Hodkinson's claims that goth fashion rarely has anything to do with its wearers' sexuality. Weinstock's view is that goths do not "abstract" objects of fetish attire "from the physical bodies they adorn."[18] Not only does he refuse the idea that goth is about style not sex, he provides an alternative history:

> although emphasis on sexual provocation and transgression, including fetishism and S-M themes and imagery, was a part of goth subculture from the start, this pattern of erotic rebelliousness increasingly has been elaborated upon via the explicit and highly visible incorporation of S-M and fetishistic sexual practices to the point that fetish attire and fetish play have now become almost de rigueur at many goth events.[19]

He lists goth bands that explicitly connect their music and performances to S/M, including the Genitorturers, Love Like Blood, Type O Negative, Lacrimosa, Die Form, Sleep Chamber, More Machine than Man, Spanking Machine, and Athamy.[20] Perhaps it is their sense that such behavior is now required of them, whether they are attracted to S/M or not, that makes some goths so angry with those who claim to see connections between goths and S/M practitioners. Yet surely when a goth, for example, appears in public wearing bondage gear, it is a bit unreasonable for him to complain that others assume he is interested in bondage. Therefore, it would be easy to dismiss such complaints as silly. However, a deeper examination of the current mainstream cultural understandings of S/M suggests that those who angrily reject the idea that goth has some meaningful relation to S/M are not being foolish or prudish, but are, instead, reflecting the ambiguity with which S/M is regarded.

The sex/gender politics of S/M are inherently ambiguous. As Gilles Deleuze points out, sadism and masochism in their purest forms, as exemplified by the practitioners for whom they are named, The Marquis de Sade and Leopold von Sacher-Masoch, are about power and control in fairly unambiguous ways—so much so that he rejects the Freudian conflation of the two sexual economies into sadomasochism.[21] As he describes them, and as they are represented in De Sade's work and in many popular cultural artifacts, sadists react to the problem of feeling aroused by another person's physicality or behavior by asserting control over that person. The practices of the sadist, in effect, say, you may have the power to excite me sexually, but I have the power to force you to gratify my desires. Inflicting pain and/or humiliations on an unwilling victim confirms the sadist's possession of this power. In popular culture, such sadists are generally depicted as psychopathic serial killers, and often offered up as ego ideals through whom audience members can vicariously enjoy ultimate sexual power. Hannibal Lecter, as played by Madds Mikklesen, in the television series *Hannibal* is a recent example.

The unambiguous masochist is surprisingly similar as understood by Deleuze, via Theodore Reik, in that he asserts his power not through controlling others but through being absolutely immune to their efforts to control him.[22] Reenacting scenes of punishment in childhood by parents or teachers or by authority figures later, such as police or jailers, he turns their attempts to control him into affirmations of his ability to take sexual pleasure from pain and humiliation. His ability to feel aroused, and in some cases to achieve orgasm, in response to actions meant to intimidate him and force his compliance is his power. This figure is less frequently represented in popular culture, but such responses to abuse were once a mainstay of films in which men reacted to a woman slapping their faces by indicating their resultant sexual excitement, usually by kissing their abuser.

These pure, unambivalent sadists and masochists trouble gender categories only when their identities oppose current, conventional views of the attributes assigned either to males or to females within gender binarity. The unambivalently sadistic male simply enacts the role patriarchal culture deems appropriate to men, although in the case of the torture killer of women, he does so excessively. He dominates and controls a woman, or weaker male, for sexual purposes, exerting his will in a show that he has the power to make satisfaction of his own desires primary. Likewise, the unambivalently masochistic woman finds her pleasure in submission, just as misogynistic culture expects of her. But even in such cases while the desires of the individual may be unambivalent, cultural interpretations of them render ambiguous the actions that result.

Current debates about the sexual politics of the book and film series *Fifty Shades of Grey* engage the important distinctions between a masochism compliant with mainstream values and one disruptive of them. In short, while the heroine of the series exerts considerable control over her sadistic lover's behavior, ultimately they both accept conventional roles: his as the sexually dominant and financially supportive husband and head of household, hers as the sexually responsive, child-bearing, and financially dependent wife. Fans of the series frequently claim that this is an exercise of power on the part of the female submissive, that she manipulates her lover in the only way she can to satisfy her need for romantic and economic security, and that, as the recipient of his sexual attentions, she establishes her greater value and importance in their partnership. For feminist interpreters of the series, like myself, the heroine seems far less resistant to patriarchal scripts. While she does determine how much painful punishment she is willing to accept from her suitor, their marital agreement at best rewrites traditional female domestic subordination as a consensually negotiated arrangement. Nothing in conventional gender roles is troubled, the sexual subtext of male dominance and female submission is merely brought to the surface. Sex radical feminist theorists contend that only when the male steps out of his conventional role to enjoy being hurt or the woman rejects hers and instead enjoys inflicting hurt do they trouble gender categories. And even here one might well say that there is no real ambiguity, only a reversal that, through its status as abnormal, reestablishes gender norms because submission continues to be articulated as a forcibly imposed (although in fact desired) femininity and dominance as the masculinity appropriated by the phallic woman.

However, masochism and sadism can be much more complexly enacted, allowing the development of greater, gender-troubling ambiguity. As Deleuze notes in his brilliant close reading of texts by Sacher-Masoch, the sexual economy of masochism is far more likely to involve a person playing the role of sadist in order to give pleasure to a masochistic partner than a dominant who prioritizes his or her own desires above those the subordinate.[23] In actual practice the sadist in the masochistic scenario has in the past been most likely to be a prostitute, who is very unlikely, for obvious financial reasons, to be acting out her or his own sexual feelings and much more likely to be doing what he or she was paid to do.

As sexual mores have loosened and the putatively perverse become more socially acceptable, the masochist's sadist may now be a romantic partner or a casual sexual play partner met through a club or an advertisement. But such cases, as again Deleuze notes, are almost always governed by some sort of contract or agreement. This is why it has become a truism of discussion of S/M that the masochist is the one in control. The use of safe words, for instance, in organized S/M scenes, ensures that the masochist will have clear control of what transpires in the encounter. Because most frequently in actual practice the masochist has the power to determine what will happen and what the limits will be, it is easy to assume that the masochist's sadist is a mere instrument. And this assumption is made by Deleuze. But a somewhat less unambiguous vision of the masochist's power is provided by contemporary situations in which romantic love renders the S/M relation less contractual than an ongoing negotiation in which each exercises some agency.

And when the masochist and sadist both have agency, both taking power to control their encounter to some extent, ambiguity enters. If both desire what is happening between them, things become even more ambiguous and complex. Now a woman who enjoys submitting and negotiates the terms of her submission to a man, who may be as excited by pleasing her as he is by "punishing" her, no longer seems to be enacting a traditional female role, especially if (as is *not* the case in the *Fifty Shades* franchise) she remains independent of his financial support and their relationship is not structured by enactment of traditional domestic roles determined by gender. And the more so if her partner's dominance of her is determined by her openly expressed desires. Similarly, a man who requests domination by his partner may be, in fact, reversing nothing traditional but instead following convention in asking the woman who loves him to gratify his sexual desires. But when his partner identifies as sexually dominant and finds direct pleasure in "topping" him, then there seems no way to clearly and unambiguously describe what happens between them in terms of conventional gender roles.

It is within the context of these ambiguities surrounding S/M identifications that the ambiguousness of goth's relation to gender is most apparent.

Weinstock observes that within goth depictions of S/M scenes, "women are almost always presented as doms, while the men are submissive."[24] This does not mean, however, that goth S/M defies gender categories. Instead, in "project[ing] a sexualized image of feminine power," goth affirms the main-stream cultural view of gender as a binary opposition between femininity and masculinity,[25] and even more troublingly privileges male femininities over those belonging to women.[26] Therefore goth cannot be said to be a cul-ture that clearly and deliberately resists conventional gender identifications. It can only be said to be one that is successfully transgressive of gender norms in its ambiguity.

The goth woman for whom femininity—and even as many describe it hyper-femininity—of personal style is used to signify sexual superiority/dominance (the ability to not only attract but also control others) is both following the traditional woman's route to power and foregrounding the role of artificiality and theatricality inherent in that tradition. Even more so, the goth man who claims femininity as part of his personal style, who makes submissive effeminacy key to his public persona and private identity, both reinforces the conventional view of femininity as the binary opposite to masculinity, holding in place gender binarity as the foundation of hu-man identities, and troubles the connections conventionally made between biological sex and gender. The very fact that these goths' gender and sexual identifications and stylings are ambiguous in their relation to conventional valuations and understandings of sexuality makes these identifications and stylings subversive because the ambiguity opens up gender as a field of play in which multiple, and highly variable, interpretations are always available.

To illustrate how S/M content in goth songs functions both in apparent alignment to traditional representations of gender difference and to im-plode their meanings through the introduction of an overwhelming amount of ambiguity, one might look at a range of songs that bring together images of heterosexuality and eroticized violence. I begin with a band whose goth credentials no one can call into question, the one generally considered the first true goth band, Bauhaus. Their song, "The Passion of Lovers," can easily be read as referencing S/M. The song begins with a description of a woman who "sought cracked pleasures," and her lascivious, lip-licking pro-nouncement that "The passion of lovers is for death." This Belle Dame Sans Merci would be right at home in Keats' eponymous poem, or any of Swin-burne's later nineteenth-century masochistic poems, such as "The Garden of Proserpine." The singer watches her "from underneath," signaling his subordinate position. And we learn that she "gets the better of" her "bigger" (presumably masculine) lovers. This is a vision perfectly compatible with the Decadent period art so popular among goths, in which evil, animalistic women thrill men with their threatening sexual voraciousness. But the mi-sogyny of such a view is disrupted by the opening attribution of the femme fatale's sexual predilections to "her fear." Here S/M becomes a strategy for managing the vulnerability love and passion bring, and in this way the gendering of each partner in the S/M pair is left open, flexible. The woman in the song dominates the singer (and other men) because she is aware of the potential they have to dominate her, but this potential to dominate is attributed to the passion one evokes in the other, not to gender difference. It is their sameness in relation to the disempowerment caused by love and their sameness in relation to the power of sexual attractiveness (which the goths' high valuation of androgyny always insists can be equally wielded by males and females) that scramble codes of gender difference.

Another band generally, although not universally, deemed goth, Alien Sex Fiend, uses lyrics that also disrupt gender roles within S/M in a representative song, "Wild Women." Possibly responding to Ida Cox's famous (and much quoted by feminists) song, "Wild Women [Don't Get the Blues]" in which wild and tame women are compared, to the disadvantage of the latter, Alien Sex Fiend's song asserts that "all women are wild." But the song is hardly straightforward in its attributions of power and violence. The singer's presentation of himself as "a child in [the] hands" of a woman "like heroin" is complicated by the subsequent chorus in which he cries out his "urgent need for flesh." The last stanza about lions hunting the wildebeest, leaves completely open who is to be considered predator and who prey. We might interpret it as narrating an ironic role reversal in which the frighteningly wild women are redefined as wild animals to be hunted and consumed, but that very frightening quality suggests that—again echoing iconography of nineteenth-century Decadence—they are not cowering wildebeests, but the lions (which are referred to in the *plural* in the song, not as individuals, like the singer). So in this song, as well as Bauhaus's, sex is about the connection of desire and pleasure to violence, pain, and even death, but not in any way that can be clearly tied to masculine/feminine gender binarity or the conventional association of male bodies to masculinity and female ones to femininity.

Explicitly S/M songs by groups often classified as goth, but whose status in relation to gothic music culture traditions is more frequently debated, such as the Genitorturers, may seem more conventional in their typically singing about women taking the submissive position, but, as with the songs discussed above, theirs fairly frequently contextualize S/M activities within a vision of love and sexuality as painful violations for everyone involved. One of the Genitorturers' most infamous songs, "120 Days," obviously references De Sade's novel *120 Days of Sodom, Or the School of Libertinage*. In the novel, and Pasolini's notorious film adaptation, the victims, or as De Sade would have it the students, of this school are both male and female, in the song they are represented androgynously. The line "You rise in the presence of our libertinage, taste all the pleasures of sin," suggests penile erection, thus coding the submissive as male, while the submissive's request "fill my hole with your affection" suggests vaginal hunger, yet it could also, of course, refer to a desire for anal penetration. In any case, that Gen, the vocalist who fronts and organized the band, always appears in dominatrix gear, often carrying a whip, slants interpretation toward imagining the song as being ultimately about female dominance, which both responds to male desire—"compelled by lust within"—and schools it through the man being "made to serve." Still the meanings remain outside a simple gender binary because sexual submission, as in consensual S/M scenes, is both imposed against the apparent will of the submissive and administered in response to submissive's stated desires, and the S/M practices are both shattering and transformative in a positive way, allowing the submissive sexual self-actualization. Are the subject positions associated with this process masculine and feminine? Not in any conventional sense.

I end this chapter with discussion of a song from the band many believe was one of the primary inspirations for goth music and fashion styles: The Cure. The lyrics are derived from a poetic prose piece, "The Eyes of the Poor" by Baudelaire, a major nineteenth-century influence on the development of goth. In both versions, this is a narrative describing an initially romantic, rainy evening in Paris when the speaker/singer goes out with his beloved, both exquisitely dressed. He ruminates on their closeness and his sense that love makes the lovers of one mind. They sit outside a beautiful café, where they are approached by an impoverished man and his two children who stare in near stupefied admiration. The speaker/singer feels shame at his privileged position, but his companion is merely annoyed and demands that the poor people be chased away. In response to this revelation of her selfishness and lack of compassion, he declares that he hates her.

Although Baudelaire is indisputably misogynistic and also inarguably a poet much concerned with representing S/M, as numerous of his writings reflect, his version actually gives a less negative portrayal of the female companion than The Cure's does. He begins by saying that he will explain why he hates her *today*, while The Cure's version lacks any reference to temporality—the singer hates her now and presumably forever. In Baudelaire's prose poem, it is the café itself that evokes the admiration, not the woman, while in The Cure's version, she seems much worse because the admiration of the poor wretches she scorns is all for *her*, "all six eyes stared fixedly on you," "How beautiful! she shimmers like a star!" If we stop at these differences, it would seem that The Cure's song is decidedly misogynistic and traditional in its depiction of women as vain and cruel and men as their victims, at least to the extent that men allow themselves to feel love and admiration for women rather than the hatred women deserve. However, the official music video for the song introduces a heavy dose of ambiguity that troubles any definitive interpretation of the lyrics.

The lyrics describe a small group of poor people (a father, son, and another, younger child with no gender assigned) who worship the beauty of the singer's female companion. But the video shows only one observer of the couple, a ragged young girl. The object of the impoverished observer's worshipful gaze, the singers' beautiful partner, who is identified as a woman in the song lyrics, is represented in the video by a series of statues of beautiful *male* youths. These images take the singer's terrible realization that the difference in their responses to the poor means that "understanding is a dream" and "no one ever knows or loves another" out of the realm of a battle between the sexes and universalizes it. Love is pain because we cannot reach true oneness, and so we mourn "the way we are." Much of goth music eroticizes that pain, just as S/M does, in ways that so inundate it with conventional, anti-conventional, and simply unconventional images of gender. As a result, gender itself becomes ambiguous, and in its ambiguity transgresses by undermining any fixed meanings one might try to attach to real human bodies and their assigned sexes. The gender ambiguity of both goth and S/M combine to articulate a dynamic of desire, agency, and power that confounds heteronormative logic. Goth resists gender binarity in many ways, but perhaps most powerfully and completely in its uses of S/M.

Notes

1 Lauren M. E. Goodlad and Michael Bibby, "Introduction," in *Goth: Undead Subculture*, ed. Lauren M. E. Goodlad and Michael Bibby (Durham, NC: Duke University Press, 2007), 19.
2 Dick Hebdige, *Subculture: The Meaning of Style* (New York: Routledge, 1993), 90.
3 Paul Hodkinson, *Goth Culture: Gender, Sexuality and Style*, 34.
4 Djuna Brill, *Goth Culture: Gender, Sexuality and Style* (Oxford: Berg, 2008), 177.
5 Ibid., 182. Despite Brill's claim that her ethnography was well-researched, she seems unaware that people often lie in response to survey questions about their sexual practices, and thus that one might regard as somewhat overstated her certainty that the vast majority of goths are not attracted to S/M nor do they practice any form of it.
6 Lauren M. E. Goodlad and Michael Bibby, "Introduction," in *Goth: Undead Subculture*, 15.
7 In this they agreed with feminist theorists such as Laura Kipnis who argues against S/M as a form of sexual expression that requires expensive equipment and thus encourages consumerism in *Ecstasy Unlimited: Sex, Capital, Gender, and Aesthetics*.
8 The term was first used by Richard North in an essay entitled, "Punk Warriors" in *NME Magazine* (19 February 1983).
9 Paul Hodkinson, *Goth Culture: Gender, Sexuality and Style*, 54.
10 Ibid., 197.
11 Ibid., 51.
12 Ibid., 134.
13 Nancy Kilpatrick, *The Goth Bible*, 147.
14 Ibid., 138.
15 Karmen MacKendrick's still unsurpassed study of contemporary S/M communities, *Counterpleasures*, gives plentiful evidence to contradict the view that the majority of public S/M practitioners eschew role switching.
16 Micah L. Issitt, *Goths: A Guide to an American Subculture*, 35.
17 Ibid., 130.
18 Jeffrey Andrew Weinstock, "Gothic Fetishism," in *Goth: Undead Subculture*, ed. Lauren M. E. Goodlad and Michael Bibby, 390.
19 Ibid., 381.
20 Ibid., 381–386.
21 Gilles Deleuze, "On Coldness and Cruelty" in *Masochism*, passim.

22 Ibid., 74–76.
23 Ibid., 41–42.
24 Jeffrey Andrew Weinstock, "Gothic Fetishism," in *Goth: Undead Subculture*, 386.
25 Ibid., 391.
26 Joshua Gunn, "Dark Admissions," in *Goth: Undead Subculture*, 56–57.

Bibliography

Brill, Djuna. *Goth Culture: Gender, Sexuality and Style*. Oxford: Berg, 2008.

Deleuze, Gilles. "Coldness and Cruelty." In *Masochism*, translated by Jean McNeil, 9–138. New York: Zone Books, 1991.

Goodlad, Lauren M. E. and Michael Bibby. "Introduction." In *Goth: Undead Subculture*, edited by Lauren M. E. Goodlad and Michael Bibby, 1–37. Durham, NC: Duke University Press, 2007.

Gunn, Joshua. "Dark Admissions: Gothic Subculture and the Ambivalence of Misogyny and Resistance." In *Goth: Undead Subculture*, edited by Lauren M. E. Goodlad and Michael Bibby, 41–64. Durham, NC: Duke University Press, 2007.

Hebdige, Dick. *Subculture: The Meaning of Style*. New York: Routledge, 1993.

Hodkinson, Paul. *Goth: Identity, Style, and Subculture*. Oxford: Berg, 2002.

Issitt, Micah L. *Goths: A Guide to an American Subculture*. Santa Barbara: Greenwood, 2011.

Kilpatrick, Nancy. *The Goth Bible: A Compendium for the Darkly Inclined*. New York: St. Martin's, 2004.

Kipnis, Laura. *Ecstasy Unlimited: Sex, Capital, Gender, and Aesthetics*. Minneapolis: University of Minnesota Press, 1993.

MacKendrick, Karmen. *Counterpleasures*. Albany: State University of New York, 1999.

North, Richard. "Punk Warriors." *NME* (19 February 1983).

Weinstock, Jeffrey Andrew. "Gothic Fetishism." In *Goth: Undead Subculture*, edited by Lauren M. E. Goodlad and Michael Bibby, 375–397. Durham, ND: Duke University Press, 2007.

Part II
Ambiguity of reception

5 Flower in the mirror and moon in the water

The ambiguity of gender, genre, and politics of Li Yugang

Qian Wang

In March 2013, I attended a gathering at a friend's place. When someone turned on the television, "Chang'e" (Goddess in the Moon) performed by Li Yugang on CCTV's (China's Central Television) Spring Festival Gala was rebroadcasted. A foreign friend was attracted by Li's performance, mistook Li as a female artist, and praised Li's feminine beauty and elegance. When I corrected him, he was amazed, claimed that Li could easily outclass many drag queen performers in the West, and asked several questions: How on earth could a drag queen performer get on the biggest TV show in China? Was this a signal that the Chinese government had really embraced queer culture in the public sphere? Was "Chang'e" a modernized version of Peking opera? Finally and the most importantly, was Li gay?

I could not give him yes or no answers but explained to him who Li was, what genre his music might be categorized into, how and why he produced his music in such style, and what impact his fame had generated on China's society. I made no conclusions in the end due to the ambiguity of Li's music, identity, and significance, which is the foundation of his success, and offers Li the vital flexibility to travel between different social spaces and hierarchies, and to convert all types of texts, symbols, and capitals into cultural and commercial resources for his stardom.

Ambiguity in China's context

Ambiguity has been analyzed and defined through multidisciplinary approaches, such as the identification of seven types of ambiguity.[1] Ambiguity can be troublesome as Walton has juxtaposed it with vagueness and obscurity in applied logic studies.[2] Burke suggests a social-rhetorical approach to understand the culture of ambiguity, which covers extensive issues, including class, race, family, gender, and sexuality.[3] From the much broader perspective of society, ambiguity can never be trivialized; Shapiro, for instance, highlights the importance of moral ambiguity in his analysis of national culture and the politics of family.[4] Mahoney and Thelen have developed a theory of gradual institutional change to analyze politics and power distribution: there are four types of ambiguity in institutional change— displacement, layering, drift, and conversion.[5]

Regardless of being an academic theory or social-cultural practice in daily life, the philosophy and culture of ambiguity has been rooted in Chinese tradition and culture for thousand years. An example is the traditional eclecticism of *zhongyong zhi dao*—the golden mean of the Confucian School which stresses the vital balance between a peaceful home and an orderly state, ruler and subject, superior and inferior, prominent and ordinary. The renascence of Confucianism in the mid-1990s is not a historical accident, but due to an urgent demand for constructing a common vision to promote social stability after an exciting, utopian, confusing, and chaotic decade: the 1980s was marked by the clash of ideologies, wholesale and radical westernization versus conservative forces, which contributed to the bloody end of the student movement in 1989.[6] No matter which category China's political system might be identified as communism, state capitalism, neoconservatism, or neoliberalism, the lack of transparency in power distribution, policy making, and implementation still colors China as a totalitarian or authoritarian nation in comparison with Western democracy. The ambiguity of the Chinese system increases as various hegemonic social forces, not only the government but also business giants, control, manipulate, and "disambiguate" one thing as another. What Schick has explained about the disambiguating process in decision theory suggests two facts: the difficulty of controlling this disambiguation process and the diversity of recontextualizing social rhetoric.[7]

Because of the difficulty of controlling gender and sexuality, policies touching on these issues evidence political ambiguity. When permitting the first gay parade in Shanghai in 2009, for instance, the policy of "No Support, no opposition, and no advocacy" (*bu zhichi, bu fandui, bu tichang*) had no explicit indications or instructions of what would be allowed or prohibited with reference to China's laws and regulations. But this ambiguity cleverly reserves the possibility of intervention for the government to step in and terminate any queer activities whenever they want to and for whatever reasons. *Speak Out* TED conference, with the slogan "let the world hear the voice of Chinese gay[s]," for example, was forced to terminate in December 2014 in Chongqing. I personally experienced how the local police officers put pressure on the theatre owners instead the TED team, avoiding direct confrontation with the queers, but nevertheless succeeding in the termination of the event. The ambiguity of policy has thus become a practical strategy of control, which gives the prerogative of disambiguating or interpreting related issues to the government.

Queer is an imported academic term from the West, but like the question (or actually, a rather thrilling statement) proposed by Liu: "Why does queer theory need China?"[8] The local development and variation of queer politics, identities, activities, and ideologies in China under the influence of global queer culture might offer something back to the West to rethink the queer theory, cultural comparison, and comparability related to sexual difference in the twenty-first century. Shifting the emphasis of Marxism from economy and labor to philosophy and methodology, this chapter resonates with

Liu's opinion to examine how issues including constitutive sociality, cultural materialism, queer transformability, and geopolitical practicality in Li's ambiguous case queers the cultural variability of China's communism and Marxism, and vice versa.

The population of queer people in China is estimated to be between 39 and 52 million by sexologist Li Yinhe,[9] which determines the impossibility of homogenizing the definition, implication, and context of gender, sexuality, and queer, not to mention the influence of other Sinophone countries and regions where gender and sexuality social movements have run ahead of the mainland. *Tongzhi*—the Chinese term for gay men cleverly and satirically recontextualized by Hong Kong artist Edward Lam in 1989, for example, originally refers to communist comrades; the fusion of two conflicting terms symbolizes the ambiguous situation of queer politics between suppression and tolerance, controllability and uncontrollability, the central and the marginal. Driven by the creative industries to target the massive mainland market, artists and producers need to carefully hide, disguise, or multiply the meaning of their works in order to deal with the censorship system. For instance, the first Chinese gay anthem released by Taiwan pop star Zhang Huimei in 2009 changed its name from the original "My Gay Friends" to the metaphoric "Rainbow." The queer phenomenon of Lady Gaga also hit China in the same year, but her sophisticated queerness is defined in internet jargon as weirdo (*leiren*), and she has been called the Godmother of weirdoes (*leiren jiaomu*). This local recontextualization of queerness runs counter to its original meaning structured through the queer social movements in the West, which exceeds the sexual meaning of homosexuality, and indicates "a constitutive sociality of the self that counters the neoliberal imagination of formal rights, electoral competition, and economic growth."[10] Whether deliberate or accidental, the mix of Queer (*ku'er*) and Cool (*ku*) has generated two opposite effects on society and culture in terms of queer avant-gardism and commercialism: we observe the advocacy of one form of queerness while ignoring the other.[11] The rapid development of the pink economy further demands ambiguous policies which allow the creative industries to tentatively touch some gender and sexuality taboos, stimulate the desire of queer consumption, and transform the millions of queer people from passive "victims" to active consumers. To a certain degree, this removes the social and cultural power of contextualizing or defining queerness from queer people, and converts queerness into a new form of capital.

Li's case is more complicated and significant than pop stars. Even in comparison with a few influential queer icons, including Leslie Cheung and Chris Lee, Li's style of gender, arts, and personality is distinctive. Borrowing the concepts of performance and performativity from Butler,[12] where Li could be positioned between the two terms is highly ambiguous and subject to manipulation. Comparatively, performance as the presentation of a static identity or visual image that may suggest queerness but that ultimately does not have the ability to influence society and culture in a profound way.

Performativity, by contrast, integrates image with a self-conscious political commitment to a productive process of identity making at the societal level. The androgyny, cross-dressing, homoeroticism, and queer aestheticism presented in Leslie Cheung's music and stage or screen performances demonstrate his greatness as a brave forerunner of gender performativity in Greater China. Unlike Cheung's affirmative self-identification of bisexuality,[13] there is only one choice for mainstream celebrities in China—heterosexuality, which represents the heteronormativity of politics and social order.

Being a first-class artist of the state-run China National Opera & Dance Drama Theatre and sometimes referred as national treasure, Li has to prove his gender and sexual normativity. In order not to clash with his female role on the stage and lose appeal to the fans, ambiguity is Li's only option, as well as other mainland queer stars'. Whether or not this paradox of presence and absence of the queers in the public sphere can be labeled as "new homonormativity" in postsocialist China,[14] Duggan's opinion on homonormativity—"a politics that does not contest dominant heteronormative assumptions and institutions but upholds and sustains them, while promising the possibility of a demobilized gay constituency and a privatized, depoliticized gay culture anchored in domesticity and consumption"[15] exactly reflects the status quo of queers in China. The government maintains its control over gender and sexuality politics while permitting domestic sexual pleasure and the development of pink economy. An example is the unexpected development of *Danlan* from a struggling personal gay website in 2012 to the biggest openly gay business organization in China valued at more than $300 million in 2014.[16] Blued, the mobile gay dating app run by *Danlan* has 22 million global users,[17] and Geng Le, the founder of *Danlan,* has transformed from a former police officer to a well-known gay celebrity. This win-win strategy of being selectively ambiguous or temporarily blind satisfies the interests of most parties. The commercialization, materialization, and consumerization of queerness trivialize the embodiment of queer politics in ordinary people's daily life. But will this situation also trigger the enlightenment, dissemination, and accumulation of queer cultural capital for potential social movements? It is still too early to conclude.

The pattern of ambiguity

In their philosophical and anthropological study of Sophocles' *Antigone*, drawing on theories from scholars like Levi-Strauss, Oudemans and Lardinois have suggested two oppositions and four categories, fusion and fission, and culture and nature, to examine the ambiguity of tragedy.[18] Unlike their approach of listing the complicated kinship under each category in the myths connected with the Theban royal house,[19] with reference to the paradigm of social space structured with cultural and economic capital by Bourdieu,[20] I cross the two oppositions to structure a pattern for the analysis of Li's ambiguity (Figure 5.1).

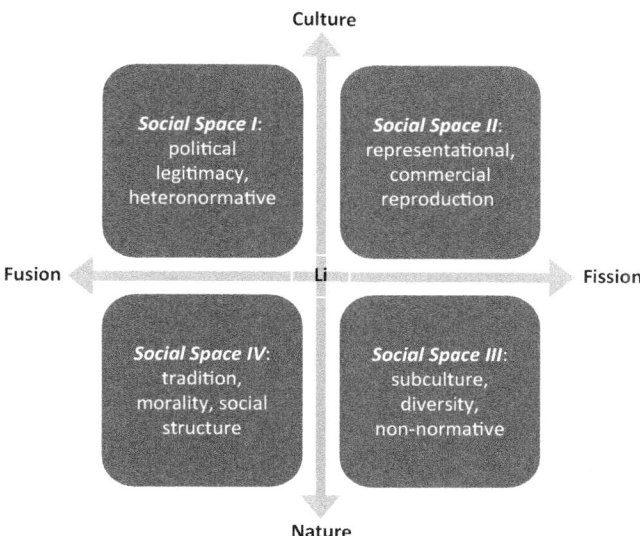

Figure 5.1 Structural analysis of Li Yugang's ambiguity.

Considering political, economic, social, and cultural factors, the four cat-egories need to be clarified in China's case. Fusion is a convergence progress driven by multiple forces for different purposes and agendas, not only the government and business giants from a top-down approach, but also the involvement of numerous creators/consumers empowered by new technol-ogies from a bottom-up approach. The existence of purposes or agendas means that convergence will be likely result-oriented, and controlled and manipulated by multiple forces. Hence, fusion signifies the intensity or con-centration of social powers.

Fission symbolizes the divergence or diversity of cultures also under the influence of multiple forces, but in contrast to the standardization or homog-enization of fusion, this process is oriented to the direction of individualism and liberalism which implies the potentiality of challenge and rebellious-ness. In accordance with Liu's suggestion of linking queer and Marxism,[21] the public (re)emergence and presentation of queers and queer cultures is tightly linked with the substantial transformation of Marxism in postso-cialist China under the slogan of "socialism with Chinese characteristics." The continuity of stratification, urbanization, and regionalization triggered by economic reforms displays the inevitable lift of totalitarian control over cultures and personal lives. Nevertheless, though the Cultural Revolution may never recur, president Xi Jinping's speech at the forum on literature and art on October 15, 2014 symbolizes the firm demand of cultural and politi-cal consensus which means that the fissions of marketing economy may be restricted to a certain degree of industrialized cultural liberalism.

Culture with a large number of subgenres or subcategories needs to be defined both generally and specifically. Levi-Strauss employs his famous culinary triangle—raw, cooked, and rotten—to explain the difference between culture and nature in early human societies.[22] In Li's case, the authenticity of politics, versus art woven into the constitutive sociality of sexuality and gender, separates culture, politics, tradition, morality, and gender in one group, and nature, art, instinct, humanity, and sexuality in the other. Culture thus needs to be addressed within the light of politics, which represents the official ideologies and attitude towards the queerness of gender and sexuality, and further consolidates governmental reign. In opposition to the strict and restricted social structure of culture, nature surely cannot represent the naturalness of the world since nature is under the social structure of human societies and forces too. But nature embraces the difference of individuals, and offers a much bigger space for artists to create comparatively more genuine, authentic, and human works at the level of constitutive sociality.

Where is Li's position in this pattern? He is right in the middle of the cross where the interrelationship between the two oppositions falls into a condition of ambiguity, which enables Li to simultaneously assimilate into and differentiate from the others as the circumstances may require. What Li's production of music, visuals, texts, and symbols evinces the separation of social spaces in the production of cultures, which is conducted by the government while being supported by many parties for different reasons.

Social space I: Culture and fusion structure the social space for political, legitimate, and heteronormative control and propaganda, where the "main melody" (*zhu xuanlü*)—the correctness of ideologies and themes in cultural products is strongly demanded.[23] Li has become a hijacked symbol of cultural heritage and innovation in this social space. "Chang'e," for example, is indeed not a song dedicated to the Goddess of the Moon in Chinese folktale for its romance, but a propaganda song. My foreign friend did not understand Chinese, so he could not read the political messages in the lyrics: "… now you let the 'Chang'e' fly, it has flown to my side and accompanies me, it carries the sentiment of all Chinese descendants, and it carries the prayer for thousands of years of all Chinese people…" Evoking the romance of folktale, this song is written to praise the achievement of CNSA (China National Space Administration) and the launch of Chang'e space detector landed on the moon. That an astronaut flew across the stage during Li's performance confirmed the message, which aimed to publicize the achievement of China's space technologies while subtly appealing to the audiences' passions of nationalism and patriotism. Li's artistic pursuit of *nan dan* (men play female roles in Peking opera) has been deeply buried under the intention of political propaganda.

Social space II: The combination of culture and fission signals the transfer of control from politics to economy. The symbolic capital of Li is representational, commercial, and duplicate. The reduction of political control does not imply the withdrawal of political intervention, but a deliberate decision in which the government tries to balance politics and economy. In his analysis of the political economy of music, Attali has identified four types of networks—sacrifice, representation, repetition, and composition—to explain the varying functions of music during different historical periods of human societies when music, the rulers, and the audiences are engaged in distinctive consumption patterns because of the new technologies and business models.[24] Hall has his interpretation on representation, and stresses the uncontrollable process of communication where the meaning of messages is not solely determined by the senders or the audiences, and the message itself can never be transparent.[25] In the process of encoding and decoding, messages will be encoded into various forms of culture to articulate the thoughts of certain social groups while the reception is unpredictable. The popularity of "new" forms of culture often triggers commercial reproduction. Li's fame has led many performers to impersonate him on TV entertainment programs; for example, there are over 3,300 clips impersonating Li on Baidu Video.[26] Because of the unevenness of artistic accomplishments, except for a few, the majority of impersonators do look like unskilled drag queen performers, but due to their viewing rates, they are popular at various talent shows. In this social space, the basic rule is to ensure that cross-gender performances are not engaged with homosexual and queer eroticism. As far as these performances are desexualized, they are safe for broadcasting.

Social space III: Fission and nature structure a marginal space for diversified and nonnormative subcultures in contrast with official and highbrow cultures approved by the government and elite classes in social space I. Though possessing less power to influence mainstream cultures, people at the low social strata can still generate impact on society through their gender performance and performativity in daily practices and consumption. The difference is that Li can hold his personal concert in the Hall of the People and have a solo performance on Chinese Spring Festival Gala as an innovative artist of traditional arts, but the rest of cross-gender performers play at clubs, bars, or temple fairs as commercial entertainers. Li's symbolic capital has become a protection umbrella for cross-gender performances, but since Li maintains his ambiguity of sexuality with a mysterious ex-girlfriend, symbolically, Li makes no direct contribution to the LGBTQ communities. An informant at a drag queen club in Beijing, for example, feels no essential similarities between drag queen performers and Li. The former is the practice of performativity at the very basic level of constitutive sociality while having some fun, but Li is just doing his stereotyped performance for his career and rewards.

Social space IV: Fusion and nature form a social space for communities and artists who put emphasis on the traditional and moral value of arts, and structure criteria, rules, or systems to make judgments for the sake of art more than politics and economy. Forces behind the fusion tendency are generally artist associations or communities, which may or may not represent the government, involved in the protection and innovation of traditional arts. Forces behind the nature tendency are individual artists who are keen to modernize or innovate traditional arts. Various forms of arts will be structured into artistic hierarchies, genres, and categories with government acquiescence. Though innovations on traditional arts might be seen as provocation or rebellion from the perspectives of those in power at the top of hierarchies, this is a comparatively liberal space for artistic experiments. Li has transformed from an amateur club singer into a first class professional artist, and produced the majority of his performance repertoires here, such as "The New Drunken Beauty" (*xin guifei zuijiu*).

This pattern of ambiguity is somehow similar to the famous BCG Matrix developed by Boston Consulting Group for business organizations to analyze their business units and product lines, which is divided into four parts: cash cows, dogs, question marks, and stars, cross structured by market growth and relative market share. It is too hasty for me to suggest that the two paradigms could be overlapped to analyze, for example, social space I is the "stars" for the potential benefits from fast-growing industries of queer products, social space II is the "question marks" for the uncertainties of consumption in high growth queer markets, social space III is the "dogs" for the profitless demand of commercialization in slow-growing industries, and social space IV is the "cash cows" for the high quality of cash generation in "mature" gender markets. But the similarities between two paradigms demonstrate the merit of ambiguity strategy in an attempt to balance the demands of arts, politics, and business. If we introduce Bourdieu's concepts of capital into Li's pattern,[27] social space I is for accumulating and consolidating his social capital with the government and dominant forces, social space II is for capitalizing his economic capital in the growing gender and queer markets with various business organizations, social space III is for disseminating his symbolic capital to the grassroots with their strong desire for gender and queer consumption, and social space IV is for certifying his cultural capital as the number one *nan dan* entertainer and celebrity. This pattern of ambiguity allows Li to walk the dangerous gender and queer high wire safely.

The ambiguity of gender

Butler points out that gender is not an immutable essence of a person but a reiterative series of acts and a citational practice of norms with certain cultural variations.[28] The emphasis on the variability of culture is vital for understanding the social structure of gender; local historical, cultural, and political factors have to be taken into account to define and contextualize related terms.

The trajectories of gender structure in twentieth-century China can be roughly divided into three periods: the enlightenment from the May Fourth Movement in 1919 to the establishment of China in 1949; the politicization from 1949 to the economic reform in 1979; and commercialization since the 1980s. Queer culture eventually entered into the public sphere with the queer phenomenon created by Chris Lee in 2005. The success of Li is undoubtedly built on the historical accumulation of gender and sexual cultural capital, which legitimates the possibility of queer visibility in the mainstream market, supported by the creative industries in today's China.

Hu Wenge—the pioneer cross-gender performer fusing Peking opera and popular music—could help us to understand how the progress of society affects the formation and transformation of cultures. Hu is the only official apprentice of the Mei Lanfang School for decades. Hu was appointed as chief *nan dan* of Beijing Peking opera Theatre in 2013. Hu started his cross-gender performance in 1987, won a pop song singing competition in Shaanxi province in 1988, was invited to present his cross-gender performance on CCTV in 1993, and experimented the fusion of Peking opera and jazz with Japanese artists in 2001. Li is in fact inspired by Hu's performance in his pursuit of *nan dan* style, and regards Hu as an important mentor. Since the musical, performing, and gender style of Hu and Li are almost identical, this raises the question of why has Hu not reached the achievement of Li. The understanding of and attitude towards gender, sexuality, and queer at different historical periods is certainly a key reason.

In his monograph on the cultural history of "her," Huang carefully explores the vital and subtle differences between modernity and Western culture, and gender equality and gender distinction,[29] which resonate with the cultural variability stressed by Butler. Other gender terms, phrases, and jargons experience the same glocalisation process, which is generally determined by the progress of society and the recontextualization of fusion with local cultures. When being questioned about his failure in comparison with Li's success, Hu firmly believes that it is the historical time period, not the difference of artistic merit, which determined their fates. Fans send countless flowers and gifts wherever Li tours nowadays, but Hu was welcomed by stones, water bottles, stinky eggs, and swear words as a pervert in the 1980s and 1990s. The same artistic style of *nan dan*, and its associated gender and sexual resonances, has unsurprisingly generated and accrued different meanings in different historical periods.

Though Hu is also unmarried and his sexual orientation has been questioned for years, after he generally restricts his performance to Peking opera, his gender and sexuality has been disambiguated from homosexuality or queerness in the form of entertainment into the role of woman in the form of traditional arts. The cross-gender performance style of *nan dan* has legitimated his queerness from the perspective of heteronormativity. By contrast, since Li travels between Peking opera and popular music constantly, the label of first-class artist does not guarantee him the privilege of being a respected artist in classic art and aesthetics. According to the artistic criteria of Peking opera, Zhu carefully analyzes the same repertoire performed by Li and other *nan dan* masters, and identifies Li's mistakes and errors. Zhu points out that Li's glamour and fame stem from gender and queer consumption, in the guise of Peking opera, rather than Peking opera consumption in the form of *nan dan*, in Li's innovative approach to traditional art.[30] Zhu's criticism on Li is debatable in that it may be regarded as a form of aesthetic formalism which ignores Li's experiment in queering the formalism, purism, and conservatism of traditional cultures. But while cross-gender performance is no longer an issue for conventional *nan dan* artists in relation to the separation of gender between artistic performance and real life, it is still a big one for Li who has to prove his gender normativity constantly.

Li demonstrates his gender and sexual normativity in three dimensions: vocal, visual, and heterosexual romance. Li is famous for his falsetto skill, delivering the aural beauty of feminine elegance, but a large number of his songs, such as "Lotus," are purposely arranged so that the vocal transfer in performance from male to female voice or vice versa confirms his masculine identity and gender normativity. Visually, Li's male images always appear together with his female images in the designs of CD covers, posters, and music videos. Li would usually wash off his female makeup, change from his female costumes back to male clothes (often traditional Chinese male long robes) in the final section of his concert to display his maleness and masculinity. If his personal life is questioned on occasion, Fan Xiaoning will be briefly mentioned as proof of a previous heterosexual romance (of which nothing can be proved beyond doubt except his unconvincing or ambiguous heteronormativity).

The ambiguity of gender allows Li to avoid governmental interventions in his career, and LGBTQ communities benefit from his fame, which creates opportunities for queers to show off their differentiated cultural taste and style on mainstream TV programs. This ambiguity, however, distances Li from the LGBTQ communities, who see it as self-denial and cowardliness, as related to me by many queer informants during fieldwork. What Li has offered is depoliticized and desexualized gentility, but the LGBTQ communities often regard the presentation of politicized sex, lust, and desire as a political stance. Hence, the relationship between Li and queers is a paradox as queers love to impersonate or imitate Li while being hostile to Li's gender and sexual politics. Surprisingly but understandably, the majority of Li's fans are middle-aged women who have suffered the hardship of social transformation, lost their youthful beauty and feminine elegance, and are finally in the social position and life stage of pursuing something for themselves. In the continuous process of forming a psychological and unconscious relationship between Li and them as performers and spectators,[31] Li's ambiguous gender has been contextualized as a simultaneously real and unreal, collective and individual symbol for multi-functional usage. Gentility in historical China[32] is exactly what has been lost in extremely materialized and savage China today. The genuine or ostensible quest for gentility by certain social groups demonstrates the further stratification of China's society. Specific forms of cultures are selected to represent their social status. Li's gentility is artistic, cultural, and illusionary, and attracts those middle-aged women, but it also meets the demand of the government to structure and maintain a harmonious society for a modernized image of cultural China.

The ambiguity of genre

Genre, as an indicator of musical style, aesthetics, ideology, value, and market, is vital for musicians and fans in identifying their communities, forming alliances, and attacking rivals. Green tells the truth that no genre can progress within an isolated cultural ecological environment, but always survive and develop through the fusion of genres.[33] Nevertheless, genres still produce their own aesthetics, criteria, rules, and regulations in order to clarify their artistic and social uniqueness. Musicians who cross the conventional genre border could be treated as traitors.

Li is generally recognized and labeled as a *nan dan* performer, but Li is not a conventional Peking opera artist judged by artistic criteria. His incompetency or more likely unwillingness to master all required skills of Peking opera to become a qualified artist for a tiny market is due to multiple industrial forces, and the ambiguity of genre produced in his stardom can demonstrate the exciting queerness of cultural diversification on one hand and the worrisome situation of cultural shallowness on the other. This ambiguity of genre is helpful to create the myth of Li's attractiveness. Barthes regards myth as a cultural construction, and believes that "it is this constant game of hide-and-seek between meaning and form that defines myth."[34] The hide-and-seek game is exactly Li's strategy of ambiguity in the construction of his myth and market. His experiment in fusing various genres, such as Peking opera, Chinese folk music, Western opera, Western musical, Chinese, and Western popular music (e.g. jazz, Mandarin pop, gothic rock, tango, R&B, and rap), into one of his own creation enriches his mysteriousness as a queer artist. The richness of genres and styles offers Li the ease of performing the most suitable repertoires on different occasions.

From the perspective of the aesthetic, cultural, and ideological criteria of genres, Li might be easily disqualified by Zhu criticisms of his Peking opera performances.[35] But Zhu's elitist cultural preference does not represent the cultural taste of the general public, who are more interested in easy listening and entertaining than classical arts. Examples of the former include the popular cult of Phoenix Legend's "The Most Dazzling Folk Style" and Chopsticks Brothers' "Little Apple." Li's individual success and the comparative failure of conventional Peking opera artists have exemplified the dominance of entertainment over art in cultural consumption by the masses nowadays.

The ambiguity and versatility of Li's genres does not substantially challenge the catègorization of Chinese popular music or indicate a model of artistic innovation, but displays a strategy of how to satisfy the demands of multiple parties through a safe approach. With reference to Halperin's definition of queer, "there is nothing in particular to which it necessarily refers. It is an identity without an essence."[36] Li's ambiguity of gender and genre is queer, regardless of his real sexual orientation and gender identification. That Li has succeeded in fusing numerous elements into his own performances means that he possesses sameness and difference from both heteronormativity and homonormativity, showing unfixed possibility in the multiplicity of both discourse and practice. Li is unlikely to be recognized as an innovative Peking opera artist, but rather, an incontrovertibly iconic figure in Chinese popular music history who has innovated the productive relationship between tradition and modernity, politics and entertainment, heteronormativity and homonormativity.

The ambiguity of politics

Analyzing the interrelationship between politics and popular culture, Street suggests that politics

> refers to many dimension of social interaction... politics extends beyond the formal boundaries of the constitution and the political processes... and it is this broader view of politics that establishes the place in politics occupied by popular culture, making the consumption and production of popular culture a political act.[37]

The relationship between Chinese popular culture and politics has varied with the transformation of society. As a once heavily politicized genre, for example, Chinese rock music has gone through three stages of political contextualization: party politics, state politics, and self-politics from 1980s to 2000s, which displays the transfer of interpretative rights of politics from the government to the people due to the rapid redistribution of social power.[38] In recent years, politics in Chinese popular cultures has been characterized by the politicization of entertainment and the entertainization of politics, in an ambiguous balance in which artists, opportunists, and industrial professionals constantly adjust their products.

Though Li's music and performance are generally depoliticized, he can never escape from political manipulation of himself and his music. What Li has contributed to the politics of cultural China as advocated by the government is his trademarks of tradition and Chineseness, which both are problematic. Since tradition has constantly been reinvented by modernity through human histories and "much of modernity is, was, and will be, traditional in its make-up,"[39] and Chineseness is a questionable term challenged by the Sinophone approach (which emphasizes the commonality of sinitic languages instead of the cultural centrism of mainland China),[40] the political significance of Li is more symbolic than material. Since Li has often toured and performed abroad as a cultural ambassador and as a political symbol, however, Li's symbolic capital still carries weight. Li's *Beautiful Costumes in the Flourishing Age* (*shengshi nishang*) concert performed at Sydney Opera House in 2009, for example, is divided into four chapters. The last chapter "The Romantic Charm of the Orient" (*dongfang shenyun*) consisted of songs such as "On the Golden Mountain of Beijing," which is sung from the perspective of emancipated Tibetan slaves, and "Today is Your Birthday, My China" written for the national day as the last song of the entire concert. Li performed all these songs in his natural male voice, which confirmed for the government his heteronormative gender, sexuality, and politics.

Beauvoir explains the subtle difference between ambiguity and absurdity, and moral idealism and political realism in her discussion on the ethics of ambiguity.[41] The pursuit of personal freedom, whether by ordinary people for the sake of body and soul or by artists for the sake of expression and autonomy, is conducted in search of a solution for the unending debate on existentialism. Li's ambiguity of gender, genre, and politics is also affected by commercial utilitarianism, which guides him to various social spaces according to the demands of government, market, and industry. Cross-gender in morality and politics is condemned and often prohibited, but the legitimation of *nan dan* as underpinned by Peking opera guarantees Li the political correctness and ability to custom fit his repertoires and performances to various ideals. Commercial utilitarianism often clashes with tradition and politics, but the government will compromise to a certain extent in return for economic rewards and other benefits. In comparison with conventional Peking opera artists who dedicate their entire lives to mastering all the requisite skills for the preservation and protection of Peking opera's aura (as conceptualized in Benjamin[42] and as appreciated by Peking opera fans), Li gives more visual pleasure and stage spectacle to the audiences. Both approaches to art are welcomed by the government, but Li can reap larger financial rewards in a much bigger market than the others.

Ambiguity is a political, moral, and economic strategy for the representation of gender, sexuality, and queerness in Li's music and performances, as well as a flexible strategy use to ensure Li's suitability for and marketability in a society geared towards "harmony" by the government. Politically, Li has succeeded in experimenting with and demonstrating how the strategy of ambiguity can help LGBTQ communities to find their social spaces, and a number of queer artists or entertainers have followed Li's path of ambiguity to enter into the mainstream market where a culturally policed boundary between homosociality and homosexuality[43] is closely monitored by the government.

Conclusion: the ambiguity of *play—xiyan*

Butler's concepts of performance and performativity have been translated as *biaoyan* and *caoyan* in Chinese scholarship, and have profoundly influenced

Chinese gender, sexuality, queer, and feminist studies. These two concepts are powerful in analyzing gender, sexuality, and queer issues in relation to social movements, gender politics, and identity making, but in the context of entertainment and popular cultures in China, I would like to introduce the concept of *play—xiyan*—to capture the significance of ambiguity in the production and consumption of Li's music and performance as well as that of other queer artists at large.

The ambiguity of *play—xiyan*—echoes Turner's understanding that play occupies a threshold between reality and unreality,[44] and also Sutton-Smith's opinion that "almost anything can allow play to occur within its boundaries."[45] But the term of *xi* not only indicates the ambiguous theatricality of entertainment, which blurs the boundaries between real and fictional, political and entertaining, flattering and satirical, subdued and rebellious in cultural works, but also means theater, especially social and political theater, which differentiates from theatricality in Butler's "performance" (e.g. cross-dressing in camp). As social and political theatre, *play—xiyan*—thus is the opposite of merely stage theater. *Xi* is an especially ambiguous, highly visible, social and political, media performance and performativity that extends beyond gender performativity in the everyday.

Neither performance nor performativity can fully explain the phenomenon of Li, who has progressed from a jobless grassroots amateur to a "national treasure" by employing the strategy of *play—xiyan*. What Li offers to the creative industries and society is his artistic relativism and ambiguity perfectly reflected by the name of his gala concert "Flower in the Mirror and Moon in the Water" (*jinghua shuiyue*). The illusion created by Li is like a kaleidoscope in which fans can see what they desire to see, when reality and imagination interact with the relationship between Li and the audiences. Performer and spectators converge, but this convergence will soon diverge in numerous cultural fissions due to social diversity, and recontextualize the new realities and illusions of Li for different pleasures and purposes. Li has touched gender, genre, and politics issues in his music and performances, but only in an imaginary reality of his own.

Notes

1 Empson, William. *Seven Types of Ambiguity.* London: Chatto and Windus, 1949.
2 Walton, Douglas. *Fallacies Arising from Ambiguity.* Dordrecht: Springer-Science+Business Media, B.V., 1996.
3 Burke, Sean D. *Queering the Ethiopian Eunuch: Strategies of Ambiguity in Acts.* Minneapolis: Fortress Press, 2013.
4 Shapiro, Michael J. *For Moral Ambiguity: National Culture and the Politics of the Family.* Minneapolis and London: University of Minnesota Press, 2001.
5 Mahoney, James and Thelen, Kathleen (eds.). *Explaining Institutional Change: Ambiguity, Agency, and Power.* Cambridge: Cambridge University Press, 2010.
6 The renascence of Confucianism is due to two reasons: firstly, the rethining of the 1980s by intellectuals and elites who were keen to find realistic and pragmatic

approaches to achieve social transformation; secondly, the government realized that communism on its own could no longer formulate official ideologies, and Confucianism was hugely adapted to construct new nationalism, more discussions see Gries, Peter Hays. *China's New Nationalism: Pride, Politics, and Diplomacy.* Berkeley: University of California Press, 2004.

7 Schick, Frederic. *Ambiguity and Logic.* Cambridge: Cambridge University Press, 2003.

8 Liu, Petrus. *Queering Marxism in Two Chinas.* Durham and London: Duke University Press, 2015.

9 Quoted in Mei Jia, "My Wife, Your Husband", *China Daily,* June 8, 2010. P. 18.

10 Liu. 2015:9.

11 Wang, Qian. "Queerness, Entertainment, and Politics - Queer Performance and Performativity in Chinese Pop", in *Queer/Tongzhi China: New Perspectives on Research, Activism and Media Cultures,* edited by Engebretsen L, Elisabeth and Schroeder F, William, 153–178. NIAS Press, 2015.

12 Butler, Judith. "Critically Queer", *GLQ: A Journal of Lesbian and Gay Studies* Vol. 1, No. 1 (1993):17–32.

13 Luo, Feng. *Leslie Cheung: Butterfly of Forbidden Colors (Zhang Guorong: jinse de hudie).* Guilin: Guangxi Normal University Press (Guilin: Guangxi shifan daxue chubanshe), 2009.

14 Liu. 2015.

15 Duggan, Lisa. *The Twilight of Equality?: Neoliberalism, Cultural Politics, and the Attack on Democracy.* Boston, MA: Beacon Press, 2003. P. 50.

16 Data is from Danlan's official website (accessed on January 26, 2016): www. danlan.org/disparticle_52741.htm.

17 Data is from Danlan's official website (accessed on January 26, 2016): www. danlan.org/disparticle_52645.htm.

18 Oudemans, Th. C. W. and Lardinois, A. P. M. H. *Tragic Ambiguity: Anthropology, Philosophy and Sophocles' Antigone.* Leiden: E. J. Brill, 1987.

19 Ibid., 17–21.

20 Bourdieu, Pierre. *Distinction: A Social Critique of the Judgment of Taste,* trans. Richard Nice. Cambridge: Harvard University Press, 1984. P. 128.

21 Liu. 2015.

22 Lévi-Strauss, Claude. "The Culinary Triangle", in *Food and Culture: A Reader, Third Edition,* edited by Counihan, Carole and Van Esterik, Penny, 40–47. New York: Routledge, 2013.

23 Wang, Qian. "Red Songs and the Main Melody – Cultural Nationalism and Political Propaganda in Chinese Popular Music", *Perfect Beat* Vol. 13, No. 2 (2012):127–146.

24 Attali, Jacques. *Noise: The Political Economy of Music,* trans. Brain Massumi. Minneapolis and London: University Minnesota Press, 1985.

25 Hall, Stuart. *Representation: Cultural Representations and Signifying Practices.* London Thousand Oaks, CA: Sage in Association with the Open University, 1997.

26 data is from Baidu Video (accessed on March 22, 2016): http://v.baidu.com/v? word=%E6%9D%8E%E7%8E%89%E5%88%9A+%E6%A8%A1%E4%BB% BF&ct=301989888&rn=20&pn=0&db=0&s=0&fbl=800&ie=utf-8&oq=%E6%9 D%8E%E7%8E%89%E5%88%9A+&f=3&rsp=0.

27 Bourdieu, Pierre. "The Forms of Capital", in *Education: Culture, Economy and Society,* edited by A. H. Halsey (et al.), 46–58. Oxford: Oxford University Press. 1997.

28 Butler, Judith. *Bodies That Matter: On the Discursive Limits of "Sex".* New York: Routledge, 1993.

29 In Chinese language, "he" and "she" – two different characters share the same pronunciation of "Ta". "She" was invented during the May Fourth Movement in 1919 for the demand of female identity and detachment from men and male authority heavily influenced by western ideologies, more discussions see Huang, Xingtao. *The Cultural History of "Her" – Research on the Invention and Recognition of New Female Pronoun ("Ta" Zi De Wenhuashi – Nüxing Xin Daici De Faming Yu Rentong Yanjiu).* Beijing: Beijing Normal University Press (Beijing Shifang Daxue Chubanshe), 2015.

30 Zhu, Xingyan. "How Much Artistic Value Does Li Yugang Possess in His Performance?" (Li Yugang Jiujing You Duoshao Hanjinliang), 2010, article is from the Internet (accessed on March 16, 2016): www.chinawriter.com.cn/bk/2010-12-20/49480.html.

31 Claid, Emilyn. *Yes? No! Maybe… Seductive Ambiguity in Dance.* London and New York: Routledge, 2006.

32 Berg, Daria and Starr, Chloe (eds.). *The Quest for Gentility in China: Negotiations Beyond Gender and Class.* London and New York: Routledge, 2007.

33 Green, Lucy. "Ideology", in *Key Terms in Popular Music and Culture*, edited by Horner, Bruce and Swiss, Thomas, 5–17. Blackwell Publishers Ltd., 1999.

34 Barthes, Roland. *Mythologies.* London: Palladin, 1973. P. 128.

35 Zhu. 2010.

36 Halperin, David M. *Saint Foucault: Towards a Gay Hagiography.* Oxford: Oxford University Press, 1995. P. 62.

37 Street, John. *Politics and Popular Culture.* Cambridge: Polity Press, 1997. P. 42.

38 Wang, Qian. *Rock Crisis: Research on Chinese Rock Music in the 1990s (Yaogun Weiji: Ershi Shiji Jiushi Niandai Zhongguo Yaogun Yinyue Yanjiu).* Shanghai: Shanghai Bookstore Publishing House (Shanghai Shudian Chubanshe), 2015.

39 Luke, Timothy W. "Identity, Meaning and Globalisation: Detraditionalisation in Post-modern Space-time Compression", in *Detraditionalisation: Critical Reflections on Authority and Identity*, edited by Heelas, Paul, Lash, Scott and Morris, Paul, 109–133. Cambridge, MA: Blackwell Publishers, 1996. P. 117.

40 Shih, Shu-mei. *Visuality and Identity: Sinophone Articulations across the Pacific.* Berkeley and Los Angeles: University of California Press, 2007.

41 Beauvoir, Simone. *The Ethnics of Ambiguity*, trans. Bernard Frechtman. New York: Citadel Press, 1948.

42 Benjamin, Walter. *The Work of Art in the Age of Its Technological Reproducibility, and Other Writings on Media*, eds. by Jennings, Michael W., Doherty, Brigid and Levin, Thomas Y., trans. by Jephcott, Edmund (et al.). Cambridge, MA: The Belknap Press of Harvard University Press, 2008.

43 Sedgwick, Eve Kosofsky. *Epistemology of the Closet.* Berkeley: University of California Press, 1991.

44 Turner, Victor. *The Ritual Process.* New York: Aldine, 1969.

45 Sutton-Smith, Brain. *The Ambiguity of Play.* Cambridge, MA: Harvard University Press, 1997. P. 3.

Bibliography

Attali, Jacques. *Noise: The Political Economy of Music*, trans. Brain Massumi. Minneapolis and London: University Minnesota Press, 1985.

Barthes, Roland. *Mythologies.* London: Palladin, 1973.

Beauvoir, Simone. *The Ethnics of Ambiguity*, trans. Bernard Frechtman. New York: Citadel Press, 1948.

Benjamin, Walter. *The Work of Art in the Age of Its Technological Reproducibility, and Other Writings on Media*, eds. by Jennings, Michael W., Doherty, Brigid and Levin, Thomas Y., trans. by Jephcott, Edmund (et al.). Cambridge, MA: The Belknap Press of Harvard University Press, 2008.

Berg, Daria and Starr, Chloe (eds.). *The Quest for Gentility in China: Negotiations Beyond Gender and Class.* London and New York: Routledge, 2007.

Bourdieu, Pierre. *Distinction: A Social Critique of the Judgment of Taste*, Trans. Richard Nice. Cambridge: Harvard University Press, 1984.

————— "The Forms of Capital", in *Education: Culture, Economy and Society*, edited by A. H. Halsey (et al.), 46–58. Oxford: Oxford University Press. 1997.

Burke, Sean D. *Queering the Ethiopian Eunuch: Strategies of Ambiguity in Acts.* Minneapolis, MN: Fortress Press, 2013.

Butler, Judith. "Critically Queer", *GLQ: A Journal of Lesbian and Gay Studies* Vol. 1, No. 1 (1993):17–32.

—————. *Bodies That Matter: On the Discursive Limits of "Sex".* New York: Routledge, 1993.

Claid, Emilyn. *Yes? No! Maybe... Seductive Ambiguity in Dance.* London and New York: Routledge, 2006.

Duggan, Lisa. *The Twilight of Equality?: Neoliberalism, Cultural Politics, and the Attack on Democracy.* Boston, MA: Beacon Press, 2003.

Empson, William. *Seven Types of Ambiguity.* London: Chatto and Windus, 1949.

Green, Lucy. "Ideology", in *Key Terms in Popular Music and Culture*, edited by Horner, Bruce and Swiss, Thomas, 5–17. Blackwell Publishers Ltd., 1999.

Gries, Peter Hays. *China's New Nationalism: Pride, Politics, and Diplomacy.* Berkeley: University of California Press, 2004.

Hall, Stuart. *Representation: Cultural Representations and Signifying Practices.* London Thousand Oaks, CA: Sage in association with the Open University, 1997.

Halperin, David M. *Saint Foucault: Towards a Gay Hagiography.* Oxford: Oxford University Press, 1995.

Huang, Xingtao. *The Cultural History of "Her" – Research on the Invention and Recognition of New Female Pronoun ("Ta" Zi De Wenhuashi – Nüxing Xin Daici De Faming Yu Rentong Yanjiu).* Beijing: Beijing Normal University Press (Beijing Shifang Daxue Chubanshe), 2015.

Lévi-Strauss, Claude. "The Culinary Triangle", in *Food and Culture: A Reader, Third Edition*, edited by Counihan, Carole and Van Esterik, Penny, 40–47. New York: Routledge, 2013.

Liu, Petrus. *Queering Marxism in Two Chinas.* Durham and London: Duke University Press, 2015.

Luke, Timothy W. "Identity, Meaning and Globalisation: Detraditionalisation in Post-modern Space-time Compression", in *Detraditionalisation: Critical Reflections on Authority and Identity*, edited by Heelas, Paul. Lash, Scott and Morris, Paul, 109–133. Cambridge, MA: Blackwell Publishers, 1996.

Luo, Feng. *Leslie Cheung: Butterfly of Forbidden Colors (Zhang Guorong: jinse de hudie).* Guilin: Guangxi Normal University Press (Guilin: Guangxi shifan daxue chubanshe), 2009.

Mahoney, James and Thelen, Kathleen (eds.). *Explaining Institutional Change: Ambiguity, Agency, and Power.* Cambridge: Cambridge University Press, 2010.

Oudemans, Th. C. W. and Lardinois, A. P. M. H. *Tragic Ambiguity: Anthropology, Philosophy and Sophocles' Antigone.* Leiden: E. J. Brill, 1987.

Schick, Frederic. *Ambiguity and Logic.* Cambridge: Cambridge University Press, 2003.

Sedgwick, Eve Kosofsky. *Epistemology of the Closet*. Berkeley: University of California Press, 1991.

Shapiro, Michael J. *For Moral Ambiguity: National Culture and the Politics of the Family*. Minneapolis and London: University of Minnesota Press, 2001.

Shih, Shu-mei. *Visuality and Identity: Sinophone Articulations across the Pacific*. Berkeley and Los Angeles: University of California Press, 2007.

Street, John. *Politics and Popular Culture*. Cambridge: Polity Press, 1997.

Sutton-Smith, Brain. *The Ambiguity of Play*. Cambridge, MA: Harvard University Press, 1997.

Turner, Victor. *The Ritual Process*. New York: Aldine, 1969.

Walton, Douglas. *Fallacies Arising from Ambiguity*. Dordrecht: Springer-Science+Business Media, B.V., 1996.

Wang, Qian. "Red Songs and the Main Melody – Cultural Nationalism and Political Propaganda in Chinese Popular Music", *Perfect Beat* Vol. 13, No. 2 (2012):127–146.

———. "Queerness, Entertainment, and Politics - Queer Performance and Performativity in Chinese Pop", in *Queer/Tongzhi China: New Perspectives on Research, Activism and Media Cultures*, edited by Engebretsen L, Elisabeth and Schroeder F, William, 153–178. Copenhagen: NIAS Press, 2015.

——— *Rock Crisis: Research on Chinese Rock Music in the 1990s (Yaogun Weiji: Ershi Shiji Jiushi Niandai Zhongguo Yaogun Yinyue Yanjiu)*. Shanghai: Shanghai Bookstore Publishing House (Shanghai Shudian Chubanshe), 2015.

Zhu, Xingyan. "How Much Artistic Value Does Li Yugang Possess in His Performance?" (Li Yugang Jiujing You Duoshao Hanjinliang), 2010, article is from the Internet (accessed on March 16, 2016): www.chinawriter.com.cn/bk/2010-12-20/49480.html.

6 What counts as "queer" in an historical context?

Cross dressing in nineteenth-century theater

Gillian M. Rodger

One of the fundamental problems encountered in looking for the "queer" in the past lies in determining what counts as queer. In current scholarship, there is a tendency to conflate "queer" with homosexuality, and to read same-sex relationships as intrinsically resistant against hegemonic social forces. This is not always the case. For example, in cultures that do not conform to a binary gender model, but rather make room for "third sex" people such as fa'afafine or berdache, can people who fall into that category be considered as "queer," or do they just queer the Western expectation of a binary gender model? Similarly, in cultures in which homosexual age-grading is practiced, the "queer" child is the boy who either refuses to engage in this process, freezing himself culturally at the status of a "child," or the young man who refuses to move into adulthood and procreate with a woman.[1] Where homosexual behavior is a normal part of the culture, declaring that this behavior is really "queer" in a Western sense becomes an act of colonization that erases particular sets of relationships that are forged at the local level. It is equally true that applying contemporary definitions of sexuality into the past also risks erasing subtle differences between past and present behaviors in any culture. For this reason, I advocate a careful consideration of any moment that appears to be "queer" in the most complex cultural context possible.

Historically, the term "queer" came to be associated with homosexuality in the English-speaking world by the turn of the twentieth century, but older uses of the term carry deeper meanings that also linger on in contemporary usage. This is particularly true for the association between "queer" and challenges to the status quo. In the Oxford English Dictionary, the term queer used as an adjective has carried these associations since the sixteenth century, denoting something or someone with an odd, eccentric, or doubtful character. The term was also used in criminal slang to denote someone untrustworthy, and to refer to counterfeit goods or money. All of these usages carry the sense that the thing or person who bore the marker "queer" went against the norm. These definitions also make it clear that in challenging that norm, the queer person or object represented something bad or untrustworthy, meaning that the term could also be used by members of wider society to locate, contain, or warn against such transgressions.

In order to determine what counts as "queer" in the past, one first needs to fully understand the social relations and power structures of past societies and then to locate those people who are seen as representing a challenge to those structures, or isolate moments when power relations seem to be challenged or disrupted. It is also worth noting the strategies used to foreclose the threat of disruption and to examine who gains and who loses as a result of the intervention. This has the potential to open the concept of "queer" to a broad range of people, and to identities forged from something other than same-sex desire, but there is also evidence that communities that found themselves at odds with hegemonic power structures have historically provided safe space for people who sought nonconforming relationships. For example, George Chauncey notes that working-class and immigrant sections of Manhattan were also home to saloons that catered to homosexual men by the 1880s.[2] Harlem functioned in a similar way in the 1920s.[3]

While Chauncey's work concentrates on the gay male world, and the ways in which entertainment venues catered to this population, there were also places that women could find relationships with each other and live independently. Lillian Faderman's work has documented the ways in which middle- and upper-middle-class women forged domestic partnerships, hiding in plain sight because they were protected by the wider social construction of women as "sexless" and a sense of pity for unmarried women. There is also a small but compelling body of anthropological work that documents working-class lesbian communities.[4] It is more difficult to learn about the lives of working-class or minority women before the twentieth century, and finding the lesbians among them is even harder. Similarly, the voices of working-class and minority men are also difficult to find in the historical narrative, and the voices of all indigenous people are almost completely absent.

Fragmentary evidence for portions of these populations survives in legal cases, and in documents associated with reform or missionary movements, but finding it often requires reading against the grain. When this evidence is combined with surviving evidence of popular or vernacular culture that survives in scholarship, and in reporting in newspapers, surviving sheet music, performance reviews, and police and legal records, it is possible to gain insight into portions of past cultures that are otherwise difficult to find in the official historical record. Pioneering historians who began to document lesbian and gay history in the late-twentieth century pushed back against the charge that private lives should remain private, and that one could not conduct research via what amounted to gossip and innuendo, to show the rich and varied ways in which people who did not conform to normative heterosexual lives found safe spaces in which to create a sense of community within an often hostile broader culture.[5] Similarly rich work that draws on queer theory and cultural studies as well as anthropology and history has followed in musicology and ethnomusicology.

This essay seeks to explore the question of what counts as "queer" by focusing on theatrical performances, performers, and their audiences in the US during the nineteenth-century. It is easy to believe that the difference between people of the past and the present is less significant than differences between people from different cultures, but when one confronts evidence of Victorian America, the past becomes very foreign indeed. Through two case studies of cross-dressed performance I will show the ways in which performers challenged and sometimes reimagined middle-class Victorian American values and culture. I will consider how performances queered Victorian American values, but also show that performances that appear to be transgressive actually worked to reinforce hegemonic power relations.

While cross-dressing had come to be associated primarily with homosexual populations in the US by the mid-twentieth century, this was not the case a century earlier. During the nineteenth-century, cross-dressed performance was a standard feature of a number of popular comic theatrical forms in both the US and England. Much of the comic theater of the nineteenth-century relied on inverting social relations, and cross-dressing contributed to the topsy-turvy world presented through comedy. Men appeared in female character in burlesque and minstrelsy, and to a lesser extent variety, while women appeared in male character in both burlesque and variety.

It is tempting to view theatrical cross-dressing on the popular stage as deeply subversive, but a very different picture emerges when one considers the ways that comic cross-dressed figures worked in different theatrical contexts. The most common cross-dressed male-to-female roles included the "dame" role found in pantomime and burlesque, in which a man portrayed an older woman, portraying her as ugly and grotesque or as delusional. Performers like Richard Sheridan, William Mestayer, and George Fortescue specialized in performing "dame" roles, and, in the case of Fortescue, the comedy was heightened by his corpulent physique. Fortescue performed as the "dizzy dame," an aging woman who imagines that she is still beautiful and who chases younger men angling for a marriage proposal. Wench roles in blackface minstrelsy operated in a similar way, except that the depiction was even crueler and more grotesque and served to both sexualize and dehumanize women of color. Even the minstrel role of the glamorous octoroon, which was not a comic role at all, served to reinforce the idea that beautiful women were the most valuable, and that light skinned African American women were destined to be exploited by men. This role wrapped the illicit sexual allure of miscegenation and homosexual desire—because the men in the audience knew that they were watching a man on the stage—into extreme sentimentality in order that the all-male audience could revel in both rape and rescue fantasies (Figure 6.1).[6]

Female-to-male cross-dressing was considerably more common in the nineteenth-century than it is today. My work has focused on cross-dressed performance in the context of variety entertainment, examining the ways that women who performed in male character were understood by their

Figure 6.1 George K. Fortescue dressed as "Buttercup" in a burlesque of H.M.S. Pinafore, ca. 1879. Photograph by Dana, New York. Author's collection.

largely male audience, but female-to-male cross-dressing was also present in burlesque, pantomime, operetta, musical comedy, and even in serious spoken drama and opera during the nineteenth-century.[7] When skilled and ambitious actresses in spoken drama sought to display the full range of their acting skills, they often did so in male roles; Hamlet and Romeo were two roles taken by the actress Charlotte Cushman, and both Sarah Bernhardt and Maude Adams portrayed Napoleon II in Edmond Rostand's play *L'Aiglon*. In burlesque and pantomime, casting conventions meant that the principal and second boy roles, the male lead and his sidekick, were most often written for women in pants. This convention continued into the twentieth century in British pantomime, and the specter of multiple women in male roles was popularized in the US by Lydia Thompson's burlesque troupe in the late 1860s.

Gender and cross-dressing in burlesque

Burlesque began as a literary form that catered to the urban elite and it was popular in both English theater and in the US before the Civil War. Scripts were written by well-known English literary figures such as W. S. Gilbert, Robert Reece, and H. J. Byron. These men set mythological and literary topics that appealed to a sophisticated and educated audience, and were full of puns, wordplay, and topical references; scripts included double-entendres that were obvious to men in the audience but escaped the notice of their wives and daughters. Burlesque's music was just as chaotic as its stories, and it included arias from opera and operetta as well as minstrel and variety tunes, blurring the lines between respectable and indecent. An equally broad range of dance was present on the burlesque stage, including classical ballet, popular jigs, and the increasingly scandalous Can-can. The fun in this form lay in the mixing of high and low, and the parody of the most straightlaced middle-class values. Burlesque's appeal lay in its absurdity and lack of coherence, and cross-dressing added to the nonsense and the preposterous ways in which familiar stories were set.

In the period after the Civil War, burlesque underwent a resurgence in the US and it was transformed into a form that was dominated by women and that presented a fragmented and chaotic entertainment that made a mockery of the standards of polite society. While purportedly featuring mythological or supernatural stories, burlesques commented on fashion and on topical subjects, and they featured women smoking, swearing, and striding around the stage, while also breaking the fourth wall to interact directly with the audience. In a world in which the majority of the roles on the stage were written for men, the critical mass of women present in burlesque represented both increased sexual appeal, and a kind of chaos that some contemporary writers found disturbing. Actresses in respectable drama in both England and the US were expected to embody the "true woman," the middle-class feminine ideal, behaving in a restrained and modest way; it was unacceptable for actresses to address their audience directly in the context of a play. Robert Allen notes that the dramatic heroine was responsible "for providing social and moral stability in a rapidly changing world..."[8] The heroine in American melodrama was both virtuous and vulnerable. She was not only at the mercy of the events depicted in the drama but reliant on the men around her for rescue. When actresses in spoken drama sang, and they often did, they chose sentimental fare that heightened this impression. Burlesque inverted these ideals by allowing women to dominate the stage, to speak directly to the audience, to perform broad and low comedy, to sing broadly comic songs that were associated with male performers, and to otherwise mimic masculine behavior.

The English actress Lydia Thompson was closely associated with this new style of burlesque that was dominated by women, and she and the other actresses who were cast in male roles were the antithesis of ideal femininity. The author William Dean Howells described the cross-dressed women in Thompson's troupe as being

> not like men, [but they] were in most things unlike women, and seemed creatures of a kind of alien sex, parodying both. It was certainly shocking to look at them with their horrible prettiness, their archness in which was no charm, their grace which put to shame.[9]

The combination of the feminine appearance of the cross-dressed actresses, whose costumes emphasized the curves of their bodies and revealed their legs, with a masculine style of performance made burlesque all the more exciting and shocking for the audience, and in the case of Howells elicited a deep sense of horror and shame. The behavior of the women on the stage reinforced the sexualized chaotic appeal of the form and over time burlesque became a genre that targeted a primarily, and later exclusively, male audience.

Lydia Thompson's troupe proved to be hugely successful, and the company was well reviewed during their season in New York stay. By the end of their time in the city, however, their reception had begun to wear a little thin, and when subsequent plays failed to garner the success of the opening work, *Ixion*, it was inevitable that some theatrical reviewers began to predict the troupe's downfall. Thompson also suffered from competition from a number of other English burlesque companies, who had headed to New York when news of her success reached England. The influx of burlesque troupes prompted editorials in the city's newspapers that expressed concerns that burlesque was pushing serious drama out of New York theaters. In addition, the troupe's manager found himself in a public conflict with the theater reviewer for *Wilkes Spirit of the Times* and the *New York Herald*. The feud played out in the pages of the *Herald* and cast doubt on Thompson's decency by comparing her to a prostitute. The conflict and scandal attracted crowds to the theater to for the troupe's performances and scandal and legal conflict increasingly came to characterize burlesque in the 1870s and 1880s. By the 1890s, burlesque was considered as a disreputable form that catered to low, male tastes and was unfit for a polite audience that included women.

The chaotic nature of burlesque, its irreverence and inversion of social hierarchies and its mockery of bourgeois values would appear to represent a challenge to hegemonic power relations, but when one examines the scripts, the music, and surviving photographs of the performers, it becomes evident that burlesque's challenges were minimal, and that they grew weaker as the form lost status. Burlesque of the 1860s through the 1880s, certainly took pleasure in its subversive refusal to conform to middle-class values, but this subversiveness increasingly served the interests of the men in the audience, and did little to undermine or question hegemonic power structures. As late as the 1880s, the comedy in burlesque relied heavily on literary allusions that were not always immediately obvious to all of the men in the audience, but the form united men of an elite class with working-class men in their shared pleasure in viewing the women on the stage. The brief costumes worn by those women, particularly those in male roles, added to that pleasure. By the 1890s, men in the burlesque audience bonded over a shared libidinal experience in which men's tastes and desires were the primary concern and the primary purpose of the women on the stage, no matter how active and anarchic, was to serve the desires of the audience. As burlesque came to be seen as more sexually explicit and less decent, the status of the form fell.

There were two results of this fall in status. First, respectable middle- and upper-middle-class women could no longer be part of the burlesque audience, and second, as women withdrew from the audience, men were even freer to express their desires in the auditorium by whistling, yelling, and otherwise interacting with the performers.

Images of burlesque actresses that circulated widely in the last third of the nineteenth-century reinforce the multiple meanings that were attached to women in burlesque. Images circulated in multiple forms including cabinet cards that were sold by both actresses and by theatrical photographers, and on the covers of sheet music that was intended for use in the bourgeois parlor. Lithographed images of the same actresses appeared in the pages of men's sporting newspapers such as the *National Police Gazette*, which also sold photographs via advertising placed in its pages. These images varied greatly, depending on their target audience. The images on the covers of sheet music that was sold to a middle-class audience for parlor performance showed the actresses dressed in the fashionable gowns worn by upper-middle-class women in this period. The same actresses also appeared in less respectable photographs that were sold to men of all classes, and in these they were dressed in risqué or revealing stage costumes. For example, an image of Lydia Thompson and a number of her actresses and dancers appeared on the cover of a series of songs that were published by G. D. Russell in Boston in 1872 to be sold to a middle-class audience for parlor performance.[10] The image shows Thompson dressed in a respectable but somewhat matronly gown and surrounded by younger women, all of whom were also dressed in the height of respectable fashion. At first glance, she looks like a mother surrounded by her daughters (Figures 6.2 and 6.3).

However, for those men who were aficionados of a different kind of theatrical photograph, this image may have taken on a second level of meaning. The women gathered around Thompson were members of a particularly notorious group of ballet dancers, the Colonna Troupe, who had caused public scandal in England due to their performance of the Can-can. Photographs of these women in professional costume also circulated commercially, as did a series of photographs of the same women in what can only be interpreted as soft pornographic poses. Risqué images such as these were circulated via advertising placed in men's sporting newspapers. This allowed merchants to sell sheet music of sentimental songs associated with the troupe to middle-class women who were ignorant of the fact that their husbands may well have owned less respectable images of the same actresses that they kept in their studies to be enjoyed in private moments (Figures 6.4 and 6.5).

These contrasting images indicate the presence of multiple worlds that coexisted during the nineteenth-century and overlapped very little. Middle- and upper-middle-class women lived in a domestic world that was certainly affected by events in the wider world, but was intended to represent an escape from its hardships for the men of the household. The culture of the home centered on family, domestic order, and maintaining domestic space

Figure 6.2 Lydia Thompson in stage costume. Photograph by Richard Fox, Police Gazette, ca. 1880. Author's collection.

Figure 6.3 Lydia Thompson in a day dress. Studio unknown, but likely Sarony, New York, ca. 1870s. Author's collection.

Figure 6.4 Colonna Troupe. Stereoview from unknown studio, ca. 1870s. Author's collection.

as a source of piousness and purity. Parlor music, which was sentimental and also sometimes had a religious or spiritual message, contributed to this mood. When men wanted a different kind of escape in which they bonded with other men in a rowdier ambience, they sought it in all-male spaces such as men's clubs, saloons, and certain kinds of theaters.

While early feminists began to push back against the idea of separate or complementary spheres for men and women in the mid-nineteenth-century, the older, restrictive ideas persisted for the vast majority of the population into the early-twentieth century. During the second half of the nineteenth-century, upper-middle-class women who sought more freedom transformed the city during the daylight hours into a relatively safe space for women,

Figure 6.5 Sarah Wright, also known as Wiry Sal. Stereoview, Stereoscopic Gems, ca. 1880s. Author's collection.

particularly in area in which stores and the most respectable theaters and concert halls that staged matinee performances were located. By the 1890s, urban planning and zoning laws created vice or theatrical districts into which men's entertainment could be segregated in order to keep other parts of the urban landscape safe for women, and the advent of electric street lighting also made urban space safer for respectable women. But inside vice districts and in the late evening hours, women were much less safe in public and working-class and minority women disproportionately bore the burden of this danger.[11]

In the same period, changes in the workplace, including a push towards mechanization and the dismantling of older artisanal patterns of work, meant that men, who had once proved their worth through skilled work and the ability to found their own business, increasingly occupied less skilled positions and worked in a more and more regulated workplace. In addition to these changes, the prolonged economic depression of the 1870s and continuing instability during the 1880s and 1890s, meant that insecurity and uncertainty had begun to dominate men's work lives in the late-nineteenth-century. Men also had to compete for work against immigrant populations, and some felt pressured by the revival in women's activism for increased participation in the public sphere through suffrage.[12] While the sons of wealthy families could prove their manhood through success in business, or adventures in the interior of the country, working men had fewer options and were more likely to turn to male leisure and convivial pursuits to prove their mettle. Sexualized variety, also known as female minstrelsy, increased during the Long Depression of the 1870s and the turbulent 1880s. This form was based in part on burlesque of the 1860s, but it dispensed with the literary allusions and language play, and concentrated on variety and minstrel acts and formation dancing such as the Can-can. Female minstrelsy catered exclusively to men and in the early-twentieth century it grew into modern burlesque that focused on low comedy and sexualized performance.

Men's culture was present in the urban spaces occupied primarily or exclusively by men. In these spaces, men could express themselves freely and did not have to worry about offending the sensibilities of women. Spaces offering men's entertainment and leisure became places where men could gather to affirm their masculinity in the presence of other men, and together fight the increasing evidence of the feminization of public space, and its deleterious effect on masculinity.[13] Saloons, which had long been all-male spaces where men could practice rituals of conviviality, became even more central to men's culture. As Michael Kimmel notes in his history of masculinity in the US: "Drinking was a form of masculine resistance to feminization."[14] Saloons and theaters catering to an exclusively male audience hosted male pastimes such as boxing matches and feats of strength. In these spaces, men tested themselves against each other, and, when young scantily dressed women were present on the stage, men not only bonded in their shared desire for these women but also reinscribed a system of gender in which men achieved masculinity through action while women occupied a lesser position and their primary role was to defer to and serve men. Women who refused to conform to those standards were described as being "unsexed" and were treated with scorn. This category of women included older and unattractive women, who were figures of pity, as well as women who sought a public role or who were considered public women. Both prostitutes and actresses fell into this category, and were thus presumed by men to be available for sex (Figure 6.6).

Female performers in low-class men's entertainment such as female minstrelsy or burlesque context had little agency.[15] They were often paid very little and their only option for supplementing their income was by inducing men to drink in wine rooms attached to the auditorium or by engaging in prostitution. Their performance skills were insufficient to allow them to

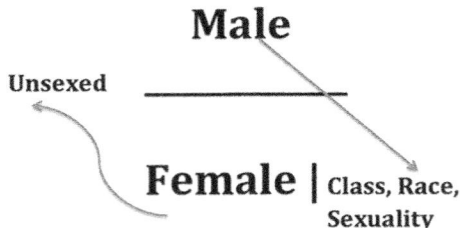

Figure 6.6 Diagram showing complementary gender model in the 19th century.

move into more respectable performance. Successful actresses who performed in burlesque had the power to refuse to participate in the rituals of the wine room because of their value to male managers, but this was less true for local women hired to perform in the chorus. While the women in burlesque did not adhere to polite middle-class standards of femininity, their performance did little to challenge or undermine gender construction of the period, and in many ways functioned to reinforce a conservative model of gender that privileged men, and helped construct space in which men's concerns were primary.

Gender and cross-dressing in variety entertainment

While variety and burlesque came to be linked in the popular imagination by the end of the nineteenth-century, the two forms had developed separately and only came to be linked as the amount of sexualized performance increased during the Long Depression of the 1870s.[16] Variety had been staged in saloons in New York and Philadelphia from the late-1840s, and by the 1860s it had spread to other cities. The Civil War spurred the growth of this genre, as young men sought entertainment in mobilizing centers and on their way to the battlefield. By the 1870s, the form had become associated with an urban audience comprised primarily of working-class men, although enterprising managers had also begun to reach out to new audiences, including working-class women and families. Variety's status slowly rose during the second half of the nineteenth-century, and by the early twentieth century the most respectable form of variety, known as vaudeville, sought to appeal to an expanding American middle class.

Variety theater made no efforts to present a coherent entertainment that was shaped by a narrative or overarching theme. Instead, it presented a series of performers in different kinds of acts, from singers and comedians to dancers and acrobats. In the period before 1900, the only consideration for organizing the sequence of acts on the stage was the personnel needed for each. In the 1870s, it was not uncommon for the variety theater's stock company to assist in sketches and to present acts in between the star performers, who toured from theater to theater, staying for a week or two at a time. At the end of the evening, the whole company and visiting stars participated in a short, one-act burlesque or parody of a topical subject or fashionable play. Scripts for some of these burlesque afterpieces survive and it is clear that they relied heavily on comedy improvised by the performers on the stage. The stock company gave the afterpiece some level of coherence, but its structure was flexible enough to accommodate whatever nonsense the touring stars provided. The comedy of the variety afterpiece shared a delight in puns, wordplay, and other forms of nonsense with burlesque, and it also made fun of middle- and upper-middle-class culture.

Much of the comedy that was fundamental to variety sought to reassure the working men in the audience that they were not at the bottom of the social hierarchy. Almost all of the comedy relied on someone else—whether immigrant or African American—serving as the butt of the joke. Unlike blackface minstrelsy, female performers were active in variety from its earliest days but their function was, for the most part, to be pretty and tuneful. Women sang a style of songs known as serio-comic; these presented a lightly humorous situation that often centered on courtship, and young women became so identified with this repertoire that they were known as "serio-comics." Women in variety also sang sentimental songs, and some of these were also published and sold to middle-class households for parlor performance (Figure 6.7).[17]

Figure 6.7 Jenny Hughes, dressed as a serio-comic in variety, reprint by unknown studio, ca. 1880s. Original photograph by Sarony, New York, 1870s. Author's collection.

When one compares the music sung by members of Lydia Thompson's bur-lesque troupes with songs sung by serio-comic singers in variety, significant differences are evident. I have found about fifty songs and three sonsgters associated with members of Thompson's 1868 troupe that were published during the later 1860s and early 1870s. The vast majority of the songs that were published in sheet music form were sentimental and came with lavishly illustrated covers suitable for use in the bourgeois home. The few comic and serio-comic songs I have found in sheet music form came with unillustrated covers typical of songs produced for the theatrical profession. The covers in this case were either plain or consisted of a long list of the titles of other songs that were available from the same publisher. I have also found a small number of songs that were associated with two of the leading variety serio-comics, Jennie Engel and Jennie Hughes. Engel was active from the late-1860s into the 1880s, while Jennie Hughes moved from burlesque to variety in the 1870s and then moved into musical comedy as it emerged in the 1880s. Both women sang a similar repertoire of sentimental and serio-comic songs and specialized in sentimental Irish songs. Despite their popularity, I have found only two pieces of sheet music associated with Hughes and nine songs associated with Engel. Both women had multiple songsters with their names on the cover, and their songs were also published in song-sheets that provided the lyrics but no melody, which were the formats that the working-class men in the variety audience most often bought songs.

The songs sung by Jennie Engel that were published for the home mar-ket are very similar in subject to those sung by Thompson's troupe, but the musical features of Thompson's repertoire show that the performers associ-ated with her troupe possessed greater singing skills. All of the sentimental and even the serio-comic songs sung by Thompson and the actresses in her troupe had ranges of over an octave as well as disjunct melodic movement and melodic embellishment. These features indicate that the women who were members of Thompson's troupe had a degree of vocal training and were capable of singing light operatic material in addition to popular songs designed for untrained singers. Engel's songs, on the other hand, indicated that she had less sophisticated singing skills. The major difference between burlesque and variety in the late-1860s and early 1870s, lay in burlesque's inclusion of more musically challenging material, which indicates the higher expectations of a portion of burlesque's audience.

The comic songs sung by Thompson's troupe were, on the other hand, very little different to those sung by male performers in variety. In 1868, Thompson sang the song *Captain Jinks of the Horse Marines*.[18] This song had been published in England in 1862 and also appeared in a number of different editions in the US between 1867 and 1870. American editions of this song named a number of different performers on their covers, including the minstrel Billy Emerson. *Captain Jinks* demands significantly less singing skill than any of the sentimental or serio-comic songs sung by the troupe. While the melody jumps at times, most of the movement is conjunct and the rhythms are simple. When performed by a male comic performer, the lyrics would likely have been spoken or performed in heightened speech. For male singers, singing skill was less important than comedic delivery, and the music indicates places at which spoken interpolations could interrupt the song. In variety and music hall performance, these spoken interpolations directly before the chorus slowed the pace of the performance, and heightened audience's anticipation of the chorus when they joined the soloist in communal singing. Interpolations also allowed the soloist on the stage to remain in control of the performance.

The lyrics of *Captain Jinks* present a military man who is a little too fond of socializing and fine fashions, but he is fairly incompetent on the military parade ground and runs away from the enemy in battle. *Captain Jinks* is a member of the English upper class and fails every standard for manhood. The lyrics give ample room both for improvised comic interpolation and physical comedy to further undercut this man's shaky manhood. There is little indication of how Thompson performed this song, and she may well have delivered it in a style more appropriate for a male performer, speaking directly to the audience and ad-libbing before each chorus. This style of performance was very different to performance conventions employed by women in respectable forms of theater, and would have added a layer of illicitness to Thompson's delivery of what was otherwise a fairly silly comic song that made fun of men not unlike those in her audience.

While songs such as *Captain Jinks* were typically performed by male comics in variety, there was also one kind of female variety performer who sang these comic songs. Known as male impersonators, these women performed in a male style, speaking their way through songs or singing in an alto range, as well as interrupting songs with long comic monologues. This was the one comic role open to women in variety from the late-1860s until the mid-1880s, although relatively few women had the experience to perform in this style. The earliest and most successful American male impersonators were mature women, some of whom had already had long careers as dancers. Their performances were compared to those of male performers, and they were among the highest-paid variety performers during the 1870s. In most respects, male impersonators were exceptional women who were granted honorary male status as a result of their popularity with male audiences.

In sharp contrast to cross-dressed burlesque performers, the costumes worn by male impersonators aimed for realism. These women dressed in the height of men's fashion that obscured their feminine curves, and they cut their hair short. At first glance, male impersonators could be mistaken for men, which was a fact frequently noted in reviews of their performances. At times, male impersonators acted as though they were equal to the men in their audience, advocating working-class solidarity and offering men advice on courtship. They also sometimes teased younger men in their audience, suggesting that they knew more about women than these inexperienced men. At the same time, they also sang about failed courtship, allowing the men to laugh at their mistakes in order to learn how to interact with women. Through performance, male impersonators worked to construct working-class masculinity in a way that depicted it as being as good as or even superior to middle- and upper-class manhood of the period. They pointed out the hypocrisy of middle- and upper-middle-class culture, emphasizing the honor of working-class men who shared scarce resources and enjoyed leisure without shame. In other words, male impersonators queered hegemonic constructions of middle-class manhood to benefit the men in their audience (Figure 6.8).

Remarkably few images of male impersonators survive from the 1870s, but those that do support my contention that men did not view these women in explicitly sexual ways. Ella Wesner was the most successful male impersonator in American variety during the last three decades of the nineteenth-century, and multiple images of her survive to the present. In each she is depicted in her stage costume, and her appearance is realistically male. She wears fashionable male clothing, and at first glance is indistinguishable from her male colleagues. Given the broad range of images of burlesque actresses, ballet dancers, and variety serio-comics that circulated, men who bought images of Wesner likely did so for similar reasons that they bought images of male performers—because they admired them and wanted to emulate their sense

Figure 6.8 Ella Wesner, in stage costume, at the age of 47. Photograph by Elite, San Francisco, 1887. Author's collection.

Figure 6.9 Ella Wesner, in stage costume, at the age of 32. Photograph by Sarony, New York, 1872. Author's collection.

of style or appearance. It is also possible that sexual desire for the male figure Wesner represented played a role in the purchase (Figure 6.9).

The sharpest contrast between cross-dressed performance in variety and burlesque lay in the appeal of the actress. While Wesner helped shape and reinforce working-class manhood, Lydia Thompson's performance became a moment when men of all classes could bond through their shared desire. As noted above, women who did not conform to middle-class expectations of gender in this period became "unsexed." This can be seen in Howell's description of Thompson's troupe as a thing of horror and as being neither men nor women but a parody of both. Women who were viewed as being unsexed were considered to be little different to public women, including prostitutes. So, a moment in variety performance that allowed working-class men to bond with the performer on the stage became a moment in which the men in the burlesque audience bonded with each other through their shared desire for the performer.

Male impersonators in variety certainly undermined middle-class standards of gender through their performances. They reimagined masculinity in a way that made fun of higher-class men and presented working-class masculinity as an ideal. The women who performed as male impersonators gained a degree of independence and a great deal of status in the profession because their performances were extremely popular with audiences. In a limited sense, male impersonators can be seen as queering the culture of the period.

The best-known and most successful male impersonators active in the US were also women whose primary emotional and likely physical relationships were with women. Annie Hindle and Ella Wesner established the ideals for this performance specialty and were emulated by several generations of actresses who followed them in American variety. Ella Wesner risked her career by abandoning performance commitments and traveling to Paris with the notorious actress Helen Josephine Mansfield who had been embroiled in the murder of the businessman James Fisk. The New York *Clipper* described this as an elopement, and included coded and joking commentary on the relationship. Annie Hindle caused even more of a furor when she married her female dresser in 1886.[19] Both women were able to salvage their careers because they were active in a period before celebrity gossip, and because the wider profession in which they worked did not care about their offstage lives.

Neither of these women had much effect on the ways that women were portrayed on the variety stage, however, and very few women chose to work as male impersonators despite their success. Hindle and Wesner were among a small number of prominent and powerful women in the theatrical profession who were tolerated because of their value, and because they could be seen as exceptional. These women gained status precisely because so few women were willing to step out of traditional roles. And when the audience no longer wanted to see women parodying upper-class men, both Hindle and Wesner lost status and, like many aging women, struggled to maintain employment.

In the twentieth century, male impersonation came to be seen as an English specialty and only a small number of American performers embraced the style, emulating imported English talent. These young women did not sustain long careers in this specialty, but rather used it as a way of distinguishing themselves from other young women in vaudeville, and all moved into female roles as they aged. By the 1890s, male impersonators in variety and vaudeville sang the same kind of lightly amusing songs that all female variety performers sang, and their acts avoided the extreme realism that had been the ideal in the 1870s.

Conclusion

None of the cross-dressing I have described in this chapter subverted gender norms of the period entirely; even male impersonators such as Hindle and Wesner catered to the men in their audience. I have long argued that male impersonation had subversive potential because it undermined the hegemonic middle-class male ideal, but in doing so it also reinforced working-class constructions of manhood. When Ella Wesner, Annie Hindle, and other male impersonators active in the 1870s and 1880s defied the ideals for working-class women, these transgressions were tolerated by the men in their audience because of the service they performed to working-class men. Because there were relatively few male impersonators active on the variety stage, they were always an oddity and were seen as exceptional rather than typical women. The vast majority of women in variety performed acts in which they were pretty and tuneful and offered themselves to their audience as objects of male desire, and they represented a working-class ideal of femininity that was more active than the middle-class ideal, but was still in a subservient position to men. Similarly, all women in burlesque performed in this way, offering little or no commentary on masculinity at all. The actresses in male roles acted in scandalous ways, but their costumes exposed their female curves and this only made them seem more available to men in the audience because it made them indecent and served to unsex them. In an all-male audience, men of all classes could bond through a shared libidinal experience watching scantily dressed women perform. At the end of the day, despite its topsy-turvy nature, burlesque served to reinforce the gender hierarchies of the period and was, if anything less subversive than variety entertainment.

Theatrical culture in this period was distinct enough from a respectable middle-class world that it could serve as a haven for lesbian and gay actors and actresses. Few of these performers traded on their personal identity in their performances, however. It was much more common for them to perform respectable middle-class roles on stage, and to present the façade of a respectable offstage life to the magazines that had begun to trade in theatrical gossip by the 1890s. Queer life was private and confined to the safety of homes and small circles of intimate friends. As vaudeville began to cultivate a polite and respectable reputation, gay and lesbian vaudeville performers similarly cultivated the appearance of respectable offstage lives.

What becomes evident through a close examination of a single performance style is that while it had the potential to undermine and challenge definitions of gender and sexuality, for the most part, these challenges were minimal and they were allowed to continue as long as men in the audience were served. The trend towards feminized performance by male impersonators in the last decade of the nineteenth-century occurred as white working-class men were beginning to identify with middle-class values, and desired to see songs depicting leisure activities and fashion rather than songs that tore down men of a higher class.

Discovering this rich and complex history required moving beyond first impressions to examine the ways in which these acts worked in the cultural context of which they were a part. In some ways, this is like conducting ethnographic fieldwork in an unfamiliar culture—one learns about the culture through academic study and then, in the field, tries to reconcile the impressions gained through existing scholarship with the more complex world of a living culture. Conducting research in the past allows one to consider much broader spans of time than one can cover in a lifetime of fieldwork, but the interconnected networks of people, processes, and institutions are still present and simple, linear narratives often do not serve to describe them sufficiently. Finding queer moments, whether embodied in homosexual subcultures, or in moments of resistance against hegemonic power structures, takes time and extreme sensitivity and it requires deep and complex cultural knowledge. And, at the end of the day, even resistant moments may be considerably less radical than a superficial examination might suggest, but it is worth noting these moments, people, and subcultures, because over the long term, they may add up to the potential for real and fundamental change and, at the very least, they effectively counter reactionary narratives that seek to maintain a repressive status quo. The construction of a diverse and complex historical past through careful and sensitive historical work can also be used to justify the continuing efforts to create a diverse multivocal society in the present.

Notes

1 See, for example, David Menasco, "Pederasty," *Gay Histories and Cultures*, edited by George Haggerty (New York: Garland Publishing, 2000), pp. 672–673. While this author does not cite Gilbert Herdt's anthropological work with the "Sambia" people in Papua New Guinea directly, the section on pederasty in a cross-cultural perspective draws on works that draw on his study.
2 George Chauncey, *Gay New York: Gender, Urban Culture, and the Making of the Gay Male World, 1890–1940* (New York: Basic Books, 1994), pp. 33–45.
3 Ibid., 248–267.
4 See, for example, Lillian Faderman, *Surpassing the Love of Men: Romantic Friendship and Love between Women from the Renaissance to the Present* (New York: Quill, 1981) and *To Believe in Women: What Lesbians Have Done for America – A History* (New York: Houghton Mifflin, 1999) for discussions of upper-middle-class women's relationships. Lillian Faderman, *Odd Girls and Twilight Lovers: A History of Lesbian Life in Twentieth-Century America* (New York: Penguin Books, 1992) and Elizabeth Lapovsky Kennedy and Madeline D. Davis, *Boots of Leather, Slippers of Gold: The History of a Lesbian Community* (New York: Penguin Books, 1994) for discussions of lower-middle-class and working-class women's communities.
5 See, for example, *Hidden from History: Reclaiming the Gay and Lesbian Past*, edited by Martin Duberman, Martha Vicinus and George Chauncey (New York: Meridian, 1990).
6 Annemarie Bean discusses this potent attraction in "Transgressing the Gender Divide: The Female Impersonator in Nineteenth-Century Blackface Minstrelsy," in *Inside the Minstrel Mask: Readings in Nineteenth-Century Blackface Minstrelsy*, edited by Annemarie Bean, James Hatch and Brooks McNamara (Hanover, NH: Wesleyan University Press, 1996), pp. 245–256.
7 See, for example, Gillian M. Rodger "'He Isn't a Marrying Man': Gender and Sexuality in the Repertoire of Male Impersonators, 1870–1930," in *Queer Episodes in Music and Modern Identity*, edited by Sophie Fuller and Lloyd Whitesell (Urbana, IL: University of Illinois Press, 2002), pp. 105–133.

8 Robert C. Allen, *Horrible Prettiness: Burlesque and American Culture* (Chapel Hill, NC: Duke University Press, 1991): 84.
9 Quoted in Allen, *Horrible Prettiness*, p. 25.
10 The song, *Courting in the Rain*, is held by the Lester Levy Sheet Music Collection at Johns Hopkins University and can be accessed at: http://levysheetmusic.mse.jhu.edu/catalog/levy:132.085 (Accessed March 24, 2016 7:23 p.m.).
11 Remnants of "safe" public space for women could be found in urban areas in Australia into the 1980s. For example, public benches could be designated as a "safe space" in which women could sit and wait for a friend without fear of harassment from men. See http://lostwomynsspace.blogspot.com/2012/04/ladies-only-bench-outside-st-pauls.html (accessed April 9, 2016, 10:04 p.m.).
12 Michael Kimmel, *Manhood in America: A Cultural History* (New York: The Free Press, 1996), pp. 81–89.
13 Ibid., 117–141.
14 Ibid., 124.
15 Small regional halls offering sexualized variety sometimes offered the services of prostitutes in rooms off the auditorium. Chorus girls from the stage were also expected to encourage men to drink in the bar after performances. Bordwell's Opera House in East Saginaw, Michigan practiced this custom, which eventually forced the city to close this venue. See, Gillian M. Rodger, *Champagne Charlie and Pretty Jemima: Variety Entertainment in the Nineteenth-Century* (Urbana: University of Illinois Press, 2010), pp. 178–189.
16 Gillian M. Rodger, *Champagne Charlie and Pretty Jemima*, pp. 158–167.
17 Ibid., 85–97. The discussion of Jennie Engel on pp. 88–89 notes a series of sentimental songs from her repertoire that were published to be sold. All feature a portrait of Engel dressed in fashionable day clothing, looking like an extremely reputable woman.
18 The sheet music for *Captain Jinks* can be found at: http://levysheetmusic.mse.jhu.edu/catalog/levy:046.054 (accessed 26 March 2016, 10:50 p.m.). This is not the edition of the music associated with Thompson, but it is identical to the music published with her name on the cover, and they both appeared with a plain cover indicating that the music was printed for trade rather than for sale to a home audience.
19 See Gillian M. Rodger, *Champagne Charlie and Pretty Jemima*, pp. 142–146.

Bibliography

Allen, Robert C. *Horrible Prettiness: Burlesque and American Culture.* Chapel Hill, NC: Duke University Press, 2000.
Bean, Annemarie. "Transgressing the Gender Divide: The Female Impersonator in Nineteenth-Century Blackface Minstrelsy." In *Inside the Minstrel Mask: Readings in Nineteenth-Century Blackface Minstrelsy*, edited by Annemarie Bean, James Hatch and Brooks McNamara, 245–256. Hanover, NH: Wesleyan University Press, 1996.
Chauncey, George. *Gay New York: Gender, Urban Culture, and the Making of the Gay Male World.* New York: Basic Books, 1994.
Duberman, Martin, Martha Vicinus and George Chauncey (eds). *Hidden From History: Reclaiming the Gay and Lesbian Past.* New York: Meridian, 1990.
Faderman, Lillian. *Surpassing the Love of Men: Romantic Friendship and Love between Women from the Renaissance to the Present.* New York: Quill, 1981.
———. *Odd Girls and Twilight Lovers: A History of Lesbian Life in Twentieth-Century America.* New York: Penguin Books, 1992.

————. *To Believe in Women: What Lesbians Have Done for America – A History.* New York: Houghton Mifflin, 1999.

Gänzl, Kurt. *Lydia Thompson: Queen of Burlesque.* New York: Routledge, 2002.

Herdt, Gilbert H. *Rituals of Manhood: Male Initiation in Papua New Guinea.* Berkeley: University of California Press, 1982.

Kennedy, Elizabeth Lapovsky and Madeline D. Davis. *Boots of Leather, Slippers of Gold: The History of a Lesbian Community.* New York: Penguin Books, 1994.

Kimmel, Michael. *Manhood in America: A Cultural History.* New York: The Free Press, 1996.

Menasco, David. "Pederasty." In *Gay Histories and Cultures,* edited by George Haggerty, 672–673. New York: Garland Publishing, 2000.

Rodger, Gillian M. "'He Isn't a Marrying Man': Gender and Sexuality in the Repertoire of Male Impersonators, 1870–1930." In *Queer Episodes in Music and Modern Identity,* edited by Sophie Fuller and Lloyd Whitesell, 105–133. Urbana, IL: University of Illinois Press, 2002.

————. *Champagne Charlie and Pretty Jemima: Variety Entertainment in the Nineteenth-Century.* Urbana, IL: University of Illinois Press, 2010.

7 Funny girls and nowhere boys
Reversing the gaze in the popular music biopic

Matthew Bannister

Some recent popular music biopics, for example *Nowhere Boy* (2009) (about the young John Lennon) and *Walk the Line* (2005) (about Johnny Cash), might also be described as "chick flicks."[1] In these films, the gaze is reversed and the male lead is eroticized, sensitized, and his career or life revealed as dependent on the agency of female characters. There are various ways of interpreting this—it could be a way of courting a broader audience (rock biopics have not generally been considered "mainstream"), or it could reflect shifting demographics around the consumption of popular music. At the same time, it could also be seen as recuperating the original ambiguity of rock and roll—the ways in which it mixed up gender and ethnic identities to create a new art form—albeit one that was rapidly normalized as white and masculine.

Both *Walk the Line* and *Nowhere Boy* can be regarded as revisionist popular music biopics to the degree that their male stars are mediated through a female or queer gaze, which, in formal terms, follows the structure of the male gaze, but reverses the subject positions.[2] Certain editing and cinematographic conventions are used to highlight sexual difference: in a shot reverse shot sequence showing gendered subjects in relationship in the same diegetic space, male and female subjects are viewed differently by the camera. There is a fetishization of particular gendered subjects: face and body are presented to the audience as pleasurable objects through the use of big close-ups, soft lighting, and a shallow focus to minimize distracting background, thus constructing the object of the gaze as spectacular, passive, emotionally receptive, isolated/removed from the world, "nowhere," fixed by and thus available exclusively for the spectator's desiring gaze. These objects may also be subject to gazes within the diegesis—seen as desirable by other characters. Moreover, just as the male gaze is, in Mulvey's account, deflected from male characters by their continuous activity—their driving of the narrative, their refusal to become spectacle—so with the reverse gaze, we expect female characters to be more active, and males more passive. But are these films "revisionist" (in the sense of modifying a "classic" genre, as in Metz) or do they rather draw on a hidden history of gender-ambiguous music biopics?[3] To what degree has the reverse gaze always been part of the popular music biopic?

The queer or female gaze has become commonplace: TV programs like *Queer Eye for the Straight Guy*, sports stars like David Beckham modeling underwear, metrosexuality, and pop and rock stars. It is often interpreted in relation to neoliberalism—the self-fashioning, conspicuously consuming man who has, in Foucauldian fashion, internalized the gaze, continuously refashioning himself in ways traditionally regarded as the domain of women and gay men.[4] Mulvey's gaze has been universalized—everybody, Foucault argues, in modern society is gazing or being gazed at, involved in complex circuits of power and pleasure, and consequent negotiations of identity.[5] However, whereas neoliberalism dates from the 1980s, gaze reversal features in music biopics from the 1960s onwards. Musical performance, by exposing all performers to a gaze, can challenge masculine hegemony.[6] Rock and roll music raised the stakes further by highlighting a spectacular and sexualized masculinity, deeply influenced by African American culture. The subsequent 1960s emergence of rock as cultural discourse can be viewed as an attempt to manage the potential queerness and racial Otherness of early rock and roll by elevating rock music to the status of art (thus minimizing its bodily, performative aspects) and by normalizing heterosexual white masculinity.[7] Thus the films discussed chronologically in this essay show masculinity moving from the wings to the stage—the subject of the gaze becoming the object. But additionally, the object changes from non-white to white masculinity. The gaze, then, is not just about gender, it is also about race.[8]

The films can also be read as mapping the emergence of a masculinized rock culture out of feminized pop culture. The 1960s youth counterculture sought to differentiate itself and its music from the entertainment industry.[9] To do so, it employed mass culture critique derived from folk music Romanticism, equating commercialism and popular culture with fakery and hence "inauthentic" femininity: female audiences, viewed as passive consumers; female or feminized performers, viewed as manufactured idols, selling the spectacle of their sexuality rather than memorable music or convincing performances: "Pop music is... prefabricated, and used for dancing, mooning over teen idols and other 'feminised'... recreations."[10] This is represented in the films as a changing relationship between "funny girls" ("funny ha ha" but mainly "funny peculiar" in their lack of conventionally feminine qualities) and pretty "nowhere boys" (to be subject to the gaze is to be "nowhere," Mulvey noting how it places the object in a fantasy space).[11] Nowhere boys gradually replace funny girls as protagonists and performers. This narrative parallels how the rock discourse marginalized woman performers, but at the same time male performers become subject to female or queer gazes (Richard Dyer discusses gay identification with "ugly duckling" female heroines like Judy Garland, who pine for handsome leading men)[12] Ethnicity is another kind of "funny" otherness which gradually gets appropriated and normalized by white men.

Tracing the evolution of the reverse gaze in the music biopic shows the influence of earlier music biopics that often focused on ethnically "Other" female entertainers, e.g. *Funny Girl* (1968), about singer Fanny Brice, and *Lady Sings the Blues* (1972) about Billie Holiday.[13] Films about women are not analyzed in recent literature on the popular music biopic.[14] Although Marshall and Kongsgaard state that popular music biopics reproduce the ideologies of popular music stardom, i.e. the "rock discourse" discussed above, they also endorse this discourse in their tacit acceptance of a male rock "canon."[15] Where the films have been read specifically as biopics, gender is discussed, but the fact that they are about popular music is not taken into account.[16] The biopic requirement of "truth-to-life," "accuracy,"[17] or more accurately, correspondence to other relevant sources, is complicated by the generic heterogeneity of the female entertainer biopic. But the biopic requirement of "accuracy" fits with the rock discourse insistence on "authenticity," while ignoring the degree to which both music and gender are performances that create their own kinds of truth which cannot be reduced to correspondence to reality. The insistence of rock discourse and biopic theory on authenticity has meant that these earlier films' associations with "entertainment" (the musical, theatrical performance, variety shows),[18] or "feminine" genres, such as romance and melodrama, has been overlooked. These conventions are present in all the films discussed in this essay: *Funny Girl, Lady Sings the Blues, What's Love Got to Do with It?* (1993) (Tina Turner), *Walk the Line*, and *Nowhere Boy*.

Funny Girl

Funny Girl (1968) is an old-style Hollywood musical comedy-melodrama based (loosely) on the life of US Jewish comedian singer actress Fanny Brice, starring Barbra Streisand in her film debut. Fanny is "funny" both in that she makes people laugh and looks Jewish: not conventionally seen as beautiful. Brice has to prove continually in her performances that talent (her singing, her wit) trumps beauty. The film is both a conventional rags-to-riches biopic (she stars in the Ziegfeld Follies, marries a playboy) but also self-reflexive: continually commenting on conventional expectations about stardom and performance, especially for women. Brice doesn't submit to the gaze—she continually talks back to it. This theme is highlighted by her love interest (Nick Arnstein), played by Omar Sharif, who is "gorgeous." As Brice sings in "Sadie, Sadie": "The groom is prettier than the bride," paralleling Dyer: "Garland is not even as attractive as her leading man."[19] However, Arnstein turns to crime, initiating the melodramatic motif of doomed love (handsome men, like beautiful women, cannot be trusted). Brice's final number, the standard "My Man" (also sung by Billie Holiday), a song of slavish devotion, underlines her suffering, but the context (performing to a theater audience) suggests that "the show must go on." Streisand offers a metaperformance—impersonating someone who is acting—and this tends to upset the conventional biopic expectation of "sincerity," of art/life correspondence.[20] The film takes Brice's point of view. She appears in virtually every scene; she even has her own voiceover (sung in places). Sharif is seen through her eyes—in a series of handsome, smiling close-ups; he has no depth as a character, however. The eroticization of masculinity seems related to the "ethnic" context—Streisand as Jewish and Sharif as Arab, showing how the gaze is not just about gender; it is also racial—an imperial or postcolonial gaze, albeit mediated partly through a woman's eyes.[21]

Streisand won an Oscar, and the film is cited as a great musical, though ironically its status as a musical may be why it is not taken seriously as a biopic.[22] Dennis Bingham, in his history of the biopic, states that the character of Nick Arnstein is sanitized, and lists inaccuracies and anachronisms such as "My Man" being performed 10 years before it was written, exemplifying how discussion of such films as biopics often leads to accusations of inauthenticity.[23] Bingham further states:

> *Funny Girl* exist[s] in order to glorify [its] female [star] in… a last moment in limbo before the onset of male-skewing demographics, low-budget filmmaking, heightened realism, and New Hollywood's vehement reaction to feminism.[24]

Bingham describes how social change at the end of the 1960s marginalized films like *Funny Girl*. But he also implies that such films—melodramatic, campy, fanciful, feminine entertainments—were doomed because they did not conform to a trend towards realism (which in turn supposedly defines the biopic form). Bingham further argues that biopics of women are "weighted down by myths of suffering, victimization and failure perpetuated by a culture whose films reveal an acute fear of women in the public realm," something which can only by alleviated "by a conscious and deliberate application of a feminist point of view."[25] *Funny Girl* apparently has no place in such a scheme. Of course, Bingham's verdict echoes that of the emergent youth counterculture.[26] You won't see Barbra Streisand in rock critics' "best of" lists; she is seen as an entertainer, not a rock artist, a view further enforced by rock's emphasis on originality—Streisand doesn't generally write her own songs.[27] In rock discourse, the separate roles of singer and songwriter (as in Tin Pan Alley) were united: the rock artist had to be autonomous, like the Beatles or Dylan. The showbiz expectation of becoming an all-around entertainer, moving from popular music to films, like Frank Sinatra, Elvis Presley, or Streisand, was now perceived as a sellout. The rock counterculture suspected that Hollywood would steal its soul and commodify its image.

Lady Sings the Blues

It is unsurprising, then, that our next example has had a troubled critical history. *Lady Sings the Blues* is a 1972 biopic based (loosely) on the jazz singer Billie Holiday's autobiography, with Holiday played by Motown star

Diana Ross.[28] The film represented Motown founder Berry Gordy's attempt to make Motown respectable by "going Hollywood," exactly the kind of representation of popular music that the emergent rock counterculture abhorred. African American music historian and critic Nelson George describes it as "shmaltzy [sic], historically distorted," that is, both inaccurate and sentimental, themes echoed in other criticism.[29] The film offers, like *Funny Girl*, a standard rags-to-riches narrative, even using a similar flashback structure; however, Streisand is reflecting from a position of power, whereas we first see Holiday in a padded cell and straitjacket, racked by the agonies of heroin withdrawal, at which point she "flashes back" to her childhood. Brice has to fight racism, but Holiday has to tackle legally enforced racial segregation. Unlike *Funny Girl, Lady* essentially positions Holiday as a victim, whose only hope is to find a benevolent father figure to protect her from racism, and ultimately from her self-destructive tendencies.

The first time the young Eleanora Fagan (Billie-to-be) enters a nightclub with the ambition to sing, the (white) owner tries to remove her, insisting: "No amount of slinky and make-up is going to turn you into a female that looks like... that" as he greets an attractive woman. As in *Funny Girl*, the "plainness" of the female lead is highlighted, which fits the way Mulvey's male gaze theory plays narrative/identification against spectacle/desire. The camera does not focus on the woman, but on the African American man, immaculately clad in a white suit, with her (Billy Dee Williams). Fagan stares at him and in a single shot slowly slides down the wall to the floor, as if "slayed" by desire. So already we have a reverse gaze, though somewhat undercut by the reaction shot of Fagan swooning, which seems to construct her as a victim of love. Eventually she auditions successfully as a singer, but black women singers are mainly valued for their ability to pick up tips— bank notes—between their thighs, something the now self-anointed Billie Holiday refuses to do. There is a long shot of Holiday, slumped defeated to the right of frame after her failed performance, with the empty dance floor in front of her, and into this space from the bottom left of the frame intrudes a hand, waving a $50 bill. The reverse shot pans up from the bill to reveal, emerging from shadow, Williams in a big close-up, in full dream-boat mode, soft light on his face, background in shadow. There is a cut to Holiday's stunned reaction in medium shot and then back to Williams who smiles slowly, the same sequence repeated twice more—four consecutive shots of Williams, the man who is to become Holiday's husband and manager (Louis McKay). This is a reversal of the gaze not only in that the man is eroticized, but also in that he is in the audience, and Holiday is the performer. But it is clear who "the star" is—the man "behind the scenes." Appropriately, she then sings "Them There Eyes."

So what work is this eroticization of African American masculinity doing here? Nelson George states that the film "transformed Holiday's story into a parable of Motown's rise: a strong black man, played charmingly by Billy Dee Williams (the 'black Clark Gable')... battles to harness a female singer's headstrong energy and ambition."[30] Williams plays a role in the film similar to that which Gordy saw himself playing in life, incarnating the Motown dream of success through marketing mainly young black women singers to a mainly white audience. The film's "appeal to blacks and white women made Ross a star and Gordy a potential force in the film industry."[31] A significant amendment here to the shot reverse shot sequence is the insertion of an intermediary image that connects the two subjects—the $50 bill, which complicates the gaze by making underlying power relations visible. Desire is made visible as a commodity. In the African American music biopic, there is no such thing as a pure gaze: the attractive women could be prostitutes, and the attractive man could be their pimp. The spectacle is no longer merely erotic, the gaze no longer a matter of gender—it is also pecuniary, showing how gender links to larger power structures. In films about black musicians, money is always an issue, whereas it is hardly present in *Nowhere Boy* and *Walk the Line*, underlining white privilege while simultaneously showing how the Romantic rock ideology of art over commerce is an unaffordable luxury in the African American world.

The film charts both Holiday's rise to fame as a singer and her descent into drug addiction. The most sexualized images of Holiday occur in conjunction with addiction—for example, in a scene with her pusher in a Manhattan night club she gets big close-ups, and also when singing "Good Morning Heartache" in the same sequence. The close-up constructs her as emotional and needy (Storhoff describes her as "hysterical," unintentionally highlighting the gender connotations of the gaze).[32] Occasions when Holiday disrobes are associated with shooting up: McKay enters her dressing room and asks her to take off her clothes. Holiday thinks he wants to make love, but actually he wants to examine her for track marks. In a later scene, McKay pursues her to the bathroom after she goes into withdrawal onstage. The last shot of the scene reveals a semi-naked Holiday "nodding out" on the toilet, accompanied by a swirling crescendo of soundtrack romantic strings. Gordy described the theme of the film as "love" but it represents Holiday as a victim incapable of choosing the "love" McKay offers.[33]

Mary Ann Doane distinguishes different melodramatic narratives by the kind of gaze they use, from romance (heterosexual love, desiring gaze) to paranoid gothic and medical drama (clinical or voyeuristic gaze), elaborating on the power relations inherent in the gaze as theorized by Mulvey.[34] The male gaze has a double aspect, both desiring and censuring, projecting sexuality onto women while also condemning them for it. Accordingly, Ross looks good when she's being bad. But this double gaze also relates to how white culture views black culture, as forbidden pleasure, so it's not just about gender. The eroticism of drug addiction sets a precedent for later rock biopics about male characters (*Walk the Line, Ray*)—another way to eroticize the male subject even when (or because) he is suffering. Drugs in turn relate to repressed trauma, and this discourse of victimhood, associated with black women, comes to be associated with (white) men too. Keightley suggests that "rock historians have misinterpreted… taste for African-American music… as overt 'political' statements. Instead, white youth… adopt this music as a sign of youth's own, privileged difference, expressing… their refusal of the mainstream."[35] Blackness functions as symbolic marginality, allowing young whites to imagine themselves as an oppressed minority: e.g. Johnny Cash as the "Man in Black."[36] While Marshall and Kongsgaard discuss many of the implications of the musician as Romantic artist and how this feeds the rock discourse, they pass over the degree to which he/she becomes a symbolic scapegoat for a repressed culture that voyeuristically enjoys the spectacle of excess popularly known as "sex, drugs and rock'n'roll."

As a pioneering film about African American culture, coinciding with the first wave of "blaxploitation" films, *Lady* struggled under the "burden of representation," which meant that, given the paucity of black hero(in)es in Hollywood cinema, it was overburdened with expectation.[37] The film was dismissed as a hysterical, masochistic melodrama, as a woman's film rather than an "authentic," historically accurate biopic.[38] But just like *Funny Girl*, it did its female star no harm, and both Ross and Streisand became hugely successful and also gay icons, suggesting that these films have been recuperated as camp.[39] One person's pathetic victim is another's tragic diva. Finally, the film reveals another contradiction in rock discourse—the way that white male rock drew on a hidden history of black female performance (Presley's infamous reworking of "Hound Dog," originally performed by Big Mama Thornton, or Mick Jagger's imitation of Tina Turner's dance moves). Although blues, the supposed roots of rock and roll, has become stereotypically associated with masculinity, *Lady* reveals the importance of the original blues, performed by black women such as Holiday, Bessie Smith, and Gertrude "Ma" Rainey.[40]

What's Love Got to Do with It?

With *What's Love Got to Do with It?* (1993) the Tina Turner biopic based on her autobiography,[41] we move into a period where rock biopics have become an established genre—e.g. Oliver Stone's *The Doors* (1991). Moreover, the Turner biopic is set in the rock and roll period—the 1950s onwards. But although the film is thematically similar to earlier music biopics—female protagonist and point of view, focus on a particular ethnic group, and a charismatic non-white man—that same man (Ike Turner) turns antagonist precisely because the historical subtext of the film is that black masculinity loses out to white rock, taking Tina with it. Similar to *Lady*, Anna Mae Bullock (Tina-to-be, played by Angela Bassett) is represented as an orphan, farmed out within her extended family, continuously reminded of her "funny" status. In a parallel sequence to *Lady*, Bullock goes to a St. Louis nightclub to be enthralled by bandleader Ike Turner (Laurence Fishburne) and the Kings of Rhythm. Ike's charisma is underlined by the adoring female audience, but as in *Lady*, the female protagonist's gaze is ambiguous—does she want him, or the money and power he represents? Ike, in his set, "auditions" prospective female singers with a microphone passed around the audience. After Anna Mae impresses with her singing, Ike takes possession of her. (At one point, he asks her to open her mouth, seemingly to kiss her. But he just wants to check for cavities, similar to *Lady,* when McKay checks Holiday for track marks). Then he starts beating her. At this point, the camera ends its affair with Fishburne's face, and focuses instead on Bassett's abused body. The narrative conflates Doane's melodrama definitions: desire turns into paranoia and ultimately into a "medical" drama: Tina's female desire is perilous.[42] However, she triumphs by teaming up with a white Australian manager, symbolically usurping Ike's authentic black masculinity—the "King of Rhythm" is deposed. Ike and Tina's story marks an intermediate step in the argument in which black masculinity loses out to black femininity, transitioning into white "masculine" rock—Tina becomes "Queen of Rock."[43]

Although the film can be read as a cautionary tale about beleaguered and dangerous black masculinity, it also represents a publicly productive, albeit privately dysfunctional, partnership.[44] In it women and men are shown as working together in musical performance, also a theme in *Ray,* the Ray Charles biopic. The dialogic nature of African American music is manifested in call-response structures, often between sexes. A common gender critique of the female biopic is that the woman's primary relationship is with a man, rather than with her career.[45] But the idea of performance partnership can also challenge the traditional separation in rock biopics of private (woman) and public life (man).[46] It means that Tina can form new partnerships (with white men). This theme of partnership becomes important in the last two examples, as does Doane's other melodramatic category—the maternal melodrama.[47] In these films we see white men emerging onto the stage via the agency of a female gaze, a "maternal gaze," a gaze that is uncertainly positioned between desiring and "caring" (also a "gaze" that helps explain the importance of the childhood flashback in both these films). Rather than Mulvey's explanation of the maternal gaze as projecting frustrated desire onto the child, in these films it functions differently, because women are represented as women performing with, enabling, and guiding male characters who are "lost," "nowhere" child-men.

Walk the Line

Consistent with the idea of white men gradually taking the stage is *Walk the Line*'s opening, which teases the viewer with tracking shots moving slowly into the heart of Folsom Prison, led on by a mysterious noise, eventually recognizable as Johnny Cash's famous "chick-a-boom," played by his band, amplified by hordes of stamping male convicts. But where is Cash? Cut to the "Wood Shop" behind the stage, and we see a finger caressing a bandsaw, then finally a big close-up of Cash (Joaquin Phoenix). A male voice off-camera says "Mr. Cash? Mr. Cash?" which he studiously ignores. The sequence culminates in an apparent "no-show" and a series of questions—Who is "Cash"? Why is he playing with a saw? Why isn't he onstage? Is there going to be a riot?

This scene sets up themes that characterize the movie—extended big close-ups of Phoenix's handsome profile, generally in various states of repose, connoting a passive, elusive, dreamy, haunted child-man—an unlikely hero. A whining dobro acts as a sound bridge to a childhood flashback, in which Cash ("JR") is a round-eyed little boy, identifying with and being influenced by women while being censored by men—the dobro is interrupted by Cash's father: "JR? Turn that radio off and get to sleep!" Cash is listening to June Carter sing, foreshadowing their later relationship and establishing her precedence. The second time we see him singing hymns in the cotton fields with his mother. Later, she gives him a copy of the *Heavenly Highway Hymns*. The mother introducing her child to music is a theme in this film and *Nowhere Boy*, as is the abusive or absent father. Although rock may be patriarchal, it is represented here as a displaced or absent patriarchy, not passed from father to son, but indirectly, from "star" to "star," and this makes sense given rock's Modernist insistence on originality.[48] The childhood flashback in *Walk* (also present in *Ray* and *Nowhere Boy*) also opens up the male star to another, arguably "maternal" gaze. This "child-directed gaze" is notably lacking in films with female stars, suggesting that "childishness" is the prerogative of white masculinity (Ray Charles' mother in *Ray* takes a "tough love" approach).

The only male character JR esteems is his older brother Jack, who dies in a saw accident (explaining the opening scene). The father blames JR: "He took the wrong son! … The Devil did this!" casting JR as Cain in an archetypal "family drama." While women are associated with music and hope, Cash's father is noise and desperation, slamming doors, hissing into JR's ear that music is "nothing." Scarred by his brother's death, rejected by his father, JR remains emotionally a child, a "mama's boy," as suggested by a time transition edit—the young Cash weeping on his bed, a reverse shot of the bedroom door opened by an adolescent woman (his sister) saying "You're going to miss your bus," and a cut back to the adult Cash, in an air force uniform, "still" lying on the bed. The sympathetic, slightly playful look and tone of voice of Cash's sister, combined with the hierarchy created by the low angle, show how the female or queer gaze is defining for Cash.

When Cash first meets June Carter (Reese Witherspoon) on tour, she is already an accomplished performer, reversing the normal gender hierarchy. In their first meeting in the theatre wings, she gets tangled with Johnny's guitar strap on her way onstage. She misses her cue, but copes ingeniously, introducing herself to Johnny, while simultaneously performing that introduction for the audience with a series of offstage quips between her and the onstage MC. She is another "funny girl," not conventionally beautiful (and known as a comic). Brost discusses Witherspoon's performance of Carter as metaperformance, playing someone who is already playing a role, which can be extended into gender analysis: "A woman must continually watch herself... she comes to consider the surveyor and the surveyed within her as the two constituent elements of her identity as a woman."[49] Carter faces peculiarly intense surveillance as a performer in a genre (country) where women are expected to stay at home, exacerbated by a highly public divorce, which, as an audience member reminds her, is an "abomination." The authenticity of country, similar to that of rock, i.e. the supposed consonance between a performer's real life and their onstage persona, is impossible for Carter as a woman; equally it is perhaps too easy for Cash. Carter appears super competent in her life and work, while Cash sleepwalks to success.

A key scene in Cash and Carter's developing relationship takes place post-show, late at night in a diner (there is a similar scene between Ike and Tina Turner, also in a diner, post-show, at the start of their relationship). The use of shot reverse shot in this scene between the two lovers-to-be reveals a female gaze (similarly, Ike gets more close-ups than Tina). However, unlike Ike, Cash is no ladies' man, opening with a terrible gaffe: "I used to look at pictures of you," a comically inappropriate comment which ironically highlights the gaze reversal in this scene. Gradually the camera embraces Cash in a series of big close-ups, while mostly keeping a discrete distance from Carter. Moreover, the camera tilts subtly up at Carter and down to Cash, emphasizing her control, confirmed by her riposte to Cash's self-deprecation: "Try taking credit for something once in a while."

Indeed, the story does not reveal Cash mastering his world; rather we witness his fall and redemption. He asks June to tour with him, but mainly as a pretext for getting closer to her, and when she rejects him, he overdoses, the tour is canceled, and his first wife divorces him, calling him "a pathetic excuse for a man." As established in *Lady*, a rock biopic staple is the drug addiction withdrawal scene, attracting a gaze that is both desiring and judging. Addiction has an erotic allure—as in an intimate bedroom scene where Cash cajoles Carter with the promise of pills, only to gobble them up himself each time, stealing them from her lips like kisses. Cash's withdrawal takes place under Carter's gaze. After rescuing Cash from a tractor accident, she sits at the end of his bed, and the shot reverse shot sequence juxtaposes her cool concern with the spectacle of a semi-naked, sweating, reclining Cash, rendered in medium close-up. Withdrawal is a highly physical, visceral, bodily experience, rendered for the cinema audience through close-ups, shots of semi-naked bodies writhing, ecstasy and agony being interchangeable from the point of view of the gaze. Drug addiction for men in rock biopics is almost always related to childhood trauma—in his withdrawal nightmares Cash relives his brother's death (as also occurs in *Ray*). This is the familiar Romantic/Oedipal trope of childhood innocence disrupted by violence, the child/mother dyad disrupted by the reality principle/father, giving rise to a psychic wound that becomes both a source of creativity (catharsis) but also a barrier to achieving maturity and psychic autonomy. However, the Freudian/Oedipal model is also gendered,[50] and this is reflected in the way that biopics about women musicians rarely make this trauma/creativity link—women's trauma typically occurs in the present, not the past. The kind of help that Cash gets would probably not have been forthcoming had he been a woman. Symbolically Cash is still a child and requires a family to "raise him right," and here the Carter family gives him a second chance: June writes "Ring of Fire" and they nurse Cash through withdrawal. Finally, the narrative returns to the opening and Cash triumphantly completes his Folsom Prison performance (released as *Live at Folsom Prison*, the recording was a hit and also heralded Cash's acceptance by the rock counterculture).[51]

Of course, the Carter family is not just any family: it is a cornerstone of country music, connecting Cash not just to June, but to a matriarchal dynasty, reversing the male kinship model: Cash is an object of exchange between women.[52] The final point is that Cash and Carter perform together throughout the film, like Ike and Tina, showing a point of connection between African American and country music—the centrality of usually heterosexual family relationships; which, although often associated with country's gender conservativism, can be read in other ways. For example, the male/female duet is a recurring feature of country music (Loretta Lynn and Conway Twitty, George Jones and Tammy Wynette, Dolly Parton and Kenny Rogers, to list just a few examples). In contrast, rock discourse is predominantly homosocial, and as a result women only figure in most rock biopics as groupies or as domestic partners.

Nowhere Boy

Nowhere Boy, set in suburban Liverpool in the 1950s, continues the theme of mother love. In the film, its title a pun on the Beatles song "Nowhere Man" (like Cash, Lennon is symbolically "fatherless"), the protagonist, the young John Lennon (Aaron Johnson), is caught in a tug of love between his aunt, Mimi (Kristin Scott Thomas), who has raised him, and his birth mother, Julia (Anne-Marie Duff). This triangular structure inverts the traditional Hollywood, homosocial paradigm, in which two men compete for the love of a woman, and is similar to chick flicks about two women competing for one man, such as *My Best Friend's Wedding* (1997). As in *Walk the Line*, women take the lead, especially the flirtatious Julia, who even introduces him to rock and roll: "Do you know what it means, rock'n'roll?" she says, staring at John seductively. "Sex." Julia's lack of boundaries contrasts with Mimi's distant, sarcastic gaze, although they share a common concern. As in *Walk the Line*, there are many shots of the hero reclining, often in bed; especially notable is a close-up scene (about eighteen minutes in) of him supine and smoking, his face framed by vegetation and smoke trailing out of his mouth and nostrils. (A similar sequence occurs near the end of the movie.) These recurring shots, which serve no narrative function, construct him as a desirable object for a female or queer gaze.

One point the film makes effectively is that Lennon was, despite his claims to the contrary, no "working-class hero." He was brought up middle class, and whatever the appeal of Julia's more working-class, colorful background, his character is also decisively shaped by bourgeois values, demonstrated in a scene where John and Mimi belittle a music shop assistant into giving them a knock-down deal on a guitar. "Oh no," says Mimi, on being told the price, "That won't do *at all.*" This middle-class perspective also extends to the film itself—leafy suburban settings, grammar school uniforms, period architecture, the cut-glass accent of the very "proper" Kristin Scott Thomas, and use of classical music in places as soundtrack, all give the film a BBC period drama feel, reminding us that gender in the British context works differently to the US. The "strong" middle-class woman wins out over working-class masculinity. Gender changes in meaning as refracted through the crystal chandeliers of the British class system. At the same time, *Walk the Line*, with its high production values, upwardly mobile stars, and sheen of HBO sophistication, is also aimed at a relatively sophisticated audience, accustomed to subtle rewritings of traditional gender roles from series like *Sex and the City*.

Although Lennon is shown as mischievous and rebellious, he's beholden to women. He takes a copy of Screamin' Jay Hawkins' "I Put a Spell on You" to Julia, as if unsure of its value. She plays the record while he lies on the sofa, looking uncomfortable, even more so when Julia lies on his lap (the scene is intercut with Lennon having sex with a girl in a wood, which dispels the possibility of mother/son incest and reaffirms his "normal" sexuality). A more conventional scene might feature Lennon discovering the music with his "mates," or possibly alone. But instead the music is mediated through a woman. Julia teaches him the banjo and all of John's early musical performances are essentially for Julia (as when he sings Elvis Presley's "Teddy Bear" to her in a cafe).

Although the story progresses on traditional homosocial lines—boys, bonds, bands—the reverse gaze is maintained through the androgynous prettiness of the young male actors playing Paul McCartney (Thomas Sangster) and George Harrison (Sam Bell). In a scene where Paul and John are performing, the camera scans the audience, revealing rapt female faces but then a curiously ambiguous one—is it a boy or a girl? It turns out to be George. This returns us to a point made earlier—how rock and roll put the male body on display, making it available to both female and queer gazes. This relates to The Beatles' subsequent career: when manager Brian Epstein first saw them perform at The Cavern Club in 1961, they were wearing their Hamburg leathers, and Epstein was known to have a taste for "rough trade."[53] Simon Napier-Bell outlines the extensive homosexual culture around early 1960s British pop, in which gay male impresarios recruited "stables" of young male talent to perform musical (and other) services.[54]

Like *Walk the Line, Nowhere Boy* features the traumatic flashback structure, which refers to the central enigma of the film—John's family background, which is eventually revealed as a variant on the Oedipal family drama. The young Lennon has to "choose" between his birth parents. He chooses his mother, but Mimi reveals that Julia was not adjudged a "fit" mother by the authorities. Shortly after, Julia is hit by a car and dies, completing a fairly conventional gender narrative of punishment of the "fallen" woman, while simultaneously providing Lennon with fresh trauma to fuel future creativity (the credits roll to the accompaniment of his song "Mother") and breaking him out of the "tug of love" so he can conquer the world with The Beatles. But although the film plays out conventionally in gender terms, in life Lennon was more like Cash in that, unusually for a male rock star, he chose ultimately to share his public life with his female partner Yoko Ono (whom he habitually referred to as "Mother") in a similar way to Cash and June Carter.[55]

Conclusion

I have discussed how the reverse gaze works as a structuring device in music biopics, viewing the dominant narrative of achievement through a female or queer lens that can be both desiring and "concerned" (the gaze always includes this ambiguity). I have argued that male and female biopics, traditionally distinct in terms of subject matter and generic identifications, are in fact closely related in their use of reverse gaze—"funny girls" looking at "nowhere" boys. Viewed historically, the roles change—the protagonist starts female and turns male—but I argue that their roles (in the films at any rate) tend towards complementarity, rather than polar opposites, and to this degree the films challenge the standard homosocial rock and roll narrative. Rather than Metz's approach to film genre, by which a classic genre is revised, say, from a feminist perspective, I have argued that the female or queer gaze has long featured in music biopics. However, the influence of female music biopics has been passed over because of their associations with "feminine" or camp genres such as musicals and melodrama, which feature exactly the kind of ambiguous gaze described in this chapter, a gaze which also tends to blur fact and fiction, and so also violates biopic and rock discourses about authenticity. I also discuss how the gaze creates not just gender, but also ethnic difference. Biopics about African American musicians may question a purely "sexual" gaze, by emphasizing other discourses of power such as commodification on the one hand, but also feature musical dialogism, giving rise to a partnership model which allows for flexibility in gender negotiations around music. Finally, I have shown how the developing rock discourse had the effect of marginalizing these non-male, non-white subjects, and thus covering over their contributions to "rock."

The reverse gaze also features in more recent biopics such as *Jimi: All Is by My Side* (2013) (Jimi Hendrix) and *Love and Mercy* (2014) (Brian Wilson). Both these films feature prominent female characters—Linda Keith, who was instrumental in discovering Hendrix, and Melinda Ledbetter, who rescued Wilson from his controlling therapist Eugene Landy and helped revive his career. To some extent, we share their point of view in discovering and "learning to love" the male protagonists. Both films contain melodramatic elements and could be described as relationship dramas, and this could reflect a broader tendency, also evident in *Walk the Line* and *Nowhere Boy,* to make rock biopics accessible to a wider audience by adding human interest, rather than relying on the limited appeal of familiar ideologies of popular music stardom. Rock and roll is not simply a boys' club—for the rock biopic to have a future it needs to acknowledge and work with gender, ethnic, and other differences.

Notes

1 Suzanne Ferriss and Mallory Young, "Introduction: Chick Flicks and Chick Culture," in idem. eds., *Chick Flicks: Contemporary Women at the Movies* (New York and London: Routledge, 2008), 1–25.
2 Laura Mulvey, *Visual and Other Pleasures* (Bloomington and Indianapolis: Indiana University, 1989).
3 Christian Metz, *Language and Cinema* (The Hague: Mouton & Co., 1974).
4 Katherine Sender, "Queens for a Day: *Queer Eye for the Straight Guy* and the Neoliberal Project," *Critical Studies in Mass Communication* 23 (2006), 131–51.
5 Michel Foucault, *The Will to Knowledge: The History of Sexuality Volume One* (Harmondsworth: Penguin, 1990).
6 Lucy Green, *Music, Gender, Education* (Cambridge: Cambridge University, 1997).
7 Keir Keightley, "Reconsidering Rock," in Simon Frith, Will Straw, and John Street eds., *Cambridge Companion to Pop and Rock* (Cambridge: Cambridge University Press, 2001), 109–42.
8 bell hooks, "The Oppositional Gaze: Black Female Spectators," *Black Looks: Race and Representation*, (Boston, MA: South End Press, 1992), 115–31.
9 Keightley, op. cit.
10 Keightley, op. cit.; Norma Coates, "(R)evolution Now? Rock and the Political Potential of Gender", in *Sexing the Groove: Popular Music and Gender*, ed. Sheila Whiteley (London: Routledge, 1997), 53.
11 Mulvey, op. cit.
12 Richard Dyer, *Heavenly Bodies: Film Stars and Society* (London and New York: Routledge, 1986).
13 Other early female music biopics include *I'll Cry Tomorrow* (1955) (about singer Lillian Roth), *Love Me or Leave Me* (1955) (Ruth Etting) and *Star!* (1968) (Gertrude Lawrence).
14 Lee Marshall and Isabel Kongsgaard, "Representing Popular Music on Screen: The Popular Music Biopic," *Celebrity Studies* 3 (2012): 346–61; Ian Inglis, "Popular Music History on Screen: The Pop/Rock Biopic," *Popular Music History* 2 (2007): 77–93.
15 Norma Coates, op. cit.
16 Dennis Bingham, *Whose Lives Are They Anyway? The Biopic as Contemporary Film Genre* (New Brunswick, NJ: Rutgers University Press, 2010).
17 Ian Inglis, op. cit.
18 Richard Dyer, *Only Entertainment* (London and New York: Routledge, 1992).
19 Dyer, *Heavenly Bodies*, 165.

20 Molly Brost, "Walking the Line: Negotiating Celebrity in the Country Music Biopic," *Scope: An Online Journal of Film and Television Studies*, 18 (2010): 1–15.
21 Ann Kaplan, *Looking for the Other: Feminism, Film and the Imperial Gaze* (New York: Routledge, 1997).
22 Richard Dyer, *Only Entertainment* (London and New York: Routledge, 1992, 52, 58).
23 Bingham, 261–68.
24 Bingham, 261.
25 Bingham, 10.
26 Keightley, op. cit.
27 Marshall and Kongsgaard, op. cit.
28 Billie Holiday and William Dufty, *Lady Sings the Blues* (London: Penguin, 1984).
29 Nelson George, *Where Did Our Love Go? The Rise & Fall of the Motown Sound* (London: Omnibus, 1986), 181. Gary Storhoff, "Strange Fruit: *Lady Sings the Blues* as a Crossover Film," *Journal of Popular Film & Television* 30 (Summer 2002): 105–13.
30 George, 181–82.
31 George, 182.
32 Storhoff, 106.
33 Gordy cited in Storhoff, 113.
34 Mary Ann Doane, *The Desire to Desire: The Woman's Film of the 1940s* (Bloomington and Indianapolis: Indiana University Press, 1987).
35 Keightley, 125.
36 Johnny Cash, *Man in Black: His Own Story in His Own Words* (Sevenoaks: Hodder & Stoughton, 1977).
37 Kobena Mercer, "Black Art and the Burden of Representation," *Third Text* 4 (1990): 61–78.
38 Bingham, 260; Storhoff, 106.
39 Dyer, *Only Entertainment*, op. cit.; Dyer, *Heavenly Bodies*, op. cit.
40 Angela Davis, *Blues Legacies and Black Feminism: Gertrude "Ma" Rainey, Bessie Smith, and Billie Holiday* (New York: Vintage Books, 1998).
41 Tina Turner and Kurt Loder, *I, Tina: My Life Story* (New York: IT Books, 2010).
42 Doane, op. cit.
43 Terrence Rafferty, "Tina Turner: Queen of Rock 'n' Roll", *The New York Times*, July 27, 2008.
44 Diane Shoos, "Representing Domestic Violence: Ambivalence and Difference in *What's Love Got to Do with It*," *NWSA Journal* 15 (Summer 2003): 57–75.
45 Bingham, 61, 214.
46 Marshall and Kongsgaard, op. cit.
47 Doane, op. cit.
48 Marshall and Kongsgaard, op. cit.; Theodore W. Adorno and Max Horkheimer, *Dialectic of Enlightenment*, trans. John Cumming (New York: Continuum, 1994).
49 Molly Brost, op. cit. John Berger, *Ways of Seeing* (London: BBC/Penguin Books, 1972), 46.
50 Raewyn Connell, *Masculinities* (Berkeley: University of California Press, 1995), 10.
51 Robert Hilburn, *Johnny Cash: The Life* (Boston, MA: Little, Brown and Company, 2013).
52 Eve Kosofsky Sedgwick, *Between Men: English Literature and Male Homosocial Desire* (New York: Columbia University, 1985).
53 Mark Lewisohn, *Tune In: The Beatles – All These Years, Vol. 1* (New York: Crown Archetype, 2013), 499, 502.
54 Simon Napier-Bell, *Black Vinyl White Powder* (London: Ebury Publishing, 2001).
55 Ray Coleman, *John Ono Lennon, Vol. 2* (London: Sidgwick & Jackson, 1984), 189.

Bibliography

Adorno, Theodore W. and Max Horkheimer. *Dialectic of Enlightenment.* Translated John Cumming. New York: Continuum, 1994.

Berger, John. *Ways of Seeing.* London: BBC/Penguin Books, 1972.

Bingham, Dennis. *Whose Lives Are They Anyway? The Biopic as Contemporary Film Genre.* New Brunswick, NJ: Rutgers University Press, 2010.

Brost, Molly. "Walking the Line: Negotiating Celebrity in the Country Music Biopic." *Scope: An Online Journal of Film and Television Studies* 18 (2010): 1–15.

Cash, Johnny. *Man in Black: His Own Story in His Own Words.* Sevenoaks: Hodder & Stoughton, 1977.

Coates, Norma. "(R)evolution Now? Rock and the Political Potential of Gender." In *Sexing the Groove: Popular Music and Gender*, edited by Sheila Whiteley, 50–64. London: Routledge, 1997.

Coleman, Ray. *John Ono Lennon, Vol. 2.* London: Sidgwick & Jackson, 1984.

Connell, Raewyn. *Masculinities.* Berkeley: University of California Press, 1995.

Davis, Angela. *Blues Legacies and Black Feminism: Gertrude "Ma" Rainey, Bessie Smith, and Billie Holiday.* New York: Vintage Books, 1998.

Doane, Mary Ann. *The Desire to Desire: The Woman's Film of the 1940s.* Bloomington and Indianapolis: Indiana University Press, 1987.

Dyer, Richard. *Heavenly Bodies: Film Stars and Society.* London and New York: Routledge, 1986.

Dyer, Richard. *Only Entertainment.* London and New York: Routledge, 1992.

Ferriss, Suzanne and Mallory Young, "Introduction: Chick Flicks and Chick Culture." In *Chick Flicks: Contemporary Women at the Movies*, edited by idem., 1–25. New York and London: Routledge, 2008.

Foucault, Michel. *The Will to Knowledge: The History of Sexuality Volume One.* Harmondsworth: Penguin, 1990.

George, Nelson. *Where Did Our Love Go? The Rise & Fall of the Motown Sound.* London: Omnibus 1986.

Green, Lucy. *Music, Gender, Education.* Cambridge: Cambridge University, 1997.

Hilburn, Robert. *Johnny Cash: The Life.* Boston, MA: Little, Brown and Company, 2013.

Holiday, Billie and William Dufty. *Lady Sings the Blues.* London: Penguin, 1984.

hooks, bell. "The Oppositional Gaze: Black Female Spectators." In *Black Looks: Race and Representation*, 115–31. Boston, MA: South End Press, 1992.

Inglis, Ian. "Popular Music History on Screen: The Pop/Rock Biopic." *Popular Music History* 2 (2007): 77–93.

Kaplan, Ann. *Looking for the Other: Feminism, Film and the Imperial Gaze.* New York: Routledge, 1997.

Keightley, Keir. "Reconsidering Rock." In *Cambridge Companion to Pop and Rock*, edited by Simon Frith, Will Straw, John Street, 109–42. Cambridge: Cambridge University Press, 2001.

Lewisohn, Mark. *Tune In: The Beatles – All These Years, Vol. 1.* New York: Crown Archetype, 2013.

Marshall, Lee and Isabel Kongsgaard. "Representing Popular Music on Screen: The Popular Music Biopic." *Celebrity Studies* 3 (2012): 346–61.

Mercer, Kobena. "Black Art and the Burden of Representation." *Third Text* 4 (1990): 61–78.

Metz, Christian. *Language and Cinema.* The Hague: Mouton & Co., 1974.

Mulvey, Laura. *Visual and Other Pleasures.* Bloomington and Indianapolis: Indiana University, 1989.

Napier-Bell, Simon. *Black Vinyl White Powder.* London: Ebury Publishing, 2001.

Rafferty, Terrence. "Tina Turner: Queen of Rock 'n' Roll", *The New York Times,* July 27, 2008.

Sedgwick, Eve Kosofsky. *Between Men: English Literature and Male Homosocial Desire.* New York: Columbia University, 1985.

Sender, Katherine. "Queens for a Day: *Queer Eye for the Straight Guy* and the Neo-liberal Project." *Critical Studies in Mass Communication* 23 (2006): 131–51.

Shoos, Diane. "Representing Domestic Violence: Ambivalence and Difference in *What's Love Got to Do with It.*" *NWSA Journal* 15 (Summer 2003): 57–75.

Storhoff, Gary. "Strange Fruit: *Lady Sings the Blues* as a Crossover Film." *Journal of Popular Film & Television* 30 (Summer 2002): 105–13.

Turner, Tina and Kurt Loder. *I, Tina: My Life Story.* New York: IT Books, 2010.

Films

Funny Girl. Directed by William Wyler. United States: Columbia Pictures; Rastar Pictures, 1968.

Jimi: All Is By My Side. Directed by John Ridley. United Kingdom; Ireland; United States: Darko Entertainment, Freeman Film, Subotica Entertainment, 2013.

Lady Sings the Blues. Directed by Sidney J. Furie. United States: Motown Productions, 1972.

Love and Mercy. Directed by Bill Pohlad. United States: River Road Entertainment, Battle Mountain Films, 2014.

My Best Friend's Wedding. Directed by P. J. Hogan. TriStar Pictures, Zucker Brothers Productions, Predawn Productions, 1997.

Nowhere Boy. Directed by Sam Taylor-Johnson. United Kingdom: Ecosse Film, Film4, British Film Council, 2009.

Ray. Directed by Taylor Hackford. United States: Universal Pictures, 2005.

The Doors. Directed by Oliver Stone. United States: Bill Graham Films, Carolco International N.V., 1991.

Walk The Line. Directed by James Mangold. United States: Fox 2000 Pictures, 2005.

What's Love Got to Do with It? Directed by Brian Gibson. United States: Touchstone Pictures, 1993.

Part III
Ontological ambiguity

8 "I'ma school that bitch"

Gay rappers defying binaries and expressing fierceness

Kirsten Zemke and Jared Mackley-Crump

I'ma take that bitch to college
I'ma give that bitch some knowledge.[1]

This chapter is the result of the two authors getting "schooled" by four gay rappers: Cakes da Killa, Le1f, Mykki Blanco, and Zebra Katz. "Schooled" comes from ball culture slang meaning to be "taught a lesson" and "woken" out of ignorance. Ball culture is a black and Latino gay underground movement, whose unique stories, movements, and language are a part of these rapper's influence, repertoire and community. This "schooling" sent us down the rabbit hole of complex and confronting topics such as "no homo," "the DL" (down low), pronouns, trans*, genderqueer, drag, homophobia, black masculinity, the commodification of black bodies, homoeroticism, twerking, bounce, and queens.

To understand these artists, we explored black gay male culture, hip-hop culture, hip-hop homophobia, and the contested domain of knowledge known as queer theory. This "schooling" helped us to contextualize the performances of our rappers, showing how they destabilize gender and sexuality binaries, as well as interrogate both homonormativity and heteronormativity within gay, black, and mainstream cultures. Their manifold gender performances are also a part of the legacy of popular music as a space where queer bodies have been able to challenge dominant norms. We were also introduced to new terms and phrases from ball culture, hip-hop culture, and the queer community, highlighting how language is gradually changing to accommodate more nuanced identities and experiences.

The inadequacy of existing labels, such as queer hip-hop, led us instead to employ the popular term "fierceness," also from ball culture. "Fierceness" is an attitude that embraces difference, denotes quality, and is defiant, bold, and confident. It challenges and owns the binaries of masculine, feminine, gay, straight, hyper-masculine, and femme, and acknowledges that gender and sexuality are fluid and dynamic. Fierceness embraces ambiguity, stripping it of any connotations of indecisiveness, doubt, or apathy. While hip-hop may include nihilism and homophobia, it is also a place for fierce talent, rhymes, and attitudes.

Queer theory: "Take that bitch to college"

Our investigation axis' on the intersection of gender and sexuality and is based on the premise that identities—gender, sexual, or otherwise—are performative, movable, and constantly in flux. Following a Butlerian/ Foucauldian model of performativity and social constructionism,[2] we view sexuality and gender as two of a number of identity continuums governed by historical, cultural, and social frameworks. These identities are always in the process of becoming, and these frameworks change and are in a constant state of negotiation, meaning that gender and sexuality are neither fixed nor stable across time.[3] For instance, there is currently greater awareness around gender and sexual diversity.[4]

It is important to begin by addressing the problematic nature of gender and sexual binaries; the simplistic binaries are mocked, renovated, and transcended by these rappers, giving their performances revolutionary currency. Early theorizing in queer studies suffered a reductionist focus on binaries, and led to the reinscription of marginality through a process of "othering" by means of power.[5] Constructs like man/woman become even more repressive when they are posited as a "binary dualism positioning the woman as a negative but necessary precondition for defining man."[6] Similarly homosexuality becomes the abnormal foil when positioned in a binary, with the normative power bestowed to heterosexuality. Early queer theory was pivotal, though, in highlighting how mainstream culture was "riddled" with heteronormativity.[7] Yet, queer became initially a reactive category, positioned in opposition to heteronormative markers, which reinforced the powerful position of heterosexuality.[8] Early queer theory silenced voices not easily slotted into these simple categorizations,[9] and was Eurocentric in focus.[10] A critique of homonormativity, and the privileging of educated, middle-class, white, masculine-performing, gay males as idealized representations of queerness, resulted.

Our artists disturb conventional ideas about gender and the binary that birthed the idea of queerness. They problematize the notion of homosexual/ heterosexual.[11] The "blackness" of these artists, and ways in which gender and sexuality are impacted by race, as well as their chosen music genre, also impact the analysis. As McCune states, "black queer performance, of any type, must be understood as always informed by the interplay of race, gender, class, and sexuality."[12] The visibility of black queer performance has gradually shifted,[13] making an exploration of the ways in which some artists are "queering"[14] the genre a timely undertaking. The artists discussed here are pop culture demonstrations of a queer analytical framework where reductionist binaries take on more nuanced, intersectional characteristics.[15]

Binaries maintain defining power,[16] but in this case it can give their subversions subcultural capital. Some of the spectacle of these performances derives from their play against stereotypes, which can potentially reinscribe the binary hegemony. To create a spectacle of sexual identity outside the norm, one needs to first place oneself inside the mainstream binaries.[17] These four MCs deconstruct the idea that sexual and gender identities are fixed; but "queer" as a framework can still be problematically defined against heteronormativity.[18]

Popular music, hip-hop, and homophobia: "The library is open"

Popular music has a complicated relationship with queerness and the gender binary. While specific pop genres include particular acceptable constructions of gender and sexuality,[19] pop music has often provided spaces for "queer bodies" to "tolerably skew the margins of acceptable identity under the guide of frivolity and entertainment."[20] That popular music has the capacity to facilitate these explorations suggests that music is a vital medium through which normative sexual and gender roles can be challenged.[21]

This is more problematic when in the genre of hip-hop. While hip-hop is generally stigmatized as homophobic, this shirks the possibility of queer and "down low" fans and artists, who derive pleasure and empowerment from the genre.[22] While the notion of hip-hop as anti-queer has much truth to it, even from so-called conscious hip-hop artists, this ignores the complexities around black masculinity that, due to histories of slavery, colonization, and racism, has a problematic relationship with anything outside cis-heteronormativity. While there are countless examples of homophobic and hate speech lyrics, there are also numerous examples of queer MC's and movements. And while queer black, Latinx,[23] and minority communities may balk at the mainstream canon of anti-gay hip-hop, they can still enjoy the race politics and representation of the genre, just as women have for years been able to both disagree with yet enjoy misogynist rock stars and other pop genres and musicians.[24]

Homophobia plays a role in defining black masculinity.[25] The black church has criticized homosexuality as a white wrought disease seeking to weaken black families and the black nation.[26] This fight over black men's bodies is rooted in slavery and colonization.[27] Migrant and diaspora men suffer racist and economic assaults on their dignity and masculinity and this can result in a pronounced response of homophobia and misogyny, sometimes visible in popular music.[28] Rapper Blanco herself asserts that hip-hop and the black community's homophobia comes from misogyny.[29] She hopes that "when femininity is seen as a source of power in black culture, homophobia will no longer exist."[30] Rose[31] points out that critics of hip-hop's homophobia act as if hip-hop "smuggled homophobia" into an "innocent welcoming America." So, while not apologising for rap's harm or exclusion, the genre must be situated in the wider heteronormative context of the US and its raced communities, as well as hip-hop's position as a cultural product. Furthermore, hip-hop is not fully representative of black culture; Rose argues that it merely represents the "versions of black reality" acceptable for white consumption and which benefits white market power.[32]

Hip-hop insiders have claimed that there have always been queer people in hip-hop but they remain on the "down low." Gay female MC Syd, from the collective Odd Future, presumes to out a few lesbians,[33] for example, while Terrence Dean has written about his gay experiences in the hip-hop community.[34] He argues that there are many prominent gay, bi, and queer rappers who "have to" hide,[35] because hip-hop artists, executives, and fans "don't want to know"; hip-hop culture is not a safe environment to come out in. From a different perspective, Mykki Blanco cites Cam-ron, rappers wearing lots of jewellery, Tupac's groomed eyebrows, and Kanye's fashion sense, as examples of gay imagery in hip-hop for young gay fans to be inspired by.[36] And Coleman and Cobb explore how rapper Caushun exploited gender ambiguity, offering himself up as a "homothug," confusing the audience's ability to consume his body, which was "at once hyper-masculinized though this thug identity and hyper-feminized through his queen identity."[37] Blanco says that young gay fans have been getting turned on by this imagery all along. She points out the irony of sayings like "no-homo,"[38] while on the other hand rappers talk about "swag." She says "swag" is a "gay black attitude," and that "gay men invented swag."[39]

Despite these claims, homophobia means that this aspect of hip-hop culture has been coded and hidden. The "down low," a slang term originally meaning "hidden," has become a useful term for a certain sexuality. It describes men who do not identify as gay but have sex with men, and has been particularly important in relation to the reassessment of HIV prevention and other sexual health campaigns.[40] McCune Jr explored black gay clubs in Chicago, where down low men perform "straight" masculine identities while engaging homoerotic desires.[41] They performed a brand of heterosexist "cool": "the queer subjects who yell 'faggot ass nigga' can feel a part of a larger black masculine sphere, one that usually excludes them."[42] It is also a moment when gay men can "de-queer" themselves, aligning with a masculinity that distances from the possibility of being perceived as "femmes," thus condemning the feminine male and ridiculing those who perform the non-penetrative sexual role.

But things are gradually changing. Mainstream superstars Jay Z and 50 Cent have signaled their support of Obama's endorsement of gay marriage;[43] rap mogul Russell Simmons has called homophobia a "sickness" in hip-hop;[44] MTV executive/BET music director Darren Brin has come out;[45] and A$AP Rocky has signaled hope for more queer acceptance in hip-hop.[46] Proper respect ("props") must also be given to the pioneering 1990s movement called "Homo Hop."[47] Coined by Tim'm T. West of the Deep Dickollective, homo hop sought not to find acceptance within hip-hop but to assert that both hip-hop and queerness should be done differently than what was being prominently projected.[48] Seeing themselves as a "necessary mobilizing tool that allowed openly queer hip-hop artists to come together,"[49] they organized the PeaceOut World Homo Hop Festival, in 2001, in Oakland, although they were aware that the term "Homo Hop" was not necessarily helpful (a reservation our featured artists have also expressed about the newer term "queer hip-hop.")[50] However, the initiative was sustained, and a 2006 documentary "Pick Up the Mic" explored the underground LGBT hip-hop scene, and further PeaceOut festivals in New York, Atlanta, and London.[51]

It is over the past 10 years, though, that technology has increasingly allowed niche artists to circulate outside mainstream record labels and build global audiences.[52] There are now a multitude of out gay rappers (both black and white) producing hip-hop music, such as JBDubs, Cazwell, Big Dipper, and Sissy Rich.[53] Rapper Shamir asserts in interviews and social media that zie[54] has no gender, no sexuality.[55] Drag queens, House of Ladosha,[56] are an "artistic collective" whose raps celebrate New York ball culture and they perform a flamboyant femme identity. Also gaining some underground traction is Young Thug,[57] a Southern gangster rapper who has worked with Gucci Mane and Waka Flocka Flame. He does not deny rumours that he may be gay, and he wears skirts, dresses, and other flamboyant garb.

In other media, a gay couple are part of the reality show "Love and Hip-hop: Hollywood" (VH1),[58] and TV series "Empire" (Fox), which centres around a hip-hop mogul and his family-run record label, also features a gay character, with storylines that center around his acceptance in the family and hip-hop business. While more a singer, Frank Ocean's coming out as bisexual in 2012, although problematic in his embodiment of the heteronormative hip-hop male,[59] was arguably an important moment; many mainstream figures such as Snoop Dogg and Busta Rhymes signaled their support.[60] White rapper Macklemore released a song called "Same Love," which advocates straight acceptance of queer lifestyles. He performed the track at the 2014 Grammy Awards ceremony where, during the song, female rap pioneer Queen Latifah officiated thirty-four gay marriages live on television.[61] Ocean's authenticity and recognized artistry, though, arguably meant that his coming out had a much greater impact than Macklemore's effort, on suspicion that Macklemore has received awards over more deserving black MC's due to racism in the music industry.[62]

Deserving of a chapter itself, Bounce is a genre and movement rooted in the geography, history, and culture of New Orleans, both pre- and post-Katrina.[63] It features a particular music style and possibly originated "twerking." For some reason, this rap music was particularly gay-friendly and produced some important genderqueer and gay artists. Occasionally called "Sissy Bounce," rappers such as Katey Red (a drag queen) and Sissy Nobby (transgendered) perform the genre at both gay and straight clubs. Post-Katrina Bounce spread outside the region. Known as the "Queen of Bounce," Big Freedia is featured on Beyoncé's "Formation" song and now has her own reality TV show.

Finally, an "honourable" mention in this "reading" of queer hip-hop, is Nicki Minaj. Though not gay, she has a large gay following which she is supportive and appreciative of.[64] Academics have explored Minaj's queer aesthetics, looking especially at her use of camp, her hyper-femme gender performance, and her refusal of acceptable black feminine gender performance.[65] Smith argues that Minaj's gender performances are able to "reassure" the heterosexual hip-hop community while at the same time "giving an air of inclusivity" for queer fans.[66]

While this discussion problematizes how hip-hop is pigeonholed as homophobic, and celebrates hip hop's queer proponents, there is no intent to minimize or mitigate the malice and harm which comes from the anti-gay lyrics and comments of highly lauded MCs.[67] Even supposedly conscious rappers like Common, Brand Nubian, and Tribe Called Quest have spat gay slurs.[68]

Four artists: "We're all cunty"

Cakes Da Killa, Le1f, Mykki Blanco, and Zebra Katz are four hip-hop MCs who are not at all ambiguous with their sexualities but whose gender performances and identities destabilize stereotypes and notions around gay masculinities, hip-hop masculinity, trans, genderqueer, and drag.

Rashard Bradshaw, born in the mid-nineties in New Jersey, goes by the name Cakes Da Killa. He has released music on three digital "mixtapes": *Easy Bake Oven, Vol. 1* (2011), *The Eulogy* (2013), and *Hunger Pangs* (2014). Some of his notable songs are "I Run This Club," "Goodie Goodies," and "Living Gud, Eating Gud." His lyrics turn the braggadocio and sexual prowess of hip-hop into assertive and explicit gay stories and affirmations. He self-identifies as a gay rapper, an "older brother," a "momma's boy," and a "good friend." He further defines his identity looking at the intersections around sexuality and gender performance: "I sleep with men, sometimes, and I'm feminine on top of that, so it's just who I am."[69] He understands that, in hip-hop, he represents an anathema to the accepted versions of masculinity, but says homophobia won't affect him because "people will love me regardless." What could be a source of oppression and degradation, he instead turns into empowerment: he represents "all the feminine boys, the bottoms, the princess boys, boys who want to embrace their feminine side." His femme identity is a source of power: he is an object of desire, as well as sexual initiator. This follows the legacy of his rap idols which include hyper-femme, hyper-sexual rappers such as Li'l Kim, Foxy Brown, and Nicki Minaj. Cakes recognizes the ability of hip-hop to tell unique narratives, which in his case includes stories about "doing dick" and "sucking ass," not to shock or for political activism, but simply because those are his stories. He talks about how the black gay community has its own culture, slang, and dance moves, distinct from both the mainstream gay community and the general African American community. His lyrics are laden with multiple cultural layers: hip-hop, New York, African American, gay, and African American gay culture, and his own style and content.

Khalif Diouf, New York born and raised half African, half African American, is an MC, producer, and record label owner, who goes by the stage name Lelf.[70] A tall, dark, and muscled gay rapper, Lelf studied ballet and dance at Wesleyan University[71] and has released a number of mixtapes and EP's. His standout singles/videos include: "Wut" (2012), "Soda" (2012), "Spa Day" (2013), "Boom" (2014), and "Koi" (2015). Commenting on the title of his album *Riot Boy* (2015) he explains his version of a femme identity:

> That is something our scene [Riot Boy] has—regardless of who is in it, it has this very powerful feminine energy, like a Nefertiti head bust or Storm from X-Men. It's a woman you see as very powerful, sassy, arrogant, and dark.[72]

His lyrics confront racism in the gay community, as well as celebrate fashion and dance. The idols he cites are female Sri Lankan activist/rapper M.I.A. and female electronica punk Alice Glass and he talks about his music being influenced by Dizzie Rascal, video game sounds, and underground electronica.[73] He states that being gay is like being black: it is not something he could ever hide. He shuns the category of "queer rap" though, as it does not have any musical cohesion or definition.[74]

Mykki Blanco is the female drag persona of Michael Quattlebaum Jr. Although identifying as a man, Quattlebaum also presents and identifies as a black transvestite, a performance artist, and drag queen.[75] Although he has dressed as a woman on and off since the age of 16, he is clear in differentiating himself from transgendered people, whom he acknowledges face a different struggle and greater hardship.[76] The character Mykki Blanco began life as a teenage girl character for a YouTube video in 2010,[77] but then evolved into a musical, performance art piece. Inspired by the riot grrrl movement, her personae explodes female stereotypes by alternating through hyper-feminine, aggressive, goth, tom boy, sassy, bitchy, glamazon, and "it girl."[78] However, as a rapper, Blanco performs as both male and female, both under the name Mykki Blanco.[79]

Quattlebaum sees himself as part of a long line of pop culture cross-dressers such as RuPaul, Boy George, Freddie Mercury, Marilyn Manson, Marc Boland, and David Bowie, as an extension of glam rock and shock rock, the "rich history of weird." He says "besides RuPaul, I'm the only black transvestite that has been in *Elle*, Italian *Vogue*, or *Interview*," and that this promotes visibility "in a way that makes everything I'm doing completely normal."[80] This echoes the call by Butler (2011) for "subversive identities" that demonstrate the "constructedness" of gender, because they can normalize and destigmatize nonbinary gender presentations, allowing them to become "intelligible" instead of feared and unknown. Quattlebaum is criticized by his gay fans when he presents as masculine, who argue he is conforming to heteronormative music industry expectations; he counters that there are times when he simply doesn't feel like getting his nails done and "sorting his weave" (wig).[81]

Besides numerous art installations and collaborations (including "Gay Dog Food" with Kathleen Hanna 2014), Blanco's output includes EP's, mix tapes, and a "studio album."[82] Blanco's tracks/videos include "Join My Militia" (2012), "Head Is a Stone" (2012), "Haze.Boogie.Life" (2012), "Kingpinning" (2013), "Feeling Special" (2013), and "The Initiation" (2013). Active on social media, Blanco came out in 2015 on Twitter and Facebook as HIV positive, stating "fuck stigma and hiding in the dark, this is my real life. I'm healthy, I've toured the world 3 times but I've been living in the dark, it's time to actually be as punk as I say I am."[83] She has recently announced she is quitting music to become a journalist who highlights international gay and trans*[84] issues, starting in Nepal.[85]

Finally, Zebra Katz, the stage name of Ojay Morgan, was created while Morgan was studying at Eugene Lang College in New York City, and grew out of a performance piece called "Moor Contradictions." Morgan conceives of Zebra Katz as "the dark rapper, the dark villain, the dark lord of the fashion world."[86] He says, "I really liked the play on the Jewish last name."[87] His album, mixtape, and EP releases include *Nu Renegade* (2015), *Tear the House Up Remixes* (2014), *1 Bad Bitch* (2014), *Drking* (2013), and *Winter Titty* (2012), but his 2012 track "Ima Read" has arguably had the biggest impact.

The lyrics are drawn from ball culture slang, which he feels has enticed and confused both ball culture and hip-hop audiences. He joked that the hip-hop crowd will like that he uses the word bitch 87 times, which also saw him accused of misogyny.[88] This reading of bitch, however, misses how the term is used in ball culture: as a "challenging female" or "wicked woman," a backhanded compliment, a sly endearment when applied to drag queens (i.e. they are performing a fierce femininity). References to ball culture by gay rappers pays homage to not only the huge cultural impact of the movement, but also acknowledges its struggles and triumphs, connecting our four MCs to a lineage of communal cultural experiences shared by gay black and Latinos in New York (and now globally).

Katz does not do drag, he presents and identifies as "black," "queer," and "other":

> Creating a strong black queer male is something that really needed to happen because you don't see it that often, especially in hip-hop. But it's terrifying standing up as a queer man... But you have to use their sexuality as a tool, instead of having them use it against you.[89]

His lyrics and videos mix danger, expletives, critique, and braggadocio with fashion, fun, and pleasure. For instance, "Tear The House Up" is a colorful burst of fashion and art patterns; "Y I Do" is dark and sparse. "Blk Wiccan" exploits and celebrates multiple identities and bodies including age, gender, sexuality, ugly, and beautiful. And "Last Name Katz" is an acerbic attack on class, money, power, deviant sex, and medicine.

Besides undeniable charisma, these four artists have in common advanced educations, innovative underground electronica backing music, elaborate humorous music videos, and subversive identities. And, we argue, they embody the term "fierce" as a sexuality and a hip-hop gender performance. They express discomfort at the term "queer hip-hop," which has been used by the media to group and define these and other queer artists of this time period and sensibility. Blanco hates the term, using it only because it exists. She feels that the so-called queer rap concept is faddish.[90] Katz feels "queer hip-hop" was something created and maintained solely by journalists, while Lelf is reluctant to differentiate his and others' music on the basis of sexuality:

> I really wanted to rap about being both black and gay simultaneously and what that means... but I'm very aware that people don't want to hear preachy music. Conscious rap is not my favourite type of rap... Let's not make gay NYC rap a 'thing'... If we were straight, no one would be comparing us [himself and Katz and Blanco et al].[91]

Bailey finds the term "queer hip-hop" an oxymoron because hip-hop is too entrenched in its embrace of "patriarchy, misogyny, capitalism, and other forms of kyriarchy."[92,93] She finds, however, that her anguish around hip-hop's sexism ends up aligning her instead with hip-hop's nihilism. She concedes that hip-hop's "I don't give a fuck" attitude offers a radical plan of action for smashing kyriarchy.

Queer hip-hop can be used as a point of difference, to gain attention, and is useful as part of the "hustle" (effort for success). Gay New Orleans Bounce queens, for example, are aware that bookings outside of their home city are founded increasingly on the novelty of their sexual identities. Dee said of Bounce:

> The notion of unabashedly gay hip-hop is like catnip to some alternative-music scenes around the country. Which puts the artists themselves in something of a bind: while sissy-bounce bookings offer them a rare chance to raise their national profiles, the last thing any of them wants is to put homosexuality at the forefront of what they do.[94]

The final word on "queer hip-hop" comes from Cakes, who does not want to be pigeonholed but is resigned to the fact that, "we're all cunty, we're all gay, and we're all really out."

Fierceness

Adjective

1　A term that gay men use to describe absolutely everything that is of "exceptional quality."
2　A term used to describe objects, people, or instances that are outlandish and cannot be handled with subtlety; often with great or animated emphasis.
3　A term coined by African American gay men to describe things are extraordinary, in either a positive or negative way.

Verb

1   The act of being bold, displaying confidence, creativity or self-reliance. Relates directly to fashion, clothes, hair or makeup.[95]

In attempting to make sense of the layered presentations of our artists, we were confronted with a theoretical conundrum. While there were clear ambiguities in their gender performances and identities, there was an undeniable essence that connected them, beyond "queerness." We posit that the concept of "fierceness" can be employed to explain the processes by which hip-hop is being queered, disrupted, and its predominant sexual norms refused. Although a popular term in contemporary (black) pop culture, giving it contextual currency, the notion of "fierceness" has a much longer history with queer black idioms. Language has historically played an important role in creating queer codes for queer communities, allowing queer people to (re) claim language as an identity marker.[96] The idea of "fierceness" aligns with the aggressive, assertive performances of hip-hop, but it is an alignment that queers in the process, allowing for ambiguity, chimera, and transgression.

The term "fierce" emerged from ball culture, an underground scene where predominantly black and Latino competitors "walk" for trophies in a multitude of categories that highlight aspects of dance, gay culture, and gender play, for example butch queen, drag diva, ghetto fab, realness male/female.[97] Ball culture achieved some mainstream attention in 1990, after the release of *Paris is Burning*, a documentary about the late-1980s New York's scene. In the same year, Madonna appropriated the "vogue" style of walking in her global hit of the same name, and, in 1993, drag celebrity RuPaul also featured ball culture in her single "Supermodel (You Better Werk)." From here, "fierce" moved into widespread use in black gay culture,[98] gay culture more broadly, and now appears ubiquitously. As Hancock notes, fierce "signifies gay culture just by name alone... In the gay community, being *fierce* is a known compliment."[99]

Rather than an identity marker, which implies a fixed nature, we conceive of fierceness as a sensibility. Our acts occupy multiple positions along axes of sexuality and gender. They defy being fixed, shifting performance by performance, video by video. Fierceness becomes an amalgamation of identity markers that are queered and authenticated. It becomes a powerful assertion, the (re)claiming of power within the hip-hop and queer cultures. Fierceness becomes a defiant challenge to status quos; to heteronormative society, to heteronormativity within hip-hop culture, to homonormativity within gay culture, to those who try to attach static categorical positions.

Susan Sontag famously positioned camp as a sensibility, a sensibility that "converts the serious into the frivolous."[100] This echoes our MCs' desires to make statements without making overtly activist art. Rather than through overt political attack, the hyper-masculine, heteronormativity of hip-hop is trivialized and parodied, made frivolous through its juxtaposition with a mixture of outlandish camp, drag, hyper-femininity, and homo-normativity. "Fierceness" takes the queer/gay/effeminate labels used as a tool of disempowerment, and reacts against them by owning and incorporating them into its multiple discourses. By daring hip-hop audiences/mainstream society to gaze upon them, knowing that they control this gaze, these queer rappers disrupt and challenge, take pleasure in the confusion, revel in the possible uncomfortableness of its audience, and thus shift the dynamics of power. Fierceness is not about "gay" rappers performing "masculine," "feminine," or "gay" identities; it's about "rappers" who are gay "queering" hip-hop by disregarding its heteronormative foundations in full gaze of its detractors, making the performances inherently political, yet rebelliously pleasurable, acts.

Sashay away

Is "fierceness" a contextually appropriate alternative sensibility to camp? Certainly it has connections to, and roots within the black community, and has become ubiquitous in (black) gay culture. We offer it mostly, though, as an alternative to the term "queer hip-hop" to describe the ambiguous sexuality and gender presentations of these and other black gay rap artists. Is fierceness available to queer artists outside hip-hop? To white gay men or black females? This should be up for further exploration. Despite being often seen as intolerant of nonmainstream sexualities and genders, hip-hop is nonetheless able to provide musical frameworks, political histories, aesthetic inspiration, activist attitudes, racial solidarity, and even idols for these rap artists. Hip-hop is flexible enough as a genre to be a voice for all marginalized, even those rejected by some of its most celebrated proponents. Having drag queens, riot boys, femme males, and queens as rappers affronts gender and sexuality categories not only in the mainstream, but disrupts even residual binaries found in queer theory, hip-hop culture, the black community, and popular music.

Notes

1 Zebra Katz 2012 "Ima Read" on Mad Decent.
2 e.g. Butler, Judith. *Gender Trouble: Feminism and the Subversion of Identity*. London and New York: Routledge, 2011.
3 e.g. Namaste, Ki. "The Politics of Inside/Out: Queer Theory, Poststructuralism, and a Sociological Approach to Sexuality." *Sociological Theory* 12.2 (1994): 220–231; Spargo, Tamsin. *Foucault and Queer Theory*. Sydney: Allen & Unwin, 2000; Taylor, Jodi. "The Music of Kings and Bio Queens." *Kritikos: An International and Interdisciplinary Journal of Postmodern Cultural Sound, Text and Image* 4 (2007), http://intertheory.org/jtaylor.htm.
4 e.g. Lorimer, Stuart. "2015: The Trans Moment?" *Huffington Post*, December 20, 2015, www.huffingtonpost.co.uk/dr-stuart-lorimer/2015-transgender-rights_b_8826856.html.
5 Namaste, Ki. "The Politics of Inside/Out: Queer Theory, Poststructuralism, and a Sociological Approach to Sexuality." *Sociological Theory* 12.2 (1994): 220–231.

6 Taylor, Jodi. "The Music of Kings and Bio Queens." *Kritikos: An International and Interdisciplinary Journal of Postmodern Cultural Sound, Text and Image* 4 (2007), http://intertheory.org/jtaylor.htm.

7 Berlant, Lauren and Michael Warner. "What Does Queer Theory Teach Us about X?" *PMLA* 110 (1995): 349.

8 Grosz, Elizabeth. *Space, Time, and Perversion: Essays on the Politics of Bodies.* London and New York: Routledge, 1995.

9 Stein, Arlene and Ken Plummer. "I Can't Even Think Straight": "Queer" Theory and the Missing Sexual Revolution in Sociology." *Sociological Theory* 12.2 (1994): 182.

10 Spargo, Tamsin. *Foucault and Queer Theory.* Sydney: Allen & Unwin, 2000.

11 Ibid.

12 McCune Jr, Jeffrey. ""Out" in the Club: The Down Low, Hip-Hop, and the Architexture of Black Masculinity." *Text and Performance Quarterly* 28.3 (2008): 298–314.

13 Ibid.

14 Jagose, Annamarie. "Queer Theory." *Australian Humanities Review* (1996), www.australianhumanitiesreview.org/archive/Issue-Dec-1996/jagose.html.

15 See, [and similarly throughout], e.g. Anthias, Floya. "Intersectional What? Social Divisions, Intersectionality and Levels of Analysis." *Ethnicities* 13.1 (2013): 3–19.

16 e.g. Bettani, Stefano. "Straight Subjectivities in Homonormative Spaces: Moving towards a New, 'Dynamic' Heteronormativity?" *Gender, Place and Culture* 22.2 (2015): 239–254; Taylor, Jodi. "The Music of Kings and Bio Queens." *Kritikos: An International and Interdisciplinary Journal of Postmodern Cultural Sound, Text and Image* 4 (2007), http://intertheory.org/jtaylor.htm.

17 Namaste, Ki. "The Politics of Inside/Out: Queer Theory, Poststructuralism, and a Sociological Approach to Sexuality." *Sociological Theory* 12.2 (1994): 224.

18 Browne, Kath. "A Party with Politics?(Re) Making LGBTQ Pride Spaces in Dublin and Brighton." *Social & Cultural Geography* 8.1 (2007): 63–87.

19 Maus, Fred. "Music, Gender and Sexuality." In *The Cultural Study of Music: A Critical Introduction*, edited by Martin Clayton, Trevor Herbert and Richard Middleton, 317–329. London and New York: Routledge, 2011.

20 Taylor, Jodi. "The Music of Kings and Bio Queens." *Kritikos: An International and Interdisciplinary Journal of Postmodern Cultural Sound, Text and Image* 4 (2007), http://intertheory.org/jtaylor.htm, also Taylor, Jodi. *Playing it Queer: Popular Music, Identity and Queer World-Making.* Bern: Peter Lang, 2012.

21 Dibben, Nicola. "Gender Identity and Music. In *Musical Identities,* edited by Raymond MacDonald, David Hargreaves and Dorothy Miell, 117–133. Oxford: Oxford University Press, 2002.

22 Clay (2012).

23 Used by some publications and scholars as a gender neutral and inclusive term for people of Latin American descent.

24 e.g. Manuel, Peter. "Gender Politics in Caribbean Popular Music: Consumer Perspectives and Academic Interpretation." *Popular Music & Society* 22.2 (1998): 11–29; Whitely, Sheila. "Repressive Representations: Patriarchy and Femininities in Rock Music of the Counterculture." In *Mapping the Beat: Popular Music and Contemporary Theory*, edited by Thomas Swiss, John Sloop and Andrew Herman. Malden, MA: Blackwell Publishers, 1998.

25 e.g. Harper, Phillip. *Are We Not Men? Masculine Anxiety and the Problem of African-American Identity.* Oxford: Oxford University Press, 1998.

26 Ward, Elijah. "Homophobia, Hypermasculinity and the US Black Church." *Culture, Health & Sexuality* 7.5 (2005): 493–504.

27 Tengan, Ty Kwika. "(En)Gendering Colonialism: Masculinities in Hawai'i and Aotearoa." *Cultural Values* 6.3 (2002): 239–256.

28 Lipschitz, George. "World Cities and World Beat: Low-Wage Labor and Trans-national Culture." *Pacific Historical Review* 68.2 (1999): 213–231.
29 Kretowicz, Steph. "Mykki Blanco Interview: 'I'm Basically Just Doing Glam Rock.'" *Dummy Magazine* March 28, 2013, www.dummymag.com/features/mykki-blanco-interview-i-m-basically-just-doing-glam-rock.
30 Lamphier, Jason. "Mykki Blanco on His Origins, Queer Rap, & Homophobia in Black Culture." *Bullett Media*, September 13, 2012, http://bullettmedia.com/article/mykki-blanco-on-his-origin-story-queer-rap-homophobia-in-black-culture/.
31 Rose, Tricia. *The Hip-Hop Wars: What We Talk about When We Talk about Hip-Hop—And Why It Matters*. New York: Basic Civitas Books, 2013.
32 Ibid.
33 Domanick, Andrea. "Syd the Kyd on Odd Future, Her Sexuality and Why She Hates the Word "Lesbian"." *LA Weekly*, January 12, 2012, www.laweekly.com/music/syd-the-kyd-on-odd-future-her-sexuality-and-why-she-hates-the-word-lesbian-2409072.
34 Dean, Terrance. *Hiding in Hip-hop: On the Down Low in the Entertainment Industry from Music to Hollywood*. New York: Atria Paperback, 2008.
35 "Is Hip-Hop Homophobic?" *Hello Beautiful*, http://hellobeautiful.com/2011/04/06/mr-cee-hip-hop-homophobic.
36 Saurs, Jenna. "The Making of Mykki Blanco." *The Village Voice*, April 10, 2013, www.villagevoice.com/music/the-making-of-mykki-blanco-6437986.
37 Coleman, Robin and Jasmine Cobb. "No Way of Seeing: Mainstreaming and Selling the Gaze of Homo-Thug Hip-Hop." *Popular Communication: The International Journal of Media and Culture* 5.2 (2007): 89–108; p. 92.
38 When straight people get caught saying something of a potentially double en-tendre sexual nature to a same–sex friend; Weiner, Jonah. "Does This Purple Mink Make Me Look Gay? The Rise of No Homo and the Changing Face of Hip-Hop Homophobia." *Slate*, August 6, 2009, www.slate.com/articles/arts/music_box/2009/08/does_this_purple_mink_make_me_look_gay.html; Brown, Joshua R. "No Homo." *Journal of Homosexuality* 58.3 (2011): 299–314.
39 "Swagger" was originally a confident walk, has come to mean over style and presentation; Battan, Carrie. "We Invented Swag: NYC's Queer Rap." *Pitchfork*, March 21, 2012, http://pitchfork.com/features/article/8793-we-invented-swag/.
40 Ford, Chandra et al. "Black Sexuality, Social Construction, and Research Targeting 'The Down Low' ('The DL')." *Annals of Epidemiology* 17.3 (2007): 209–216; Wolitski, Richard J. et al. "Self-Identification as "Down Low" among Men Who have Sex with Men (MSM) from 12 US Cities." *AIDS and Behavior* 10.5 (2006): 519–529.
41 McCune Jr, Jeffrey. *Sexual Discretion: Black Masculinity and the Politics of Passing*. Chicago, IL: University of Chicago Press, 2014.
42 McCune Jr, Jeffrey. ""Out" in the Club: The Down Low, Hip-Hop, and the Archi-texture of Black Masculinity." *Text and Performance Quarterly* 28.3 (2008): 307.
43 "Jay-Z Supports Gay Marriage – Rap Mogul Backs President Obama: 'It's about People'." *Rolling Stone*, May 15, 2012, www.rollingstone.com/music/news/jay-z-supports-gay-marriage-20120515; www.bet.com/news/music/2012/07/16/50-cent-supports-frank-ocean-gay-marriage.html.
44 Morgan, Glennisha. "Russell Simmons Calls Homophobia A Sickness, Says Rappers Less Anti-Gay than Before." *Huffpost Queer Voices*, February 02, 2016, www.huffingtonpost.com/2013/02/22/russell-simmons-homophobia-gay-rights_n_2742321.html.
45 Balfour, Jay. "Former MTV & BET Executive Darren 'Buttahman' Brin Speaks On Homophobia in Hip Hop." *Hip Hop DX*, April 8, 2015, http://hiphopdx.com/news/id.33323/title.former-mtv-bet-executive-darren-buttahman-brin-speaks-on-homophobia-in-hip-hop.

46 Morgan, Glenisha. "Rapper A$AP Rocky Sounds Off On 'The Gay Thing' in Hip Hop." *Huffpost Queer Voices*, February 02, 2016, www.huffingtonpost. com/2013/03/25/rapper-asap-rocky-gay-thing-hip-hop_n_2950676.html.

47 Woo, Jen. "Homo Hop is Dead, Queer Hip Hop is the Real Deal." *FourTwoNine*, March 11, 2013, http://dot429.com/articles/1645-homo-hop-is-dead-queer-hip-hop-is-the-real-deal.

48 Spaulding, Stephany. "Margin Me: Intentional Marginality in the Queered Borderlands of Hip-Hop." In *Understanding Blackness through Performance: Contemporary Arts and the Representation of Identity*, edited by Anne Cremieux, Xavier Lemoine and Jean-Paul Rocchi, 181–195. New York: Palgrave MacMillan, 2013.

49 Woo, Jen. "Homo Hop is Dead, Queer Hip Hop is the Real Deal." *FourTwoNine*, March 11, 2013, http://dot429.com/articles/1645-homo-hop-is-dead-queer-hip-hop-is-the-real-deal.

50 Shorey, Eric. "Queer Rap is Not Queer Rap." *Pitchfork*, April 1, 2015, http:// pitchfork.com/thepitch/712-queer-rap-is-not-queer-rap/.

51 Booth, Kwan. "Peaceout Festival brings Homo-Hop to the World." *Bay Area Reporter*, Vol. 46/No. 14/7, April 2016, www.ebar.com/news/article. php?sec=news&article=2215.

52 Glass, Pepper. "Doing Scene: Identity, Space, and the Interactional Accomplishment of Youth Culture." *Journal of Contemporary Ethnography* (2012). doi:10.1177/0891241612454104.

53 For purposes of brevity, our analysis focuses on cis-gendered male rappers. It must however be acknowledged that, in recent years, there has also been a cluster of defiantly out young female MC's, such as Azealia Banks and Brooke Candy (e.g. Duffy, Nick. "Azealia Banks: I Can't Be Homophobic because I'm Bisexual." *Pink News*, July 4, 2015, www.pinknews.co.uk/2015/07/04/azealia-banks-i-cant-be-homophobic-because-im-bisexual/; Pursley, Angelica. "The Interview: Brooke Candy." *Hunger TV*, May 6, 2014, www.hungertv.com/ feature/interview-brooke-candy/; Smith, Marquita. ""Or a Real, Real Bad Lesbian": Nicki Minaj and the Acknowledgement of Queer Desire in Hip-Hop Culture." *Popular Music and Society* 37.3 (2014): 360–370.

54 A pronoun some people choose to address persons of no gender.

55 Vivinetto, Gina. "Is Shamir the Post-Gender Pop Star for Our Time?" *Advocate*, May 14, 2015, www.advocate.com/arts-entertainment/music/2015/05/14/shamir-post-gender-pop-star-our-time; Beaudoin, Kate. "The Next Big Pop Star has 'No Gender, No Sexuality and No F***s To Give'." *Huffington Post*, April 03, 2015, www.huffingtonpost.com/2015/04/03/shamir-sexuality_n_7000716.html.

56 Chapman, Alex. "Discovery: House of Ladosha." *Interview Magazine*, June 14, 2012, www.interviewmagazine.com/music/discovery-house-of-ladosha#; Out. com Editors. "Out100: House of Ladosha". Out.Com 2013-11-11, www.out.com/ out-exclusives/out100-2013/2013/11/11/out100-house-ladosha.

57 Miller-Rosenberg, Doran. "Is Young Thug The First Gay Thug Rapper?" *Elite Daily*, February 11, 2014, http://elitedaily.com/music/music-news/young-thug-first-gay-thug-rapper/.

58 Kaufman, Gil. "'Love & Hip Hop Hollywood' Specia Gets Real about Gay Rappers." MTV News, October 19, 2015, www.mtv.com/news/2354367/love-hip-hop-hollywood-gay-rappers-church/; Kennedy, Gerrick D. "Black Gay Couple in VH1's 'Love & Hip Hop: Hollywood' Breaks New Ground." *Los Angeles Times*, October 19, 2015, www.latimes.com/entertainment/la-et-ms-gay-hip-hop-hollywood-20151019-story.html.

59 Sasaki-Picou, Nayo. "Performing Gender: The Construction of Black Males in the Hip-Hop Industry." *Contingent Horizons: The York University Student Journal of Anthropology* 1.1 (2014): 103–107.

60 Markman, Rob. "Frank Ocean Is 'Impeccable,' Busta Rhymes Praises." *MTV News*, July 6, 2012, www.mtv.com/news/1689131/frank-ocean-coming-out-busta-rhymes/.

61 "Macklemore, Queen Latifah Turn 'Same Love' into Mass Grammy Wedding." *Rolling Stone*, January 26, 2014, www.rollingstone.com/music/news/macklemore-queen-latifah-turn-same-love-into-mass-grammy-wedding-20140126.

62 Menyes, Carolyn. "Macklemore Discusses Race in Hip-Hop, White Appro-priation and 'Thrift Shop' Success on Hot 97." *Music Times*, December 30, 2014, www.musictimes.com/articles/22276/20141230/macklemore-race-hiphop-white-appropriation-thrift-shop-hot-97-watch.htm; Battan, Carrie. "Macklemore Says Kendrick Deserved Grammy for Best Rap Album." *Pitchfork*, January 27, 2014, http://pitchfork.com/news/53726-macklemore-says-kendrick-deserved-grammy-for-best-rap-album/.

63 Zemke, Kirsten. "What the Genre-Bounce." *APRA/AMCOS*, September 07, 2015, http://apraamcos.co.nz/news/2015/september/what-the-genre-bounce/.

64 Gajewski, Ryan. "Is Nicki Minaj Gay? The Answer Might Surprise You!" *Wetpaint*, April 25, 2013, www.wetpaint.com/is-nicki-minaj-bisexual-the-answer-might-surprise-you-765852/; Benxi, Trish. "Nicki Minaj Says She's Not Really Bisexual." *Afterellen*, June 18, 2010, www.afterellen.com/people/74948-nicki-minaj-says-shes-not-really-bisexual.

65 McMillan, Uri. "Nicki-Aesthetics: The Camp Performance of Nicki Minaj." *Women & Performance: A Journal of Feminist Theory* 24.1 (2014): 79–87; Shange, Savannah. "A King Named Nicki: Strategic Queerness and the Black Femmecee." *Women & Performance: A Journal of Feminist Theory* 24.1 (2014): 29–45; Smith, Marquita. ""Or a Real, Real Bad Lesbian": Nicki Minaj and the Acknowledgement of Queer Desire in Hip-Hop Culture." *Popular Music and Society* 37.3 (2014): 360–370; White, Theresa. "Missy "Misdemeanor" Elliott and Nicki Minaj Fashionistin' Black Female Sexuality in Hip-Hop Culture—Girl Power or Overpowered?" *Journal of Black Studies* 44.6 (2013): 607–626.

66 Smith, Marquita. ""Or a Real, Real Bad Lesbian": Nicki Minaj and the Ac-knowledgement of Queer Desire in Hip-Hop Culture." *Popular Music and Soci-ety* 37.3 (2014): 360–370.

67 Yuscavage, Chris. "10 Rappers Who Have Gotten into Trouble for Making Homophobic Statements." *Vibe*, January 10, 2013, www.vibe.com/2013/01/10-rappers-who-have-gotten-trouble-making-homophobic-statements/.

68 Williams, Stereo. "Hip-Hop's Most Anti-Gay Lyrics." *Rolling Out*, February 5, 2013, http://rollingout.com/2013/02/05/lord-jamar-calls-kanye-west-queer-conscious-hip-hops-10-most-homophobic-lyrics/.

69 "HipHop Reborn: Cakes da Killa," uploaded January 21, 2012, by Blunted Music, www.youtube.com/watch?v=f1fYKC82swE.

70 Camp & Street, a subsidiary of Greedhead Music.

71 Oliver, Shayne. "Lelf'S Riot Movement." *Interview Magazine*, November 10, 2015, www.interviewmagazine.com/music/lelf-riot-boi.

72 Ibid.

73 Ibid.

74 "Gay Rapper Lelf on His Music, His Sexuality and the Haters." *Daily Extra*, September 29, 2014, www.youtube.com/watch?v=AZJsppUc7kE.

75 Kretowicz, Steph. "Mykki Blanco Interview: 'I'm Basically Just Doing Glam Rock.'" *Dummy Magazine*, March 28, 2013, www.dummymag.com/features/mykki-blanco-interview-i-m-basically-just-doing-glam-rock.

76 Ibid.

77 Lamphier, Jason. "Mykki Blanco on His Origins, Queer Rap, & Homophobia in Black Culture." *Bullett Media*, September 13, 2012, http://bullettmedia.com/article/mykki-blanco-on-his-origin-story-queer-rap-homophobia-in-black-culture/.

78 Hawkins, Stan. *Queerness in Pop Music*. London and New York: Routledge, 2015: 207; Saurs, Jenna. "The Making of Mykki Blanco." *The Village Voice*, April 10, 2013, www.villagevoice.com/music/the-making-of-mykki-blanco-6437986.
79 see "Wavvy" 2012 and "She Gutta" 2014.
80 Kelly, Chris. "'I Want to f**k with People'. The unstoppable rise of Mykki Blanco." *Factmag*, November 3, 2012, www.factmag.com/2012/11/03/i-want-to-fk-with-people-the-unstoppable-rise-of-mykki-blanco/2/.
81 Ibid.
82 *Michael* 2015; *White Pelle Pelle* 2015; *Spring/Summer 2014* 2014; *Betty Rubble: The Initiation* 2013; *Mykki Blanco & the Mutant Angels* 2012; and *Cosmic Angel: The Illuminati Prince/ss* 2012.
83 "Queer Artist Mykki Blanco Reveals He Is HIV Positive." *Gay Star News*, June 13, 2015, www.gaystarnews.com/article/rapper-and-queer-groundbreaker-mykki-blanco-says-he-hiv-positive130615/#gs.QEefmCI.
84 Using trans with an asterisk is still being explored in the queer community. For some it was a way to express more than specifically trans men and trans women, to include identities like gender fluid, agender, non-binary, two spirit, transsexual, transvestite, among others. We use it here to further awareness of the evolution of language around gender.
85 Villareal, Yezmin. "Why Mykki Blanco Is Quitting Rap to Become an Investigative Journalist." *Advocate*, March 24, 2015, www.advocate.com/arts-entertainment/music/2015/03/24/why-mykki-blanco-quitting-rap-become-investigative-journalist.
86 Ugwu, Reggie. "Zebra Katz Talks Busta Rhymes, Covering Tiffany's 'I Think We're Alone Now' & 'DRKLNG' Mixtape." *Billboard*, May 24, 2013 accessed April 10, 2016, www.billboard.com/articles/columns/the-juice/1563858/zebra-katz-talks-busta-rhymes-covering-tiffany-drklng-mixtape.
87 Battan, Carrie. "We Invented Swag: NYC's Queer Rap." *Pitchfork*, March 21, 2012, http://pitchfork.com/features/article/8793-we-invented-swag/.
88 Ibid.; also Hoby, Hermione. "Zebra Katz: 'Creating a Strong, Black, Queer Male Is Something that Needed to Happen.'" *The Guardian*, May 25, 2013, www.theguardian.com/music/2013/may/25/zebra-katz-interview-ima-read.
89 Ibid.
90 Saurs, Jenna. "The Making of Mykki Blanco." *The Village Voice*, April 10, 2013, www.villagevoice.com/music/the-making-of-mykki-blanco-6437986.
91 Battan, Carrie. "We Invented Swag: NYC's Queer Rap." *Pitchfork*, March 21, 2012, http://pitchfork.com/features/article/8793-we-invented-swag/.
92 Bailey, Moya. "Homolatent Masculinity & Hip-Hop Culture." *Palimpsest: A Journal on Women, Gender, and the Black International* 2.2 (2013): 187–199.
93 Kyriarchy is an expansion on patriarchy to include multiple and intersecting forms of oppression including race, sexuality, ableism, colonialism etc.
94 Dee Jonathan. "Punks under Pressure Big- Freedia and Katey Red in the Third Ward of New Orleans." *The New York Times*, July 22, 2010, www.nytimes.com/2010/07/25/magazine/25bounce-t.html?pagewanted=all&_r=0.
95 From https://wordofthegay.wordpress.com/2008/03/04/4-fierce/.
96 e.g. Green, Jonathon. "Language: Polari." *Critical Quarterly* 39.1 (1997): 127–131; Kulick, Don. "Gay and Lesbian Language." *Annual Review of Anthropology* 29 (2000): 243–285.
97 e.g. Johnson, E. Patrick. "Mother Knows Best: Black Gay Vernacular and Transgressive Space." In *Speaking in Queer Tongues: Globalization and Gay Language*, edited by William L. Leap and Tom Boellstorff, 251–278. Champaign: University of Illinois Press, 2004.
98 e.g. Weems, Mickey. *The Fierce Tribe: Masculine Identity and Performance in the Circuit*. Logan: Utah State University Press, 2008.

99 Hancock, Joseph. "Chelsea on 5th Avenue: Hypermasculinity and Gay Clone Culture in the Retail Brand Practices of Abercrombie & Fitch." *Fashion Practice: The Journal of Design, Creative Process & the Fashion Industry* 1.1 (2009): 63–86: p. 80.
100 Sontag, Susan. "Notes on Camp." *Camp: Queer Aesthetics and the Performing Subject* (1964): 53–65.

Bibliography

Anthias, Floya. "Intersectional What? Social Divisions, Intersectionality and Levels of Analysis." *Ethnicities* 13.1 (2013): 3–19.
Bailey, Moya. "Homolatent Masculinity & Hip-Hop Culture." *Palimpsest: A Journal on Women, Gender, and the Black International* 2.2 (2013): 187–199.
Berlant, Lauren and Michael Warner. "What Does Queer Theory Teach Us about X?" *PMLA* 110 (1995): 343–349.
Bettani, Stefano. "Straight Subjectivities in Homonormative Spaces: Moving Towards a New, 'Dynamic' Heteronormativity?" *Gender, Place and Culture* 22.2 (2015): 239–254.
Brown, Joshua R. "No Homo." *Journal of Homosexuality* 58.3 (2011): 299–314.
Browne, Kath. "A Party with Politics?(Re) Making LGBTQ Pride Spaces in Dublin and Brighton." *Social & Cultural Geography* 8.1 (2007): 63–87.
Butler, Judith. *Gender Trouble: Feminism and the Subversion of Identity*. London and New York: Routledge, 2011.
Clay, Andreana. *The Hip-Hop Generation Fights Back: Youth, Activism and Post-Civil Rights Politics*. New York: New York University Press, 2012.
Coleman, Robin and Jasmine Cobb. "No Way of Seeing: Mainstreaming and Selling the Gaze of Homo-Thug Hip-Hop." *Popular Communication: The International Journal of Media and Culture* 5.2 (2007): 89–108.
Dean, Terrance. *Hiding in Hip-Hop: On the Down Low in the Entertainment Industry from Music to Hollywood*. New York: Atria Paperback, 2008.
Dibben, Nicola. "Gender Identity and Music. In *Musical Identities*, edited by Raymond MacDonald, David Hargreaves and Dorothy Miell, 117–133. Oxford: Oxford University Press, 2002.
Ford, Chandra, et al. "Black Sexuality, Social Construction, and Research Targeting 'The Down Low' ('The DL')." *Annals of Epidemiology* 17.3 (2007): 209–216.
Frith, Simon and Angela McRobbie. "Rock and Sexuality." *Screen Education* 29 (1978): 3–19.
Glass, Pepper. "Doing Scene: Identity, Space, and the Interactional Accomplishment of Youth Culture." *Journal of Contemporary Ethnography* (2012), accessed April 10, 2016, doi:10.1177/0891241612454104.
Green, Jonathon. "Language: Polari." *Critical Quarterly* 39.1 (1997): 127–131.
Grosz, Elizabeth. *Space, Time, and Perversion: Essays on the Politics of Bodies*. London and New York: Routledge, 1995.
Hancock, Joseph. "Chelsea on 5th Avenue: Hypermasculinity and Gay Clone Culture in the Retail Brand Practices of Abercrombie & Fitch." *Fashion Practice: The Journal of Design, Creative Process & the Fashion Industry* 1.1 (2009): 63–86.
Harper, Phillip. *Are We Not Men? Masculine Anxiety and the Problem of African-American Identity*. Oxford: Oxford University Press, 1998.
Hawkins, Stan. *Queerness in Pop Music*. London and New York: Routledge, 2015.

Jagose, Annamarie. "Queer Theory." *Australian Humanities Review* (1996), accessed April 10, 2016, www.australianhumanitiesreview.org/archive/Issue-Dec-1996/jagose.html.

Johnson, E. Patrick, "Mother Knows Best: Black Gay Vernacular and Transgressive Space." In *Speaking in Queer Tongues: Globalization and Gay Language*, edited by William L Leap and Tom Boellstorff, 251–278. Champaign: University of Illinois Press, 2004.

Kulick, Don. "Gay and Lesbian Language." *Annual Review of Anthropology* 29 (2000): 243–285.

Lipschitz, George. "World Cities and World Beat: Low-Wage Labor and Transnational Culture." *Pacific Historical Review* 68.2 (1999): 213–231.

Manuel, Peter. "Gender Politics in Caribbean Popular Music: Consumer Perspectives and Academic Interpretation." *Popular Music & Society* 22.2 (1998): 11–29.

Maus, Fred. "Music, Gender and Sexuality." In *The Cultural Study of Music: A Critical Introduction*, edited by Martin Clayton, Trevor Herbert and Richard Middleton, 317–329. London and New York: Routledge, 2011.

McCune Jr, Jeffrey. ""Out" in the Club: The Down Low, Hip-Hop, and the Architexture of Black Masculinity." *Text and Performance Quarterly* 28.3 (2008): 298–314.

McCune Jr, Jeffrey. *Sexual Discretion: Black Masculinity and the Politics of Passing.* Chicago, IL: University of Chicago Press, 2014.

McMillan, Uri. "Nicki-Aesthetics: The Camp Performance of Nicki Minaj." *Women & Performance: A Journal of Feminist Theory* 24.1 (2014): 79–87.

Namaste, Ki. "The Politics of Inside/Out: Queer Theory, Poststructuralism, and a Sociological Approach to Sexuality." *Sociological Theory* 12.2 (1994): 220–231.

Rose, Tricia. *The Hip-Hop Wars: What We Talk about When We Talk about Hip-Hop—And Why It Matters.* New York: Basic Civitas Books, 2013.

Sasaki-Picou, Nayo. "Performing Gender: The Construction of Black Males in the Hip-Hop Industry." *Contingent Horizons: The York University Student Journal of Anthropology* 1.1 (2014): 103–107.

Shange, Savannah. "A King Named Nicki: Strategic Queerness and the Black Femmecee." *Women & Performance: A Journal of Feminist Theory* 24.1 (2014): 29–45.

Smith, Marquita. ""Or a Real, Real Bad Lesbian": Nicki Minaj and the Acknowledgement of Queer Desire in Hip-Hop Culture." *Popular Music and Society* 37.3 (2014): 360–370.

Sontag, Susan. "Notes on Camp." *Camp: Queer Aesthetics and the Performing Subject* (1964): 53–65.

Spargo, Tamsin. *Foucault and Queer Theory.* Sydney: Allen & Unwin, 2000.

Spaulding, Stephany. "Margin Me: Intentional Marginality in the Queered Borderlands of Hip-hop." In *Understanding Blackness through Performance: Contemporary Arts and the Representation of Identity*, edited by Anne Cremieux, Xavier Lemoine and Jean-Paul Rocchi, 181–195. New York: Palgrave MacMillan, 2013.

Stein, Arlene and Ken Plummer. "I Can't Even Think Straight": "Queer" Theory and the Missing Sexual Revolution in Sociology." *Sociological Theory* 12.2 (1994): 178–187.

Taylor, Jodi. "The Music of Kings and Bio Queens." *Kritikos: An International and Interdisciplinary Journal of Postmodern Cultural Sound, Text and Image* 4 (2007), accessed April 10, 2016, http://intertheory.org/jtaylor.htm.

Taylor, Jodi. *Playing it Queer: Popular Music, Identity and Queer World-Making.* Bern: Peter Lang, 2012.

Tengan, Ty Kwika. "(En)Gendering Colonialism: Masculinities in Hawai'i and Aotearoa." *Cultural Values* 6.3 (2002): 239–256.

Ward, Elijah. "Homophobia, Hypermasculinity and the US Black Church." *Culture, Health & Sexuality* 7.5 (2005): 493–504.

Weems, Mickey. *The Fierce Tribe: Masculine Identity and Performance in the Circuit.* Logan: Utah State University Press, 2008.

White, Theresa. "Missy "Misdemeanor" Elliott and Nicki Minaj Fashionistin' Black Female Sexuality in Hip-Hop Culture—Girl Power or Overpowered?" *Journal of Black Studies* 44.6 (2013): 607–626.

Whitely, Sheila. "Repressive Representations: Patriarchy and Femininities in Rock Music of the Counterculture." In *Mapping the Beat: Popular Music and Contemporary Theory,* edited by Thomas Swiss, John Sloop and Andrew Herman. Malden: Blackwell Publishers, 1998.

Wolitski, Richard J. et al. "Self-Identification as "Down Low" Among Men Who Have Sex with Men (MSM) from 12 US Cities." *AIDS and Behavior* 10.5 (2006): 519–529.

9 Queer desire is not gay, gender is a fantasy

Ways of loving Britney

Gavin Lee

In the past two decades, research has concretized the relation between gay men, disco, and dance music. Disco's earliest moments was located in African American gay clubs in New York in the late 1960s, but it became a mainstream pop culture phenomenon by the mid-1970s. A strong link between gay men and disco dancing is evidenced in autobiographies of singers and record label executives who weave together accounts of their professional and personal lives, sometimes against the background of a larger queer history.[1] The association between gay men, dance, and clubs remained strong even after the homophobic explosion of "gay" disco records at what is now known as the Comiskey Park incident in 1979 in Chicago,[2] morphing in the 1990s into weekend-long, round the clock, all gay male "circuit" parties.[3] Of note in this history is the presence of iconic female divas, particularly black divas in the 1970s, and then white divas like Madonna in the 1980s as "gay" and "black" disco was repackaged as "dance" music for mass/white appeal, repeating the history of the appropriation of black genres in popular music (ragtime, blues, jazz, rhythm and blues, rock and roll). A number of articles have addressed the prominence of female divas in the gay dance scene from the perspective of camp subversion of gender, and survival narratives common to black women and gay men in an alliance of minorities.[4]

Both normative and nonnormative identities are important analytics in examining research in gay dance music. There is the crucial intersection of gay with black and female, placed in opposition to straight, white, and male. Beyond the relatively narrow scope of gay club music and culture, more research could be conducted into the broader range of LGBTQ music, which can help us to expand beyond gay to reach lesbian, bisexual, trans, and queer cultures. This array of identities is useful both academically and politically in helping us to mark out the social terrain and to form alliances— to know both who our friends and our enemies are. However, research into alternative music culture does not employ identity solely as a conceptual anchor. For example, Mitchell Morris examines the psychical nature of gay men's fascination with female divas, going beyond narratives of subversion and survival to discuss desire, sexual abundance, fantasy, and pleasure.[5] In this chapter, I first examine how gay men discover a queer (non-normative) desire for female bodies and visual and sonic surfaces, that is not narrowly focused on masculine, muscular bodies; subsequently, I explore how Britney became a queer icon because of the psychical intensity presented by her persona, and why this intensity is so deeply destabilizing and potentially subversive. I refer in particular to white, largely cisgendered gay men who regularly visit gay dance clubs in cosmopolitan US cities, and who adore Britney Spears. I recall being caught in crossfire as two young gay men in a gay club in Raleigh around 2010 fought over Britney versus Lady Gaga. Lady Gaga has talent, but Britney is natural and doesn't try too hard—was the gist of the argument. While I do not purport to offer a resolution to that argument, I note the fierce intensity of gay men's feelings about their divas.

One can explain gay men's desire for their female divas in terms of identity: gay men identify with their divas, i.e. they identity as feminine. However, this explanation reproduces the heteronormative binary logic of effeminate gay men desiring their polar opposite, masculine men (just as women desire men). This binary logic also informs feminist criticism of drag queens who are seen as appropriating femininity. Women, Carole-Anne Tyler argues, may be positioned as figures of power who emasculate men in drag, and yet this reflects the desire of masochistic *men* who yearn for such emasculation *and* assume the powerful position of such a woman.[6] It could be argued that men who lip-synch to Britney Spears are participating in the same psychical realm. Binary logic also informs Jay Prosser's analysis of the difference between transgender and transsexual. Whereas the trans*gender* trope is a privileged, amorphous figure in Butler's queer analysis, Prosser argues, the male-to-female trans*sexual* wishes for a postoperative, *non*-transgendered state that reflects one of the binary poles.[7] The problematics of binary identity can be seen even in queer-affirming scholarship. Jodie Taylor's *Playing It Queer* opens with a personal account of queer world-making. "I was the diva one moment and a rock star the next."[8] Being a *feminine* operatic diva brings with it a sense of empowerment through being desired, while being a *masculine* rock star brings with it the entitlement of desiring other women and self-fashioning. Here, as with the previous examples, the inhabiting of femininity *and* masculinity paradoxically both affirms and destabilizes the heteronormative order.

I would like to approach the relationship between gay men and female divas not only through the lens of identity, but *also* through the lens of desire. This is not to dismiss the importance of gay identity. Stephen Amico, for instance, emphasizes the conjunction of sexuality, ethnicity, body, and place to form an affective "home" in his study of Latin house music in a gay club.[9] While recognizing the social and subjective function of identity, however, this essay demonstrates the critical salience of destabilizing dominant identities in order to defer the reification of "us" versus "them."[10] My point of departure is that many gay men do not identify as feminine, even if they love Britney. More theoretically, Tim Dean argues that a psychical object of desire has queer potential in that desire can travel across a series of objects that extends beyond heterosexual and homosexual choice of partners, i.e. beyond heteronormative, *gendered* sexual desire itself, and thus beyond gender identity.[11] *Queer*, as opposed to "gay," male-male same-sex desire, traverses beyond gendered bodies, wherein desire is freed to refocus on any and everything—a polymorphous desire that is not tied to any particular object.[12] While the assertion that gay men do not prefer other men may raise some eyebrows, this is a plausible explanation for their love of music videos in which desire is directed at the image and voice of Britney; of special salience are music videos in which men are marginalized, such as "Work Bitch" (2013) or "Gimme More" (2007). To take the issue one step back, we could ask why gay men don't desire male singers instead? A possible explanation is that straight male stars are prohibited by the social order from fraternizing with other shirtless, sexy men, such as the dancers of "Hold It Against Me" and "If You Seek Amy." "Nice" gay singers like Adam Lambert, Stephen Gately, and Steve Grand are also prohibited from associating with proliferating images of biceps and six packs. Against the taboo of gay sexual desire, however, a series of music videos from the underwear label Andrew Christian present images of the toned men, briefs, and buttocks. The video "Angels vs. Demons," for instance, features the song "Sanctus" by Edouard Andre Reny, and the plot line of star-crossed gay lovers lends itself to orgiastic scenes of combatting men in underwear enhanced with the Greek Antiquity camp of sword, shield, cape, and even wings.[13] Yet even this kind of soft porn is unable to offer the *particular* kind of release Britney lends to gay men. Why?

The question of what gay men want from female divas could be answered with recourse to the concept of identity, which is calibrated using the analytics of difference and sameness. Gay men are supposedly different from the heterosexual majority and similar to minorities. Therefore, the argument would logically go, gay men would want to subvert heteronormativity through camp and identify with the struggles expressed by black female divas. While not dismissing the import of insights and political leverage the concept of identity lend to us, this chapter teases out gay men's desire for Britney through an analysis not of substantive, stable identity, but of her aesthetics of emptiness. What gay men want from Britney is not *necessarily* quantifiable in terms of identity or identification (I want a "woman"; I want to "be a woman"), but could be lost in Britney's airy voice and glazed gaze. The gay obsession with Britney's aesthetics of emptiness could be read a sign that desire is moving beyond binary logic. This is not to diminish the criticism that Britney is problematically stereotyped as passively feminine, but to point to a silver lining within current cultural practices, however faint it may be. In the discussion in the next section, I have deliberately chosen to focus on aesthetics rather than Britney's feminine hypersexuality as far as possible, in order to avoid this stereotypical facet of her media personality.

In the second part of this chapter, I proceed to examine how Britney emerged as a gay icon in the first place, focusing on her 2007 MTV Awards performance of "Gimme More," which was an instance of the *failed* performance of femininity. To set the scene, I explicate Britney's personal "breakdown" of 2007–8 (head shaving, police standoff) and the media's "enjoyment" (*jouissance*) of her failure. Failure becomes a site for the buildup of psychic intensity and its release as *jouissance*. Furthermore, Britney's failure in the MTV performance was of *minimal* proportions—an extra inch at the waist between perfection and fat, the thin line between sexy diva and stripper whore, the split second difference that causes the illusion to crack in lip-synching. Minimal failures recast Britney for gay audiences into a drag queen, whose performance is always precisely that of a failed femininity that never fully convinces anyone. Britney's real life breakdown shows us how *gender is a fantasy*, and fantasy as an analytic sheds insights into her music videos, in which identity is queered by enjoyment (*jouissance*) and the ambiguity of alternate fantasies.

In moving from identity to desire and fantasy, this chapter responds to the recent call of *Rethinking Difference in Music Scholarship* to reexamine the politics of difference premised on oppositional, "maximally" different, inevitably essentializing (strategically or otherwise) identities, while also distancing itself from a reversal to the analytic of sameness noted in the introduction by editors Olivia Bloechl and Melanie Lowe.[14] I echo the editors' continued faith in the analytic of difference, and will not be pursuing the analytic of sameness in the form of a revamped human commonality. Humanities scholars have sought alternatives to a politics of difference as articulated through identity because of a perceived impasse: the exorcism of stereotypes in favor of proper discursive recognition in scholarship has failed to substantively alter the lives of "others." Bloechl and Lowe present an alternative of focusing on the redistribution of social and material goods as well as on the capacity for social action, a proposal which is premised on the social ideal of liberalism, wherein each subject is invested with autonomy and the opportunity to acquire said goods.[15] The redistributive framework is indirectly related to this chapter in that it silhouettes the homonormativity of US white gay male culture, within which racial and economic others are marginal, and females and femininity occupy problematic positions. Thus even as we move beyond identity to desire and fantasy, there is a broader intersectional discussion to be had, which lies outside the scope of this chapter.

Queer desire is not gay

Within the queer worlds of many of Britney's music videos, what is it that gay men are obsessed with? Extrapolating from the work of popular cultural writer Robert Greene, I argue that Britney as a "glittering object" is magnetic because we are "strongly drawn to things that have no meaning beyond their fascinating appearance."[16] Britney is a fetish media-object which consists in (her collective audience's) structure-less psychical intensity, that indicates the limits of the social order (death drive).

> The real object of fascination... was unquestionably [Marlene] Dietrich's face. What had enthralled [Austrian-American director Josef] von Sternberg was her blankness—with a simple lighting trick he could make that face do whatever he wanted... [Dietrich] could pose in a way that would most excite a man, her blankness letting him see her according to his fantasy, whether of sadism, voluptuousness, or danger... The effect worked on women as well; in the words of one writer, she projected 'sex without gender'... She was like a beautiful object, something to fetishize and admire the way we admire a work of art... Because [the fetish] is an object we can imagine whatever we want to about it. Most people are too moody, complex, and reactive to let us see them as objects we can fetishize.
>
> —Robert Greene, *The Art of Seduction*[17]

To begin to understand gay men's queer desire for Britney, we can apply the analytic of emptiness across a number of domains—the purported emptiness of pop music; postmodern aesthetics of depthless surface; the appeal of image, voice and sound; the crumbling of a substantive social order. At the core of these domains is a set of empty objects: the monotone of mostly a single repeated note in Britney choruses; the non-expressive voice without traces of subjectivity; the vacant gaze without apparent intent; the bodily movements signifying nothing; images of body parts which gender is diluted by a postmodern aesthetics of the shiny surface. These *mesmerizing* objects of queer desire—like Dietrich's face—are invested with psychical value.

Even without looking at Britney's music videos, we know from journalistic discourse that pop music has been constructed as depthless, void of the masculine agency of rock. This has been documented by Diane Railton, who outlines rock discourse as centered on the core masculine value of rationality (as opposed to feminine corporeality), which informs the "artistic, political and philosophical status of rock."[18] Rock discourse has over-determined music criticism to the extent that even dance music is appraised through the values of complexity and intelligence.[19] This can lead to misrecognition of Britney. A censored version of the dance hit "Work Bitch" blips out "bitch," leaving multiple reiterations of "You'd better work." Also, the black culture exhortation of "work it" (your sexiness, your talent) has been transformed hilariously into the criticism of Samantha Highfill of *Entertainment Weekly*: "the song is about the fact that women can and should work hard and find success."[20]

While it has been appraised by a social order that prioritizes substance (artistic value, being hardworking), "Work Bitch" can be reread against the famous aesthetics of the surface as formulated by Fredric Jameson.[21] The music video presents several scenes where depth is disrupted by the sometimes unlikely coextensiveness of often untextured surfaces: a white wall with the expanse of a pool of turquoise blue water in front and the sky above; a white square platform for dancers surrounded by desert sand in every direction, with the horizon coextensive with sky or mountain range; another white wall spot lit in the dark, coextensive with sand in front. Attention is drawn to the glittery surface of Britney's bikini and gold-plated bra, the shiny leather of the dancers' outfit and thigh high boots, the glistening surface of the pool, and the reflective surfaces of a dressing table in the middle of the desert. Musically, the first half of the verses is deliberately constructed with a minimum of pitches—just two main notes a perfect fifth apart, while the rest of the rapped song is void of pitches. When she does sing, Britney presents a light head resonance for the most part without the darker timbre of chest resonance. Aside from her voice, Britney's gaze in close-ups is also expressionless, in contrast with earlier videos like "Stronger," in which furrowed brows and narrowed eyes indicate subjective agency. Body movements merely reflect the passing of musical measures, with Britney's bodily twists in the opening chorus reflecting the accentuation of the first beat of each measure, the repetitious four-on-the-floor of the beat stretching evenly across the temporal span of the song. "Work Bitch" presents a carefully constructed mirage of seamless surface which, as Jameson argued, defers the critical hermeneutic distance that comes with surface-depth structures. The point about hermeneutic distance was made by Jameson to highlight the importance of such distance as a foundation of critical thought. However, in momentarily deferring the hermeneutics of identity, we enable the queering of desire without the regulation of what gay men *should* desire when desire is formulated through the prism of identity politics (gay men should desire subversion, alliance, etc.).

The aesthetics of surface is also expressed in "3" (2009). Untextured spatial expanse is presented in a number of scenes: close-ups of Britney against a completely white background; a blurry image of Britney in what appears to be a steamroom, behind a glass partition; Britney and dancers arranged along a single arm's-reach-height horizontal bar, against another white background; Britney on a concrete platform with everything else darkened, a black surface. In "3," Britney's flesh is on prominent display in elaborate close-ups. Face, neck, shoulders, hair, arms, thighs are all featured as Britney alternately wears a bra, exotic intimate lacey wear with lots of bareness, and a swimsuit with a neck line plunging to the navel. Admittedly, Britney has more facial expression in "3" than in "Work Bitch" but the overt sexual content of the lyrics makes interpretation of her expression superfluous. As before, spatial expanse, body parts, and gaze are coextensive with a light head voice and surface-chorus consisting almost entirely of a single repeated note.

The depthlessness of Britney's music videos allows queer desire to range over a series of surface-objects without the intrusion of subjective agency, and because of the absolute minimum of subjectivity that is expressed, a large degree of degendering is achieved. This is not to say that the bodily objects are not recognizably female, but gender expression is partially eclipsed by the attractiveness of bodily, visual, and sonic surfaces which are coextensive with the expansive walls, desert, and pool of the scenes in both songs. A queer porn of minimalist landscape, vacant voice, gaze, melody, music, and dance traverses across and beyond female bodily parts, arresting the attention of the queer inside the gay man.

In addition to empty surface-objects arousing queer desire, we can also queer Britney by examining the relation between Britney and Britney. In "Gimme More," the blond spectator-Britney finds her mirror image in the black-haired pole dancer Britney, long hair hidden in a top hat to express male gender. While the dancer is presented indistinctly—blurry images, moving hand-held camera, part objects (face, shoulder, butt, thighs)—the spectator pauses now and then, as if recognizing herself in the dancer. Britney finds a mirror reflection, which in spite of a fragmented presentation, congeals for the spectator into a unified identity (ego as an identity-*object*) with whom identification is possible. (Indeed, the dancer eventually loses the top hat and her *feminine* tresses falls, and the spectator and dancer are revealed to be of the same gender, facilitating identification.) However, the spectator-dancer identification is imaginary in so far as the unity of identity is illusory, for there is an asynchronicity of the *subject* of queer, disunified desire with its unified *ego* (an external image or identity-object). The dancer disintegrates into a series of surface-objects (face, shoulder) that arouses the queer desire of otherwise gay-identified men for images of female body parts and its metonymic surfaces. The conventional trademarks of the surface are also present: light head voice, blank gaze, a dark bar with continuous black surfaces, and the depthlessness of the chorus, which consists almost entirely of one repeated note as with "3."

"Gimme More" presents a subject-object mirror relation in the form of the two Britneys, but the mirror can also be an intermediary between the gay music video viewer and the "mirror" reflection of close-ups of Britney looking straight into the camera. In "Womanizer" (2008), too, Britney gazes into your eyes, as if you are looking at your own reflection. As with the previous videos, her body spills over to a general aesthetics of the surface, allowing queer desire to roam free; steam room Britney is all skin, and the dark grey of walls, floor, bench and sunken hot stones blends into a surface. The naked steam room Britney is presented as a recurring nexus of identification even as various other versions of Britney as office colleague, waitress, and driver taunt the "womanizer"—male model Brandon Stoughton—who doesn't realize they are all his girlfriend in disguise until the final scene when the three Britneys visually coalesce into one. On the one hand, there is good reason to argue that gay men identify with Britney, who is presented as an agential subject with a core essence (steamroom) and various disguises. As the subject in charge, she taunts and titillates Brandon, who is objectified at the same time that he is cast as objectifying women in sexy "Halloween" disguises. In this reading, Britney in the steamroom offers to gay men a mirror reflection of self and a subjective view of Brandon as object of desire. Conversely, because "Womanizer" features a conventionally attractive male model throughout the entire video, gay men might identify with and/or desire the man in the video, thus viewing Britney as other.

An answer to the identification conundrum of "Womanizer" for gay men could go along the lines of temporary alignment, now with Britney, then with Brandon, giving rise to ambiguity. However, these identifications are imaginary in that they presume stable identities to exist, when subjects are in fact unstable nexuses of desire who can never be properly satisfied or unified. So, already on this level, the interpretation premised on identity fails. Evidence of the disunity of subjects abound throughout the video. On the one hand, Britney's presence is too intense for Brandon, who, while viewing a photocopy of Britney's butt, is yanked via his tie by Britney's hand which breaks through the photocopy, and Brandon ends up smashing his face on the photocopier's glass screen. On the other hand, Brandon is continually surprised and confused as he is shoved from scene to scene following the elusive Britney. With regard to a fit between the spectator and the onscreen identities, the possibilities are even more obscure. Admittedly, there will be a significant number of Brandons among the clientele of gay clubs where Britney is pumping, who may identify with (or not) as well as ogle Brandon—but gays come in all walks of body sizes and shapes. With Britney, one could make the hoary argument that gays are tied to her by a common feminine bond, but I would argue that identification is prone to be destabilized by queer desire. In the aesthetics of the surface, Britney's naked body spills over in the steam room to the uniform marble gray of the walls, floor, and the sunken pit of rocks, and to her various campy skin-deep disguises, stoking queer desire.

The imaginary unity of Britney-identity (especially in "Gimme More") disintegrates into queer desire for a series of surface objects: this offers something *in excess* of, e.g. Brandon as an object of *gay* desire. Desire is further queered in the underlying S/M (sadomasochism) dynamics of "Womanizer," in which the hapless Brandon is alternately yanked and shoved in each change of scene and space. As theorized by Elizabeth Freeman, the eroticism of S/M is focused on delay and surprise, an active inaction on the part of the submissive, since the timing of the fall of the whip is out of the submissive's control.[22] This suspension offers potential for alternatives from a history of violence (whipped slaves), connecting with it while modifying it (master-slave role switching).[23] The suspended whip defers cultural and biological reproduction, bringing the quick time of commodity production and capital accumulation into a dialectic with *slow* temporality.[24] Even with the insistent driving acoustic beat of "Womanizer," then, *temporality* is slowed or even suspended in that Brandon's "pleasure" derives from *waiting*, always anticipating the next violent yank or shove. This is seen when at the end of a dance sequence in the main office space, Britney and her dancers suddenly vanish, compelling Brandon to leap up (whip falls) from his chair in confusion before he is yanked by the desire-leash to the photocopy room where Britney is now. The "slow" temporality of S/M anticipation redirects a male-male desire between gay spectator and Brandon into a queer desire structured around temporality and the embodied aesthetics of surprise.

It is undeniable that in a sense "Womanizer" replicates the whore narrative through the multiple faces of Britney, but desire is also queered through surface aesthetics and the temporal *deferment* (whip suspended) of the consummate reproductive act of binary, complementary sexual identities. This is a crucial point because there is something about Britney that is desirable even in excess of music videos featuring underwear-clad men. A plausible competitor to Britney videos for gay men's attention is Andrew Christian's "Angels vs. Demons," which features stylized, slow motion battle scenes with a high energy dance track set in Latin. Indeed, "Angels vs. Demons" does not only stoke gay desire but also offers its own aesthetics of the surface through a series of objects: the vast expanse of white among the clouds, then of smoke-infused darkness in the battle scene; the surface of armor and cape, of Greek Antiquity camp; the musical surface of choral and descant parts repeated without variation throughout the video, i.e. sacred choral camp; the surface theatricality and performativity of camp itself; and of course, the surfaces of torsos, crotches, and buttocks. And yet Britney offers more than that. By marginalizing men in videos like "Work Bitch," Britney offers the freedom for desire to multiply queerly across bodily, non-bodily, visual, and sonic objects. The imaginary Britney-identity disintegrates into objects of queer desire—fragmented images and sounds of Britney; her metonymic surfaces.

Perhaps the queerest manifestation of desire in Britney is not in the visual realm of gendered bodies, but in the aural equivalent of what is called "orgasm denial" or "ruined orgasm" in porn. This technique is perfected in circuit music (remixed and extended dance songs) and evidenced in "Work Bitch," in which musical buildup is observed at structural points. It has been noted that disco and circuit music is characterized by such climaxes at structural points of the 32-second beat (1 section of 8 measures) in disco and meta-structural points of 64- and 128- and 256-beats, with corresponding more intense climaxes, in circuit music.[25] At structural points in "Work Bitch," such as the end of the chorus and the breakdown, the rhythmic intensity of the snare drum is gradually increased from 8- to 16- and 30-second notes. Rather than sustaining this all the way to the climatic arrival point of the next downbeat, which coincides with the beginning of a new section, however, the buildup stops abruptly just before the climax. The climax is denied and ruined, again and again. This denial of straightforward pleasure brings us to the "dark" side of desire, and cues us for the turn to queer fantasy.

Gender is a fantasy

In what is known as her "breakdown"[26] of 2007–8, Britney Spears entered a rehabilitation clinic, only to leave after less than a day, after which she shaved her head. Subsequently, she refused to surrender her son Jayden James to the court-appointed custody of Kevin Federline, leading to a police standoff and involuntary psychiatric hold. *As* media, the significance of this sequence of events lies not so much in its verity (*Was* Britney under the influence of drugs?) but in what they tell us about the media obsession with celebrity breakdowns, and what this obsession in turn tells us about the collective psyche. What is of salience for us here is the way media represented the sequence of events as a "breakdown," and further, how this breakdown was then translated into Spears' music video "Hold It Against Me" (2011).

In "Hold It Against Me," Britney is situated between terrestrial and extraterrestrial, reality and fantasy. Shooting to earth in a meteor, "alien"-Britney in a wedding dress discovers video-images of singer-Britney and internet dating. The opening and ending dance sequences present Britney in relatively conventional stage performances. From the first chorus onwards, however, a series of odd images indicate the proximity of an unbearable psychical intensity, associated with her breakdown. The odd video images include: for the "psycho" singer-Britney surrounded by microphones, a pair of extracted lips against black background, a single, crooked long black "witch's" nail, and an eye with two irises; for the wedding-gown-Britney, "blind" eye-less dancers clawing their way out from underneath Britney's giant wedding gown, "IVs" shooting colorful streams from Britney's hands, and rapid oscillation of Britney who becomes a blur of hair and "IV" streams and stains.

In contrast to the conventional dance sequences at the beginning and end of the music video, the odd images present something so far out of the social order that their presence is more a psychical intensity than meaningful symbols that represent anything in particular. One *could* argue that the odd images "represent" Britney's crisis period of 2007–8 before her resumption of professional activity under the dictates of the social order—namely, under the terms of a permanent conservatorship by Britney's father Jamie, draining the singer of control over her assets and daily life. The way to push this reading, however, is in asking not what the odd images represent (the breakdown), but what precisely it is that is *unrepresentable*. What is unrepresentable within the rational social order is not Britney's actions, but what is called the "death drive." The death drive is the psychical point where the social order breaks down. Subjects are compelled towards this breaking point, doing things that constitute precisely this breakdown. Britney's head shaving, police standoff, and involuntary psychiatric hold all represent, for her media public, the death drive, the involuntary compulsion—more or less successfully mediated by the psyche—to push beyond the social order.

The radical power of the death drive to disrupt the social order is embraced by Lee Edelman in *No Future* to counter the reproductive, future-oriented temporality symbolized by the child, in whose name campaigns against "anti"-reproductive abortion and gay rights are waged. In the post-apocalyptic future of P. D. James' *The Children of Men*, Edelman notes, the narrator feels that because of the loss of mankind's reproductive capacity, "all pleasures of the minds and senses sometimes seem to me no more than pathetic and crumbling defenses shored up against our ruins."[27] Edelman postulates that reproductive futurity is a symptom of the social order's inability to come to terms with its own status as an edifice—not of reality—but of psychical desires, identifications, and intensities. By holding out a future for the child, the social order is justifying its own continued existence, thereby denying its psychically constructed nature. The death drive, the psychical intensity *beyond* meaningful social symbols, is an ideal concept for locating and analyzing social breaking points—not just in the instance of reproductive futurity, but in connection with *all* forms and aspects of the social order. For Edelman, the death drive is thus congruent with queer theory's anti-normative stance.

What is particularly disturbing about the death drive is not just the unexplainable, irrational psychical intensity named by the term; there is also an "enjoyment" ("*jouissance*") that indicates the presence of the death drive. Britney presents the death drive to the media public because of her apparent *jouissance* of seeking whatever she desires to the point of threatening her general well-being. This apparent lack of socialized self-control coheres problematically with hoary stereotypes of the irrational female, which is problematically reinforced by Britney's aesthetic presentation of empty subjectivity, airy voice, and glazed gaze. Her aesthetics express a strong psychical intensity without discernible meaning or narrative. Britney's psychical intensity is so unbearable that the full weight of medicine and law was applied to drain the singer of her money, autonomy, and most importantly, her *jouissance*. The main point is not whether Britney did or did not actually have medical, drug-related, or psychiatric issues (whether or not she did indeed have *jouissance*)—all this is wrapped in a tangle of media, medical, and legal discourses, and who can really know if Britney has *jouissance* other than Britney herself? What *can* be observed is the *jouissance* of the *obsessive production*—i.e. "enjoyment"—of *discourses* related to Britney. This is the unrepresentable death drive or social breaking point dissembling itself as a patchwork of discourses attempting to shore up the social order, producing and reproducing the "breakdown" or "comeback" of Britney. Following Edelman, we can understand *jouissance* not merely as "enjoyment" as manifest in the proliferation of "breakdown" discourse, but also as a figure of queer politics.[28]

There is something rather vicious about the media obsession with Britney's breakdown, as seen in the freedom with which it wields its razors on her. In the performance that is conventionally recognized as epitomizing her breakdown, of "Gimme More" at the 2007 MTV Awards, Britney provided her media public with a ripe opportunity for *jouissance*. Shortly after her performance, the comedian Sarah Silverman took to the stage and pronounced Britney's two children, then aged 1 and 2, "the most adorable mistakes you will ever see."[29] Here, Britney is castigated for not performing her proper role in reproduction, veering off instead into realms of *jouissance*—what was described in *The Children of Men* as "all pleasures of the minds and senses," or in our contemporary terms, mind-altering substances. But more disturbingly than with drug use, Britney presents these pleasures of minds and senses crucially in her new aesthetics of emptiness, first glimpsed in that MTV performance. This was a peep into the more relaxed choreography of the music video of "Gimme More" (2007), a significant departure from the earlier energetic dance routines of songs such as "Stronger" (2000). Whereas Britney's music has always been about sex, this was previously dissembled as high-energy dance virtuosity in earlier and later songs. In contrast, the MTV "Gimme More" performance disturbingly presented sex *as* sex, with Britney in stripper costume, gyrating more or less as a stripper would have, without the fiction that her performance is about dance excellence. "There was just so much that went wrong. Out-of-synch lip-synching. Lethargic movements that seemed choreographed by a dance instructor for a nursing home. The paunch in place of Spears' once-taut belly."[30] This quote from a reviewer anticipated the precise logic of the draining of Britney's *jouissance* through the law later on, using discourse in this instance to censor the MTV Award Britney's *jouissance*, which is not only that of stripper-Britney, but also of the Britney who is lazy ("nursing home") and eats too much ("paunch").

Unlikely as it may seem, this bald (hair shaven earlier), drug-using, stripper, lazy, fat Britney presents a site for alternative sociality, indicated most dramatically in the YouTube castigation of the critics of Britney's MTV performance, by openly gay fan Chris Crocker (pseudo name), who was subsequently offered his own television show.[31] Chris' impassioned plea for media commentators to curb their negative comments and instead offer sympathetic understanding of Britney's plight marks the beginning of Britney's rise as a gay icon. The Britney scorned, it turns out, was also the Britney irrevocably queered as she brought with her now the peculiar *jouissance* of alterity, offering free flow "sex as sex" content (a well-known gay political rallying call) without the denial of sex as actually dance excellence. Her stage failures from the mainstream perspective paradoxically made Britney into a symbolic drag queen, whose "femininity" is precisely a *performance* that is always on the precipice of failing.[32]

In Britney's MTV performance, we can see the minimal difference between feminine ideal and failed femininity—the smallest of difference between perfect lip-synching and being out of synch, between a taut abdomen and that extra inch in the waist line, between stripper fantasy and too much like a real stripper, between femininity and drag queen. These tiniest of differences are what caused the seismic release of *jouissance*—in Britney, in the media, amongst gay men. This is because the tiniest difference is what is most potent in calling the bluff not of day*dream* temporality (the dream sequence in "Baby... One More Time"), but of day*time* temporality itself (feminine ideal in the social order). What is the queer politics of the "minimal" difference?

We return for a minute to "Hold It Against Me," specifically to Britney's voice in the musical breakdown, which represents her real-life breakdown. The breakdown features voice-altering technologies, including splicing, repetition, and timbral distortion. While a palpable difference can be observed between the "normal" and monstrous images of Britney, and the "natural" and processed voice, an audible, (comparatively) *minimal* differentiation is detected in the timbral change of the chorus lines which are sung at the end of the breakdown, linking into the actual chorus with the resumed beat. The timbral profile of the chorus lines is initially muted through filtering out the higher frequencies, which gives the impression of distance. Then a rapid timbral modulation leading to a return of the higher frequencies gives an impression of drastically reduced distance (like a camera zooming in), as if we have flown right into the scene of the final chorus. From a psychoanalytic perspective, there is a crossing over from the breakdown with unrepresentable-as-such psychical intensity back into the social order, which is sonically all the more "real," more "here" because of the sense of arrival created by the timbral change, a minimal difference with maximal impact.

Minimal difference is also the organizing concept of the "Piece of Me" music video, in which Britney is presented both as a subject (in the sequences of her against a darkened background with only a morphing light display wall) and as an object photographed by the paparazzi. In the chorus, Britney enunciates a series of "I'm Mrs. ___," pronouncing herself as the emblem of the media image, fascinating for her fame and wealth and newsworthiness, scrutinized for her body size, castigated for being "shameless." On first look, this appears to be a postmodern stance, with subject and object flattened onto the same plane, expressing the aesthetics of the surface, of depthless emptiness. On the other hand, what of the minimal difference between "Mrs.," and "Britney" in "I'm Mrs. 'Oh my god, that Britney's shameless'"? Here, shameless Britney is situated in the normative social order, whereas "Mrs." is the *jouissance* of "breakdown." We could say that the social judgement of "shameless" functions as the necessary nexus of reality where we find excess enjoyment beyond the social order (*Mrs.* Shameless). In this reading, "I" (the haplessly disunified subject) am not embracing the social order of the shameless, but lost in the *enjoyment* of "Mrs. Shameless."

Britney has an allure which lies in the capacity of her music videos to release queer desire, roaming over the smooth surfaces of bodies and objects—in the fantasy of ideal femininity *and* the latter's breakdown into psycho drag queen *and* the *jouissance* of this breakdown; in the minimal difference between proper social ordering and Britney's psychical intensity. It is because Britney has danced on the wild side of "Gimme More" that she becomes the location of the minimal difference that separates the social order from its disorganized, unrepresentable outside. This minimal difference between the social order and its outside is theorized by Žižek as the "parallax view."[33] The parallax view necessitates "constantly shifting perspective between two points between which no synthesis or mediation is possible... [T]here is no rapport between the two levels, no shared space— although they are closely connected, even identical in a way, they are, as it were, on the opposed sides of a Moebius strip." On one side of the strip, we find Britney the feminine ideal; on the other side directly beneath, we find MTV Awards "Gimme More" Britney, the drag queen, gay icon, and object of queer desire.

The two sides of the Moebius strip are most distinctly represented in "If You Seek Amy" (2009), where Britney or "Amy" is surrounded by muscular male torsos in what appears to be a darkened study; outside the study, we see the aftermath of an orgy with men and women putting on their clothes or passed out. While gay desire could be narrowly focused on the male dancers, what *is* queer here is Amy's transformation into a WASP mum in a pale pink shirt with a white sweater tied around her shoulders, which queer not just in its Stepford camp, but also in the resultant uncertainty over which world constitutes fantasy.[34] Either the mom identifies with an inner Amy, or Amy identifies with an inner mom. The mom materializes during the musical breakdown from a white out, suggesting that this is Amy's dream of happiness. Yet reading the music video backwards from the final black and white snapshot with mother's Ken-doll husband and two kids, the orgy scene appears to be mom's obscene fantasy. There is something about the temporality of these two worlds that speaks to gay life, with its well-known metaphors of the closet and coming out. Queer temporality is theorized as sexual practice by Elizabeth Freeman (as mentioned earlier) and as amateur reading by Carolyn Dinshaw.[35] Both are opposed to dominant notions of time as clocked (as in wage labor), linear (modernist progress), and mathematically/empirically measurable. It could be said that the psychical subject is a patchwork of multiple asynchronous temporalities, as if the ingredients of smooth linear time have deliberately been disassembled. Indeed, Amy's identity is revealed to be elusive in that she seems to have lost herself—the singer Amy (perhaps channeling the mom) herself titularly "seeks" and desires "Amy" ("If You Seek Amy"). In the mom segment, queer desire focuses on the ambivalent pie with dual sexual or familial meanings, which Amy brings from the orgy inside to meet her Ken-doll husband and two kids outside. Either way, the two scenes may appear to be diametrically opposed by conventional standards, but they are in fact only minimally different in the psyche, separated by the thinnest of Moebius strips.

Desire and fantasy are not queer by nature, but they can both contribute to a queer politics. Desire can be unfixated from sexual objects and released onto unexpected sexual objects as well as musical and visual objects. The theory of fantasy can be applied to gender to break it apart in order to reveal it as fantasy. Further, the force of fantasy leads us to question the stability of the "I" of the social order, reversing moral degradation into revelry in the "shameless," and ultimately exposing the illusory nature of reality—how do you know which is reality and which is fantasy? By releasing the potential for desire to roam, and for fantasy to breakdown, we enact a queer politics.

On a speculative closing note, we might observe the relentless production and "enjoyment" of discourses about difference in recent decades and ask: What does musicology want? Extrapolating from my foregoing analysis, "difference" would be precisely the point where the academic social order encounters a psychical intensity that remains unrepresentable other than as the ethics of difference. This suggests that difference is in a critical sense an attempt to *represent ourselves* as ethical "angels."[36] In which social order, after all, can it be said that some minority or other "wants" to be the same as or different from this or that identity? Isn't this an attempt to represent something that cannot otherwise be grasped, through the classic high school exercise in "compare and contrast"? One of our responsibilities, then, is to push towards this "otherwise" through the queer concepts of desire, fantasy, and death drive. Traversing the minimal difference from the ethics of difference to this "otherwise" could be what musicology needs most at this juncture in order to redirect the conversation with its own mirror reflection.

Notes

1 See Mel Cheren, Gabriel Rotello, and Brent Nicholson Earle, *My Life and the Paradise Garage: Keep on Dancin'* (New York: 24 Hours for Life, 2000); Randy Jones and Mark Bego, *Macho Man: The Disco Era and Gay America's "Coming Out"* (Westport, CT: Praeger, 2009). Mel Cheren was a founder of West End Records, one of the most prominent disco labels of the time. Randy Jones was a member of the iconic disco group The Village People.
2 For an account of "Disco Demolition Night," a promotional stunt that took place after the first of two planned baseball games (the second was cancelled due to rioting), see Gillian Frank, "Discophobia: Antigay Prejudice and the 1979 Backlash against Disco." *Journal of the History of Sexuality* 16 (2007): 276–306.
3 See Mickey Weems, *The Fierce Tribe: Masculine Identity and Performance in the Circuit* (Logan: Utah State University Press, 2008).
4 See Nadine Hubbs, "'I Will Survive': Musical Mappings of Queer Social Space in a Disco Anthem." *Popular Music* 26 (2007): 231–44; Kay Dickinson, "'Believe'? Vocoders, Digitalised Female Identity and Camp." *Popular Music* 20 (2001): 333–47.
5 See Mitchell Morris, "'It's Raining Men': The Weather Girls, Gay Subjectivity, and the Erotics of Insatiability," in Elaine Barkin and Lydia Hamessley eds., *Audible Traces: Gender, Identity, and Music* (Los Angeles, CA: Carciofoli Verlagshaus, 1999), 213–30.
6 Carole-Anne Tyler, "Boys Will Be Girls: Drag and Transvestic Fetishism." in Fabio Cleto ed., *Camp: Queer Aesthetics and the Performing Subject* (Ann Arbor: University of Michigan Press, 1999), 378. On the theory that men appropriate women in transsexualism, see Sandy Stone, "The 'Empire' Strikes Back: A Post-transsexual Manifesto," in Patrick D. Hopkins ed., *Sex/Machine: Readings in Culture, Gender, and Technology* (Bloomington, IN: Indiana University Press, 1998), 324.

7 Jay Prosser, *Second Skins: The Body Narratives of Transsexuality* (New York: Columbia University Press, 1998), 21, 32.

8 Jodie Taylor, *Playing It Queer: Popular Music, Identity and Queer World-Making* (New York: Peter Lang, 2012), 2.

9 Stephen Amico, "Su Casa Es Mi Casa: Latin House, Sexuality, Place," in Sheila Whiteley and Jennifer Rycenga eds., *Queering the Popular Pitch* (New York: Routledge, 2006), 137.

10 Philip Brett details, just to cite one example, the fateful coalescing of homosexuality, femininity, and musicality. Philip Brett, "Musicality, Essentialism, and the Closet," in Philip Brett, Gary C. Thomas, and Elizabeth Wood eds., *Queering the Pitch: The New Gay and Lesbian Musicology* (New York: Routledge, 1994), 10.

11 Tim Dean, *Beyond Sexuality* (Chicago, IL: University of Chicago Press, 2000), 216.

12 I'm using "gay" as a convenient adjective denoting "male-to-male preferences for sexual activity" in this essay to give the appropriate meaning to terms such as gay men and gay desire—in to order to differentiate them from what I'm calling "queer desire"—although "gay" is a subculture which is more than just sex. David M. Halperin, *How to Be Gay* (Cambridge, MA: Belknap Press of Harvard University Press, 2012), 6.

13 "Angels vs. Demons." www.andrewchristian.com/index.php/angels-vs-demons.html (retrieved on 9 July 2015).

14 Olivia Bloechl, with Melanie Lowe, "Introduction: Rethinking Difference," in idem. and Jeffrey Kallberg eds., *Rethinking Difference in Music Scholarship* (Cambridge: Cambridge University Press, 2015), 35.

15 The liberal subject has been extensively critiqued in queer theory, perhaps most controversially by Gregory Tomso, who argues that unsafe sex among gay men is a *communal* means of resisting, through pleasure, the state's attempt to manage citizens. Through public health discourse and policy, the neoliberal state appropriates the liberal concept of a citizen's autonomy, casting *individuals* as being successful or unsuccessful in assuming responsibility for their personal well-being, thereby aiming to improve labor productivity. See Gregory Tomso, "Viral Sex and Politics of Life." *South Atlantic Quarterly* 107 (2002), 265–85.

16 Robert Greene, *The Art of Seduction* (London: Profile Books, 2001), 128.

17 Ibid., 122.

18 Diane Railton, "The Gendered Carnival of Pop." *Popular Music* 20 (2001), 325.

19 Ibid., 326.

20 Samantha Highfill, "Is Britney Spears' 'Work Bitch' Video the Prequel to Beyonce's 'Run the World (Girls)'?" *Entertainment Weekly* 2 October 2013. www.ew.com/article/2013/10/02/britney-spears-beyonce-work-bitch-run-the-world (retrieved on 18 May 2015).

21 Fredric Jameson, *Postmodernism, or, the Cultural Logic of Late Capitalism* (Durham, NC: Duke University Press, 1991), 8.

22 Elizabeth Freeman, *Time Binds: Queer Temporalities, Queer Histories* (Durham, NC: Duke University Press, 2010), 147.

23 Ibid., 152.

24 Ibid., 138.

25 Weems, *The Fierce Tribe*, 207.

26 The interpretation of the musical breakdown as Britney's breakdown has some currency in popular journalism, as evidenced in Bradley Stern, "Daily B: Britney Spears—'Hold It Against Me' (Video Analysis)," *MuuMuse* 18 February 2011. www.muumuse.com/2011/02/daily-b-britney-spears-hold-it-against-me-video-analysis.html (retrieved on 18 May 2015).

27 Lee Edelman, *No Future: Queer Theory and the Death Drive* (Durham, NC: Duke University Press, 2004), 12.

28 Edelman calls this figure the "sinthomosexual," a combination of "homosexual" and the Lacanian "sinthome," which (among many things) posits that *all* social reality is symptomatic of psychical propensity and fantasmatic intensity. Edelman, *No Future*, 33.

29 "Sarah Silverman Defends Jokes about Britney Spears' Children." *People* 25 September 2007. http://celebritybabies.people.com/2007/09/25/sarah-silverman-2 (retrieved on 18 May 2015).

30 Perhaps quite aptly in a study of fantasy, the critic, who is quoted in this authorless report, remains unidentified. "'I Looked Like a Fat Pig,' Says Britney after MTV Fiasco," *Mail Online* 13 September 2007. www.dailymail.co.uk/tvshowbiz/article-480947/I-looked-like-fat-pig-says-Britney-MTV-fiasco.html (retrieved on 18 May 2015).

31 Catherine Elsworth, "Youtube Britney Spears Fan To Get Own Show." *The Telegraph* 21 September 2007. www.telegraph.co.uk/news/worldnews/1563772/YouTube-Britney-Spears-fan-to-get-own-show.html (retrieved on 18 May 2015).

32 Failure is read as a "queer art" that paradoxically succeeds politically where a conventional definition of success would have meant capitulation to heteronormativity in Judith Halberstam, *The Queer Art of Failure* (Durham, NC: Duke University Press, 2011), 5.

33 Slavoj Žižek, *The Parallax View* (Cambridge, MA: MIT Press, 2006), 4.

34 The film *The Stepford Wives* (2004) (based on the original 1975 film by Bryan Forbes) is Frank Oz's parody of ideal femininity in the form of life-like robots who pass as humans to unsuspecting newcomers to the planned community of Stepford.

35 Carolyn Dinshaw, *How Soon Is Now? Medieval Texts, Amateur Readers, and the Queerness of Time* (Durham, NC: Duke University Press, 2012), 23.

36 Currie suggests that uncritical enthusiasm for Jankélévitchian ineffability represents an attempt to make our work "shiny enough to reflect back the oldest fantasy of all: that we are on the side of angels." James Currie, "Where Jankélévitch Cannot Speak." *Journal of the American Musicological Society* 65 (2012): 251.

Bibliography

Amico, Stephen. "Su Casa Es Mi Casa: Latin House, Sexuality, Place." In *Queering the Popular Pitch*. Edited by Sheila Whiteley and Jennifer Rycenga. New York: Routledge, 2006.

Bloechl, Olivia with Melanie Lowe. "Introduction: Rethinking Difference." In *Rethinking Difference in Music Scholarship*. Edited by idem. and Jeffrey Kallberg. Cambridge: Cambridge University Press, 2015.

Brett, Philip. "Musicality, Essentialism, and the Closet." In *Queering the Pitch: The New Gay and Lesbian Musicology*. Edited by idem., Gary C. Thomas, and Elizabeth Wood. New York: Routledge, 1994.

Butler, Judith. "Is Kinship Always Already Heterosexual?" *Differences* 13 (2002): 14–44.

Cheren, Mel, Gabriel Rotello, and Brent Nicholson Earle. *My Life and the Paradise Garage: Keep on Dancin'*. New York: 24 Hours for Life, 2000.

Currie, James. "Where Jankélévitch Cannot Speak." *Journal of the American Musicological Society* 65 (2012): 251.

Dean, Tim. *Beyond Sexuality*. Chicago, IL: University of Chicago Press, 2000.

Dickinson, Kay. "'Believe'? Vocoders, Digitalised Female Identity and Camp." *Popular Music* 20 (2001): 333–47.

Dinshaw, Carolyn. *How Soon Is Now? Medieval Texts, Amateur Readers, and the Queerness of Time*. Durham, NC: Duke University Press, 2012.

Edelman, Lee. *No Future: Queer Theory and the Death Drive*. Durham: Duke University Press, 2004.

Fink, Bruce. *The Lacanian Subject: Between Language and Jouissance*. Princeton, NJ: Princeton University Press, 1995.

Frank, Gillian. "Discophobia: Antigay Prejudice and the 1979 Backlash against Disco." *Journal of the History of Sexuality* 16 (2007): 276–306.

Freeman, Elizabeth. *Time Binds: Queer Temporalities, Queer Histories*. Durham, NC: Duke University Press, 2010.

Greene, Robert. *The Art of Seduction*. London: Profile Books, 2001.

Halberstam, Judith. *The Queer Art of Failure*. Durham, NC: Duke University Press, 2011.

Halperin, David M. *How to Be Gay*. Cambridge, MA: Belknap Press of Harvard University Press, 2012.

_____. *Saint Foucault: Towards a Gay Hagiography*. New York: Oxford University Press, 1995.

Hubbs, Nadine. "'I Will Survive': Musical Mappings of Queer Social Space in a Disco Anthem." *Popular Music* 26 (2007): 231–44.

Jameson, Fredric. *Postmodernism, or, the Cultural Logic of Late Capitalism*. Durham, NC: Duke University Press, 1991.

Jones, Randy and Mark Bego. *Macho Man: The Disco Era and Gay America's "Coming Out"*. Westport, CT: Praeger, 2009.

Koestenbaum, Wayne. *The Queen's Throat: Opera, Homosexuality, and the Mystery of Desire*. New York: Poseidon Press, 1993.

Morris, Mitchell. "'It's Raining Men': The Weather Girls, Gay Subjectivity, and the Erotics of Insatiability." In *Audible Traces: Gender, Identity, and Music*. Edited by Elaine Barkin and Lydia Hamessley, 213–230. Los Angeles, CA: Carciofoli Verlagshaus, 1999.

Prosser, Jay. *Second Skins: The Body Narratives of Transsexuality*. New York: Columbia University Press, 1998.

Railton, Diane. "The Gendered Carnival of Pop." *Popular Music* 20 (2001): 321–31.

Stone, Sandy. "The 'Empire' Strikes Back: A Posttranssexual Manifesto." In *Sex/Machine: Readings in Culture, Gender, and Technology*. Edited by Patrick D. Hopkins. Bloomington: Indiana University Press, 1998.

Tomso, Gregory. "Viral Sex and Politics of Life." *South Atlantic Quarterly* 107 (2002), 265–85.

Taylor, Jodie. *Playing It Queer: Popular Music, Identity and Queer World-Making*. New York: Peter Lang, 2012.

Tyler, Carole-Anne. "Boys Will Be Girls: Drag and Transvestic Fetishism." In *Camp: Queer Aesthetics and the Performing Subject*. Edited by Fabio Cleto. Ann Arbor: University of Michigan Press, 1999.

Weems, Mickey. *The Fierce Tribe: Masculine Identity and Performance in the Circuit*. Logan: Utah State University Press, 2008.

Žižek, Slavoj. "There Is No Sexual Relationship." In *Gaze and Voice as Love Objects*. Edited by Renata Salecl and idem. Durham, NC: Duke University Press, 1996.

———. *The Parallax View*. Cambridge, MA: MIT Press, 2006.

10 "Blackness in a white void"

Dissonance and ambiguity in Isaac Julien's multi-screen film installations

Ellie M. Hisama

I always see my works partly as songs.

—Isaac Julien

This essay explores British installation artist and filmmaker Issac Julien's historiographical and artistic project of rewriting cultural memory, and considers how music and sound help to manufacture the rich set of visual images across multiple screens in two of his works: *True North* (2004) and *Ten Thousand Waves* (2010).[1] Julien acknowledges that reading these words of Frantz Fanon in *Black Skin, White Masks*—"My body was given back to me sprawled out, distorted, recolored, clad in mourning in that white winter day"[2]—led to his wanting to create "an image of the black subject in a white void" and provides a metaphor for what he terms the "disalienation" of the Black subject within a transglobal, geopoetical economy.[3]

Viewers who encounter the multiple screens in both of these works inhabit a fragmented, moving visual space in which the experience of the images depends on their multiplication. These multiple roads of linearity produce an ambiguity as to how the images can be read. The flow of sound across the screens helps to bind together the disparate images the listener takes in and the perspectives she assumes. An individual's experience of the installations is thus contingent on sound to provide continuity and to propel the works forward while presenting an ambivalent set of images open to a range of orderings in time and space. The ambiguity of the artwork established through these multiple routes may produce multiple experiences of the installation across an audience or within a single viewer/auditor, which does not dilute the impact of these works or render them uncritical; it rather expands the range of experience from each set of narratives and the potential impact of each.

True north

While you never gain the power to make a different world, you can change something of how reality is experienced.

—Isaac Julien

The lure of the North Pole for early twentieth-century explorers may be difficult to fathom. Consider these words from July 6, 1908:

> We're off! For a year and a half I have waited for this order, and now we have cast off. The shouting and the tumult ceases, the din of whistles, bells, and throats dies out, and once again the long, slow surge of the ocean hits the good ship that we have embarked in. I saw the last hawse-line cast adrift, and felt the throb of the engines of our own ship... [F]rom now on it is due north.[4]

Schoolchildren who are taught the usual narrative of Captain Robert Peary's "discovery" of the North Pole in 1909 might immediately attribute these words to him, but they were, rather, written by Matthew Henson, who also reached the North Pole that year. In 1912, he wrote of himself in the third person thus:

> To-day there is more general knowledge of Commander Peary, his work and his success, and a vague understanding of the fact that Commander Peary's sole companion from the realm of civilization, when he stood at the North Pole, was Matthew A. Henson, a Colored Man.[5]

Orphaned at age 11, Henson met Peary while working as a store clerk in Washington, D.C.[6] After hiring Henson to be his assistant, Peary invited him to accompany him on numerous Arctic expeditions for the next 18 years. He had prodigious hunting and sled-driving skills and could speak Inuktitut, the indigenous language dialects of Inuits in the Arctic. By his own account, Henson reached the North Pole first: "I was in the lead that had overshot the mark by a couple of miles... We went back then and I could see that my footprints were the first at the spot."[7] *National Geographic* asserts that he arrived 45 minutes ahead of Peary and greeted him by saying, "I think I'm the first man to sit on top of the world." In Henson's words, this remark angered Peary. "Oh, he got hopping mad. No, he didn't say anything, but I could tell," wrote Henson.[8] Henson noted that Peary "fastened the flag to a staff and planted it firmly on top of his igloo."[9]

Peary and Henson became estranged, and it took several decades for Henson to receive any recognition for his historic achievement. He received a Congressional medal in 1944, and in 1954, the year before Henson's death, President Eisenhower bestowed upon him a special commendation for his work as an explorer; he was reinterred in 1988 at Arlington National Cemetery next to Robert Peary.[10] Julien learned about Matthew Henson from a trip to The National Great Blacks in Wax Museum in Baltimore,[11] after which he conceived of and created a three-screen film installation titled *True North*, the title brilliantly playing upon the multiple ways in which North can be located—through a magnetic compass, by the earth's axis, or by individuals who produce conflicting narratives about "discovery" and primacy.

True North is a three-screen film installation filmed in Iceland and Sweden that retraces and reimagines Henson's journey northward with a performance of Henson by a Black *female* actor, Vanessa Myrie. Having a woman portray Henson alters the gender dynamic in the received narrative of the expedition and disrupts masculinist assumptions about the history and dynamics of polar exploration. As Lisa Bloom notes,

> She turns the landscape of dangerous ice flows into just ice—not life or death—and enables us to see the story in a way that doesn't reduce it to merely the overwrought masculine heroics of that era and the traditional feminine positions that women tended to occupy in these narratives.[12]

Julien's *True North* not only recognizes but also foregrounds three of the four Inuit co-explorers—Ooqueah, Ootah, and Seegloo—who accompanied Peary and Henson in their 1909 journey, bringing them to visibility, and it erases Peary completely in the film narrative, flipping the script (Figure 10.1).[13]

On selecting a *woman*, Vanessa Myrie, to depict Matthew Henson, Julien has commented on her "very androgynous look, which, I felt, could be used to queer images of the Arctic explorer."[14] Myrie's short-cropped hair,

Figure 10.1 Vanessa Myrie as Matthew A. Henson (center) and two Inuit explorers in Isaac Julien, *True North*. Isaac Julien, from *True North*, DVD installation with 3 screens and 5 channel sound, 14:40. Collection of the Akron Art Museum.

intense facial expressivity, and tall, powerful, and lean frame make for a riveting, central figure. Her heavy black outerwear is shed by the end of the film after the frozen North has thawed, when she wears a diaphanous white dress while strolling next to the water's edge. Her androgyny is key to Julien's retelling of the narrative. As Monica L. Miller notes, *True North* "rejects the imperialist attitude of 'manifest destiny' attached to the landscape's penetration and displacement of the native Inuit people."[15] The gender ambiguity effected by Julien's casting of Myrie as Henson keeps the viewer always acutely aware that polar exploration has traditionally been dominated by men intent on "discovering" and then laying claim to a geographical site.

Julien agrees with interviewer Martina Kudláček's observation that Myrie has a "certain hybridity" and he expands on Myrie's appearance as it relates to his work:

> There's a gender-question aspect, and I'm attracted to her powerful and unusual appearance; there's a certain *otherness* to her look. A female-masculinity. It's something that's developed from her cyborg character in *Baltimore* [a 2003 film installation by Julien]. In most of the works she has that male-female aspect, which I am parodying and developing. You can never tell books by their covers. In my work nothing is as it seems.[16]

Julien's interest in projecting hybridity, a subjectivity of both/and rather than either/or, a "female-masculinity" and a "male/female aspect," underscores the critical role of gender ambiguity in this work. His remarks further resonate with the notion that the polar arctic may be regarded as a queer space. Of Myrie, he observes: "With her there's a definite idea of gender performativity or queering of gender, which are codes to be tampered with as well."[17] In her analysis of *True North*, Lisa Bloom suggests that Julien

> borrows the commercial aesthetics of fashion photography [to] make... the Arctic appear almost as a runway... This brazen strategy queers a discourse that otherwise inscribes and validates a highly simplified and formulaic narrative of white, masculinist, heterosexual agency prevailing over a feminized space.[18]

Although the scene with the flowing water with giant, glittering chunks of ice on land evokes the specter of global warming more strongly than fashion runways, Bloom's reading of a queered discourse and a critical view of a received history is apt. The Polar North can be regarded not only prey, but also as a space that is "pretty," to borrow a term theorized by film theorist and historian Rosalind Galt in her book *Pretty: Film and the Decorative Image*. Galt argues that "discourses of film criticism... depend on the exclusion of the pretty" and that "anti-pretty rhetoric of cinema" makes "the pretty" a problem.[19] The "pretty" and inviting quality of ice and of explorer Henson/Myrie in *True North* also contributes to a queer reading of the North, in stark opposition to the representations of ice in Peary's account as a fierce and deadly opponent. This striking focus on a Black *woman* in the film redirects our attention to the erasure of Inuit women from historical narratives about the expedition, and both Peary's and Henson's sexual relationships with Inuit women that resulted in children (Josephine Diebitsch-Peary met her husband's pregnant companion Allakasingwah when she traveled to Greenland to assist him after his toes were amputated).[20]

Lisa Bloom's 1993 book *Gender on Ice* deeply influenced Julien himself during the process of working on *True North*.[21] In her article on *True North*, Bloom offers an incisive critique of the gendered, sexual, racial, and colonial politics in the early North Pole expeditions, noting that Perry "sanctioned Inuit mistresses on his expeditions to protect against what was seen as the potential, but more dangerous, carnal relations between white men."[22] She makes a strong case that Peary's reputation was actively shored up by institutions including *National Geographic* magazine despite a mountain of evidence that he led a failed expedition and in fact may have not been the first person to reach the North Pole.

In her book *Surface: Matters of Aesthetics, Materiality, and Media*, visual studies scholar Giuliana Bruno writes of *True North*:

> Constructed as a travel diary, *True North* is… a landscape of memory accruing on the surface… it glides across a luminous landscape of mere ice, building, and an absolute, total light space… landscape is a pleated archive, a place where cultural memory and affects are themselves represented as topography, and vice versa.[23]

Bruno's conception of the "folds" or pleats between each pair of screens in relation to the traversed landscape and its topography provides a generative image for viewers to conceptualize the three images in flux.

The screens in *True North*'s triptych are configured in different relationships: we see the single screen; the double screen; the triple screen that presents a panoramic view of a unified landscape; the triple screen that presents the same image or event from different perspectives; the triple screen that presents disparate images. Imagine that you are sitting, standing, or walking in front of three screens, each some seven feet tall, and the effect can become disorienting, even dizzying for what Julien refers to as "the mobile spectator," or the traveling spectator, one who can move between and among screens, close and far back, in a gallery viewing, unlike the viewer in a traditional cinema who is fixed in her seat. In her essay on *True North* and Julien's 2005 triptych audiovisual installation *Fantôme Afrique* which depicts the phantoms of an imagined Africa in contrast to the bustling urban life in present Burkina Faso and elsewhere, art historian Christina Albu observes:

> Faced with the tripartite structure of the installation, the viewer is challenged to simultaneously adopt contrasting points of view, to follow

multiple narrative streams, and to explore richly heterogeneous spaces. The triptych formation might first appear to impose limitations upon representation through the image fragmentations it imposes, but it acts as an instrument of liberation from conventions and hierarchies. The tripartite format acts as an instrument both for separating the scenes and for fusing their diverse meanings. Through triptych juxtapositions, Julien exposes the conventions of cinematic manipulation of images.[24]

As cultural theorist James Clifford remarks, Henson's visibility was greater than the Inuit explores who accompanied Peary and Henson and who made the voyage possible.[25] In sharp contrast to the photographs of the explorers of color that appear in Peary's published account, his 1910 book *The North Pole: Its Discovery under the Auspices of the Peary Arctic Club*,[26] as a group of indistinct, barely visible figures, these same explorers conquering the frozen north appear in *True North* with head shots and unflinching, fatigued faces bearing traces of snow, ice, and wind. In so framing the faces of the non-white explorers, the filmmaker gives twenty-first century viewers the opportunity to appreciate the hardships endured by the Inuit explorers without being given sufficient recognition or payment for their labor; Peary referred to them as his "children of nature" converted into the "technology" that fuels his "traveling machine."[27]

The soundtrack for *True North* provides a kind of narrative unity, stitching together the various screens for the viewer. To quote Julien:

> In making my work, I'm very much looking at the use of sound as a way of trying to orchestrate how we might look at something but also the way in which you might try to manufacture the image…[28]

This notion of orchestration informs *True North* and others of his audiovisual installations. Julien has said that the sound precedes the visual material, and as such it is orchestrated both by Julien and film editor Adam Finch. In Julien's words: "I have to mold all of that visual information [and] all these visual spaces together. To me it's the sound design that does that, along with the parallel montage."[29]

His multi-screen installations are built upon a double choreography, of sound and of spectators: "[A]s well as choreographing the image we were choreographing the sound, making it a component that would in turn choreograph the spectators, inviting them to move from one location to another…"[30] The sonic resources thus shape and transform the visual components of the installation. Julien writes:

> Ten Thousand Waves uses 9.2 surround sound, and we had to find a large enough mixing studio (Peter Gabriel's Real World studio…) to allow arrangements of nine speakers and let us build a sound track that would complement the image and keep the work and the spectators moving.[31]

Through Julien's and Finch's mixing and editing the disparate sonic sources, the sound world is immersive but not overwhelming for the nearly hour-long work.

Three types of music are used in *True North*: (1) songs by the female Inuit throat singers Nukariik (Kathy Kettler and Karin Kettler) titled "The Mosquito" and "Love Song from Baker Lake"; (2) ambient compositions by the London-based Australian composer Paul Schütze titled "Plasma Falls," "Writing on Water," and "Sleep III"; and (3) "Lizveyou Ndeye" by the Senegalese composer and drummer Doudou Ndiaye Rose.[32] These selections help to carve out the hard sonic space explored by Myrie/Henson.[33] Paulette Gagnon identifies the "detour through the soundtrack" thus: "the splintered musical segments are statements that play upon rupture to create unity ... it is ultimately a single musical momentum that can be made perceptive and be unfurled in the image's secret depth."[34] Although I would not characterize the function of the musical selections as creating "unity," Gagnon's idea of musical momentum is suggestive as a way to understand the function of music in *True North*.

Julien's selection of performances by Nukariik—sisters Kathy Kettler and Karin Kettler from Nunavik, Quebec—to accompany scenes with the dogsleds and the sound of feet crunching in the snow beautifully gives sonic expression to those whose voices have been largely silent in previous accounts of polar expeditions and bodies that have provided native sexual labor.[35] I read *True North* as using an elastic definition of Blackness that encompasses First Nations/Native populations in a white void, a whiteness that, as Julien observes, is "denaturalized through the presence of the Black subject."[36]

Ten thousand waves

> Englishness is not a fixed identity but a series of contesting identities, a terrain of struggle as to what it means to be English.
>
> —Catherine Hall

Julien's *Ten Thousand Waves*, inspired by a tragedy in 2004, is a multiscreen installation that sprung from the tragic deaths of 23 Chinese cockle pickers in Northern England. In February 2004 in England's Morecambe Bay, a group of Chinese immigrants from Fujian province were picking cockles, the small salt-water bivalve clam, but did not leave the area by nightfall, unaware of the incoming tides that would drown most of them. Julien, whose parents migrated from St. Lucia to Britain, was deeply affected by what he characterizes not just as a tragedy, but as a crime: the cocklers were required to work at night, were not told about the tides, and did not speak sufficient English to understand the warnings from the British cocklers who saw the Chinese workers approaching the area and tapped their watches as a signal about the incoming tides.[37]

The work prompted by these events was a 49-minute, double-sided nine-screen installation with multiple story lines. The images and sounds include the recorded emergency 999 calls to the authority and video taken by helicopter about the unfolding horror; the benevolent presence of the white-robed goddess Mazu, the protector of ocean travelers, played by Maggie Cheung, who has appeared in several of Wong Kar-Wei's films including *In the Mood for Love*; and excerpts from Wu Yonggang's 1934 silent film titled *The Goddess*, about a mother who supports her son through prostitution.[38] Julien has noted

> my film juxtaposes the image of the prostitute with the words of a contemporary male cockle picker, 'I have no time to watch my son grow,' making an explicit connection between the two generations of Chinese workers and finding similarities in their plight.[39]

Just as *True North* provides an example of Julien's "blackness in a white void" includes First Nations/Native populations using a more encompassing definition of Black, Asian immigrant populations can also be regarded as Black in a politics of Blackness within a global economy underpinned by racism and transnational capital.[40] With regard to "Blackness" in these works, I am using the more encompassing understanding of the term that includes those who are regarded as "the Dark Other" such as the Inuit explorers who assisted Peary and Chinese migrants toiling in the British food industry.[41] Indeed, Julien himself has connected the drowning of the cocklers with the drowning of slaves in their passage across the Atlantic.[42]

Julien has increased the number of screens in his film installations from three in *True North* to five in *Western Union: Small Boats* to nine in *Ten Thousand Waves*, putting into play numerous events, images, and storylines at the same time. Julien notes that this "escalation in scale" in the number of screens "has always been in service to ideas and theories: film as sculpture, film and architecture, the dissonance between images, movement, and the mobile spectator."[43] In an interview, he reflected:

> Essentially I'm working in this bricolage form bringing together what would normally be incongruous materials: police footage, CGI [computer-generated images] manufactured waves, handheld video of Morecambe Bay and film footage of Maggie Cheung.[44]

Film theorist Laura Mulvey characterizes Julien's installation as having a "kaleidoscopic effect... [which] gradually extends beyond aural and visual profusion to the heterogeneity of the installation's content: fusions of fact and fiction, story and images, quotation and reference, archive and reenactment."[45] That the nine screens are double-sided effectively brings the number to 18, dramatically increasingly the material to be absorbed at any one moment.

As of this writing, *Ten Thousand Waves* has been mounted in thirty countries, including Brazil, Australia, China, Sweden, Finland, the US, and Germany.[46] The experience of the installation differs dramatically according to the available space; one setup at the Sydney Biennale allows viewers to walk around the screens, taking in several at once.[47] Julien has noted that audiences sometimes end up sitting or standing in a fixed position rather than moving around the work. As a result, when working on *Ten Thousand Waves*, he

> decided to create a configuration where there was no 'best' position: you had to move around and were encouraged to view from different points. I kind of prefer the notion of the travelling spectator, where there is an idea that as spectators follow the characters' journeys, there should be some movement and instability in their own experience—the haptic should become a part of the looking.[48]

One's polyphonic experience of the installation differs vastly depending on the venue and viewers. At New York's Museum of Modern Art's installation in one large room, the mezzanine level directly above the West 53rd Street entrance into the museum, few people spoke, and many sat or lay on the floor to view the ceiling-mounted screens; one could also view the screens from an upper floor.

One of the few writers on Julien's work to address his use of music and sound in detail is film theorist and curator Mark Nash, who observes: "There is an elaborate sonic structure to Julien's work equally as complex as the visual."[49] The music that accompanies some of scenes of contemporary China is by the white British bass guitarist and composer Jah Wobble and his Chinese Dub Orchestra. Their rich, lively sound weaves together sounds of traditional Chinese instruments including the guzheng (Chinese zither), bamboo flute, Mongolian and Tibetan vocals, bass, keyboards, percussion, pipes, and glockenspiel, to evoke modern China including the Pudong Hyatt in Shanghai's financial center from which Julien filmed some of the scenes.[50] Because the Dub Orchestra comprises musicians from both the West and East, including Jah Wobble's wife, guzheng player Zi Lan Liao, the Chinese-identified music is transnational.

Another style of composition heard in *Ten Thousand Waves* is music by composer Maria de Alvear, a student of Mauricio Kagel, in her *Equilibrio* for two pianos, flute, percussion, and strings composed to accompany Julien's work.[51] Her haunting music accompanies some of the more dreamlike sequences, and provides another sonic voice of modernism that is simultaneously of the Western classical tradition and alternative to it in its tuning—the pianos and strings are tuned a quarter tone apart. The avoidance of tonality in de Alvear's use of microtonality furthers the ambiguity of the sound-world and the fantastical elements of the Mazu narrative.

Nash further suggests that

> The soundtrack of the *Ten Thousand Waves* installation is both woven together from these different elements [Jah Wobble and the Chinese Dub orchestra, atonal compositions by Maria di Alvear, and abstract elements of sound design by Mukul Patel and ChoP (Zen Lu and Grzegorz Bojanek)] as well as sequenced together with, and in counterpoint to, the movement of the images. This gives the installation something of a symphonic structure—a series of movements of sound image and voice (poems by Wang Ping) in which shifts of musical theme and register, the editing of the sound track, move the piece along as much as the editing of the image track.[52]

Rather than providing a homogenous sound locked to a single narrative, the disparate music and sonic contributions to *Ten Thousand Waves* mold the various visual spaces together. The "cinematic rhythm," a phrase borrowed from Giuliana Bruno, creates a counterpoint between the sound features and the screen images.[53] Given the profusion of screens in *Ten Thousand Waves* and the distance between viewer and screen, the soundtrack from the nine speakers stitches the visual material together. The mobile spectator's experience is stretched multidimensionally, and the choreography can become virtuosic for those who take in the 50-minute work.

In their essay "Sound Events: Innovation in Projection and Installation," film theorists Maureen Turim and Michael Walsh propose that sound in installations "beckons the audience, suggesting that they stay with the work longer than they otherwise might."[54] They identify the call to British first responders about the tragedy heard in the opening of *Ten Thousand Waves* as "actuality sound,"[55] which contrasts with the sounds from sources both of nature (wind and waves) and of humans (streetcar wheels). Turim and Walsh note that Julien and other installation artists use sonic elements such as "fragmentation, isolation, spatial placement, and repetition in ways unique to installation."[56] At the Royal Ontario Museum's 2017 exhibition of Julien's *True North* and *Western Union: Small Boats* (also presented as a triptych), the source of sound for these installations was a speaker corresponding to each screen. Unlike the visual triptych, which requires an ocular choreography as well as a more generalized mobile spectatorship, the sound streams for each installation mold the visual spaces and the listener through an immersive auditory experience. It should be noted that the nature of the gallery space and circumstances of the viewing can in fact obliterate and minimize the installation's sound world, as took place at the opening night reception of *Ten Thousand Waves* at the Bass Museum in Miami Beach, and thus lessen the potential political impact of the installation on the audience.[57]

Isaac Julien's technique of incorporating sound into "parallel montage," or the editing of several screens at once rather than sticking to the strictly linear editing of a single screen, results in the carving out of an "architectural space" for his multiscreen installations.[58] The time between screens, or the interstice between different scenes, is filled by the sonic narrative joining disparate visual squares. The circulation of ambiguous images and subjects in these works, and the ambiguity with which a spectator/auditor experiences the work, underscore the multiple experiences it makes available, both in a single apprehension of the installation and upon repeated viewings. By opening up the installation space to mobile spectators and listeners and focusing on female protagonists in traditionally male spaces of polar exploration, subsistence fishing, and gleaming high rises in financial urban centers, *True North* and *Ten Thousand Waves* avoid the narrowness of a single, fixed experience. Through his conception of sound as inhabiting a prior compositional space, and indeed one that guides the visual material, Julien's film installations gracefully bridge image and sound, land and ocean, colonizer and colonized through multiple narratives, offering the viewer/auditor new ways to apprehend, to mourn, and to remember.

Notes

1   Versions of this essay were presented at the conference Ice Cubed: An Inquiry into the Aesthetics, History, and Science of Ice, Society of Fellows, Heyman Center for the Humanities, Columbia University, April 2016; the 2015 Music Graduate Students' Symposium, Schulich School of Music, McGill University, McGill University, March 2015; the Department of Music, Cornell University, February 2017; the Department of Music, Case Western Reserve University, December 2016; and the Department of Music, Stony Brook University, April 2015. For their kind invitations to present this work and for organizing my visits, I am grateful to Maggie Cao, Matthew Hall, Rebecca Woods, Daniel Goldmark, Laura Risk and the graduate students at McGill University, Margaretha Adams, Catherine Bradley, Ryan Minor, Sean Lorre, and Stephen Decatur Smith. For their helpful responses to and queries about this essay, I thank Lisa Barg, Vanessa Blais-Tremblay, Francesca Brittan, Georgia Cowart, Kate Doyle, Matthew Hall, Andrew Hicks, Erica Honisch, Judy Lochhead, Sean Lorre, Becky Lu, Elizabeth Lyon, Alejandro Madrid, Susan McClary, Ryan Minor, Judith Peraino, Laura Risk, David Rosen, Stephen Decatur Smith, Eleanor Stubley, Benjamin Tausig, Rob Walser, Max Williams, Lloyd Whitesell, and David Yearsley.
2   Frantz Fanon, "The Fact of Blackness," in *Black Skin, White Masks*, trans. Charles Lam Markmann (London: Pluto Press, [1952] 1986), 86; quoted in Isaac Julien, *Riot* (New York: The Museum of Modern Art, 2013), 166.
3   Julien, *Riot*, 166. I borrow the term "geopoetics" from Julien's discussion of his work. "Geopoetics" elegantly queers the term "geopolitics," mapping it onto the terrain of a poetics of vision and sound. See Isaac Julien, Mellon Visiting Artist at the School of the Arts, Columbia University, lecture at the World Leaders Forum, Columbia University, New York (November 17, 2011), www.youtube.com/watch?v=Hhks5oyH-mY.
4   Matthew A. Henson, *A Negro Explorer at the North Pole* (New York: Frederick A. Stokes Company, 1912), 15; reprinted as *A Black Explorer at the North Pole: An Autobiographical Report by the Negro Who Conquered the Top of the World with Admiral Robert E. Peary* (New York: Walker and Company, [1912] 1969). In exchange for writing the foreword, Peary exercised editorial control over

Henson's book. See Anthony S. Foy, "Matthew Henson and the Antinomies of Racial Uplift," *Auto/Biography Studies* 27/1 (2012), 25.

5 Henson, *A Negro Explorer*, 2.

6 Biographical information about Matthew Henson is drawn from Henson, *A Negro Explorer at the North Pole*; Bradley Robinson, *Dark Companion: The Story of Matthew Henson* (Greenwich, CT: Fawcett, [1947] 1967); Anna Brendle, "Profile: African-American North Pole Explorer Matthew Henson," *National Geographic News* (15 January 2003), news.nationalgeographic.com/news/2003/01/0110_030113_henson.html; and Matthew Henson, Biographies, Peary-McMillan Arctic Museum at Bowdoin College, www.bowdoin.edu/arctic-museum/biographies/henson.shtml, Julien review with received history global warming than of fashion runways, architecture narratives.

7 Matt Henson, "Who Reached Pole with Peary in 1909, Dies at 88; He Was the Only American With Explorer," *New York Times* (10 March 1955).

8 Robert H. Fowler, "The Negro Who Went to the Pole with Peary," *American History Illustrated* 1/2 (May 1966), 48–49 [final instalment of a two-part article based on several interviews with Henson in 1953 by Fowler]; quoted in *Isaac Julien* (Paris: Éditions de Centre Pompidou, 2005), 52.

9 Brendle, "Profile."

10 Henson worked as a parking attendant in a Brooklyn warehouse just before his death. Robinson, *Dark Companion*, 225.

11 Julien, *Riot*, 166.

12 Lisa Bloom, "True North: Isaac Julien's Aesthetic Wager," in *Isaac Julien: True North | Fantôme Afrique*, ed. Veit Görner and Eveline Bernasconi (Ostfildern: Hatje Cantz, 2006), 44.

13 Henson gives biographical information on Ootah, Egingwah, Seegloo, and Ooqueah, the four Inuit explorers, whom he identifies as "Esquimos." He mentions their approximate ages, marital status, character, and motivations for joining Peary and Henson, and remarks: "They had all of the characteristics of the dogs, including the dogs' fidelity." See Henson, *A Negro Explorer*, 137. Both Henson and Peary compared the Inuits to animals in their published writings.

14 Julien, *Riot*, 168. Myrie appears in several other of Julien's works, including *Baltimore* (2003), *Fantôme Afrique* (2005), *Fantôme Créole* (2005), *Western Union: Small Boats* (2007), and *Stones Against Diamonds* (2015).

15 Monica L. Miller, "Taking the Temperature of True North," *The Scholar and Feminist Online* 7.1 (Fall 2008), sfonline.barnard.edu/ice/mmiller_01.htm.

16 Martina Kudláček, "Interview with Isaac Julien," *Bomb* 101 (Fall 2007), bombmagazine.org/article/2954/isaac-julien.

17 Kudláček, Interview.

18 Lisa Bloom, "Polar Fantasies and Aesthetics in the Work of Isaac Julien and Connie Samaras," *The Scholar and Feminist Online* 7.1 (Fall 2008), sfonline.barnard.edu/ice/bloom_01.htm.

19 Rosalind Galt, *Pretty: Film and the Decorative Image* (New York: Columbia University Press, 2011), 9. My thanks to Lloyd Whitesell for suggesting the relevance of Galt's work.

20 "Josephine Diebitsch Peary," Biographies, Peary-McMillan Arctic Museum at Bowdoin College, www.bowdoin.edu/arctic-museum/biographies/jpeary.shtml. Lisa Bloom critically examines Diebitsch-Peary's position as a "mediated and subservient person" who seems to have "played little more than the role of hyphen, connective, or mere incident in this male genre," despite her travels to Greenland with Peary and her writings about her experiences as an explorer. See Lisa Bloom, *Gender on Ice: American Ideologies of Polar Expeditions* (Minneapolis: University of Minnesota Press, 1993), 39; Josephine Diebitsch-Peary, *My Arctic*

Journal: A Year among Ice-Fields and Eskimos (Philadelphia, PA: The Contemporary Publishing Company, 1893); and Josephine Diebitsch-Peary, *The Snow Baby: A True Story with True* Pictures (New York: F. A. Stokes Company, 1901).

21 Isaac Julien, Remarks made at Virginia C. Gildersleeve conference Gender on Ice, Barnard Center for Research on Women, Barnard College, November 2008; Julien, *Riot*, 166.

22 Bloom, "Polar Fantasies and Aesthetics."

23 Giuliana Bruno, *Surface: Matters of Aesthetics, Materiality, and Media* (Chicago, IL: University of Chicago Press, 2014), 181. Her discussion of the pleated archive in Julien's installations extends her meditation on Deleuze's concept of the fold as it relates to Wong Kar-Wei's films–see Giuliana Bruno, "Pleats of Matter, Folds of the Soul," in *Afterimages of Gilles Deleuze's Film Philosophy*, ed. David Norman Rodowick (Minneapolis: University of Minnesota Press, 2009), 213–34.

24 Christina Albu, "The Indexicality of the Triptych Video Constructions in Isaac Julien's Installations," in *Isaac Julien: True North and Fantôme Afrique*, ed. Veit Görner and Eveline Bernasconi (OstfildernRuit: Hatje Cantz Publishers, 2006), 77, 78.

25 James Clifford, "Remarks," in *Isaac Julien*, ed. Christine van Assche, Exhibition catalogue (Paris: Centre Pompidou, 2005), 14; quoted in Christina Albu, "The Indexicality of Tripych Video Constructions," 80.

26 Robert E. Peary, *The North Pole: Its Discovery Under the Auspices of the Peary Arctic Club* (New York: Frederick A. Stokes Company, 1910).

27 Bloom, *Gender on Ice*, 45.

28 Andrew Markaele, "Not Global, Trans-Local: Interview with Isaac Julien," Catalogue for *Isaac Julien: Ten Thousand Waves* (London: Victoria Miro Gallery, 2010), 101.

29 Ibid.

30 Julien, *Riot*, 193.

31 Ibid.

32 Credits for *True North, Isaac Julien* (Paris: Éditions de Centre Pompidou, 2005), 47.

33 For more information about de Alvear, Schütze, and Rose, see "Maria de Alvear," Other Minds: Revolutionary New Music, www.otherminds.org/shtml/deAlvear.shtml; Gary Bearman, "Tyranny of the Text: The Paul Schütze Interview," *Perfect Sound Forever* (December 1997), www.furious.com/perfect/schutze1.html; and Patricia Tang, *Masters of the Sabar: Wolof Griot Percussionists of Senegal* (Philadelphia, PA: Temple University Press, 2007), 61.

34 Paulette Gagnon, *True North* (Montréal: Musée d'art contemporain de Montréal, 2004), 77.

35 A live performance by Nurariik of "Mosquito Song" may be heard at www.youtube.com/watch?v=-fmPMrHOTLw.

36 Françoise Vergés, "Scapes," in *Isaac Julien*, 55.

37 Russell Jenkins, "Jury sees film of trapped cockler's dramatic rescue," *The Times* [UK] (21 September 2005), 16; and Hsiao-Hung Pai, "Another Morecambe Bay is waiting to happen," *The Guardian* (27 March 2006).

38 Christopher Connery, "Shanghai Waves," *Ten Thousand Waves* (London: Victoria Miro/Metro Pictures, 2010), 9. Connery notes that Fujian has served as the center for the cult of Mazu since around year 1000 (8).

39 Isaac Julien, Introduction to *The Goddess* (1930), Eye Film Institute, Amsterdam (27 September 2012); quoted in Mulvey, "Ten Thousand Waves," 206.

40 The cocklers were trafficked in containers into Liverpool, hired through local criminal agents of international gangsters, and paid £5 for 25 kg of cockles. See Eugene Henderson, "How a Musical about Morecambe Bay's Chinese

Cockle-Pickers Has Split the British Seaside Town," *South China Morning Post* (27 November 2016), www.scmp.com/week-asia/personalities/article/2049330/how-musical-about-morecambe-bays-tragic-chinese-cockle.

41 I first heard the term "the dark other" from Richard Leppert.
42 "What resonated for me was that they drowned, they drowned in the sea, and that connects with the slaves' passage across the Atlantic, in which so many were lost in the ocean." Isaac Julien in conversation with Cynthia Rose in preparation for Julien, *Riot*; quoted in Laura Mulvey, "Ten Thousand Waves," 210.
43 Julien, *Riot*, 188.
44 Andrew Markaele, "Not Global, Trans-Local: Interview with Isaac Julien," 101.
45 Laura Mulvey, "Ten Thousand Waves," in Julien, *Riot*, 202.
46 Tim Adams, "Power to... the art of protest," *The Guardian* (11 September 2016), www.theguardian.com/artanddesign/2016/sep/11/protest-art-miro-elmgreen-dragset-isaac-julien-sarah-sze-doug-aitken-interview.
47 A diagram showing the layout of the screens in *Ten Thousand Waves* at the Sydney Biennale's installation appears in Catherine Fowler and Paola Voci, "Brief Encounters: Theorizing Screen Attachments Outside the Movie Theatre," *Screening the Past* (2011), 3, www.screeningthepast.com/2011/11/brief-encounters-theorizing-screen-attachments-outside-the-movie-theatre/.
48 Julien, *Riot*, 193.
49 Mark Nash, "Electric Shadows" (Dian Ying 電影)," in *Isaac Julien: Ten Thousand Waves*, 42.
50 Laura Mulvey, "Ten Thousand Waves," 204.
51 Ibid.
52 Mark Nash, "Electric Shadows," 42.
53 Giuliana Bruno, *Atlas of Emotion: Journeys in Art, Architecture, and Film* (New York: Verso, 2007), 344.
54 Maureen Turim and Michael Walsh, "Sound Events: Innovation in Projection and Installation," in Oxford Handbook of New Audiovisual Aesthetics, ed. John Richardson, Claudia Gorbman, and Carol Vernallis (Oxford: Oxford University Press, 2013), 558.
55 Ibid.
56 Ibid.
57 Heinrich Schmidt's video of the opening reception of *Ten Thousand Waves* at the Bass Museum in Miami Beach on December 1, 2010 may be viewed at www.youtube.com/watch?v=Le4O0CXppF4.
58 Julien, *Riot*, 193.

Bibliography

Adams, Tim. "Power to... the Art of Protest." *The Guardian* (11 September 2016), www.theguardian.com/artanddesign/2016/sep/11/protest-art-miro-elmgreen-dragset-isaac-julien-sarah-sze-doug-aitken-interview.

Albu, Christina. "The Indexicality of the Triptych Video Constructions in Isaac Julien's Installations." In *Isaac Julien: True North and Fantôme Afrique*, edited by Veit Görner and Eveline Bernasconi, 77–80. OstfildernRuit: Hatje Cantz Publishers, 2006.

Bearman, Gary. "Tyranny of the Text: The Paul Schütze Interview." *Perfect Sound Forever* (December 1997), www.furious.com/perfect/schutze1.html.

Bloom, Lisa. *Gender on Ice: American Ideologies of Polar Expeditions.* Minneapolis: University of Minnesota Press, 1993.

Bloom, Lisa. "True North: Isaac Julien's Aesthetic Wager." In *Isaac Julien: True North | Fantôme Afrique*, edited by Veit Görner and Eveline Bernasconi, 42–45. Ostfildern: Hatje Cantz, 2006.

Bloom, Lisa. "Polar Fantasies and Aesthetics in the Work of Isaac Julien and Connie Samaras," *The Scholar and Feminist Online* 7.1 (Fall 2008), sfonline.barnard. edu/ice/bloom_01.htm.

Brendle, Anna. "Profile: African-American North Pole Explorer Matthew Henson." *National Geographic News* (15 January 2003), news.nationalgeographic.com/ news/2003/01/0110_030113_henson.html.

Bruno, Giuliana. *Atlas of Emotion: Journeys in Art, Architecture, and Film*. New York: Verso, 2007.

Bruno, Giuliana. "Pleats of Matter, Folds of the Soul." In *Afterimages of Gilles Deleuze's Film Philosophy*, edited by David Norman Rodowick, 213–34. Minneapolis: University of Minnesota Press, 2009.

Bruno, Giuliana. *Surface: Matters of Aesthetics, Materiality, and Media*. Chicago, IL: University of Chicago Press, 2014.

Clifford, James. "Remarks." In *Isaac Julien*, edited by Christine van Assche. Paris: Centre Pompidou, 2005.

Connery, Christopher. "Shanghai Waves." In *Ten Thousand Waves*. London: Victoria Miro/Metro Pictures, 2010.

Diebitsch-Peary, Josephine. *My Arctic Journal: A Year among Ice-Fields and Eskimos*. Philadelphia, PA: The Contemporary Publishing Company, 1893.

Diebitsch-Peary, Josephine. *The Snow Baby: A True Story with True Pictures*. New York: F. A. Stokes Company, 1901.

Fanon, Frantz. "The Fact of Blackness." In *Black Skin, White Masks*, trans. Charles Lam Markmann. London: Pluto Press, [1952] 1986.

Fowler, Catherine, and Paola Voci. "Brief Encounters: Theorizing Screen Attachments Outside the Movie Theatre," *Screening the Past* (2011), www.screeningthepast. com/2011/11/brief-encounters-theorizing-screen-attachments-outside-the-movie-theatre/.

Fowler, Robert H. "The Negro Who Went to the Pole with Peary." *American History Illustrated* 1/2 (May 1966), 45–52.

Foy, Anthony S. "Matthew Henson and the Antinomies of Racial Uplift." *Auto/Biography Studies* 27/1 (2012): 19–44.

Gagnon, Paulette. *True North*. Montréal: Musée d'art contemporain de Montréal, 2004.

Galt, Rosalind. *Pretty: Film and the Decorative Image*. New York: Columbia University Press, 2011.

Henderson, Eugene. "How a Musical about Morecambe Bay's Chinese Cockle-Pickers Has Split the British Seaside Town," *South China Morning Post* (27 November 2016), www.scmp.com/week-asia/personalities/article/2049330/how-musical-about-morecambe-bays-tragic-chinese-cockle.

Henson, Matthew A. *A Negro Explorer at the North Pole*. New York: Frederick A. Stokes Company, 1912. Reprinted as *A Black Explorer at the North Pole: An Autobiographical Report by the Negro Who Conquered the Top of the World with Admiral Robert E. Peary*. New York: Walker and Company, [1912] 1969.

Isaac Julien, edited by Christine van Assche. Paris: Éditions de Centre Pompidou, 2005.

Jenkins, Russell. "Jury Sees Film of Trapped Cockler's Dramatic Rescue." *The Times* [UK] (21 September 2005).

"Josephine Diebitsch Peary." Biographies, Peary-McMillan Arctic Museum at Bowdoin College, www.bowdoin.edu/arctic-museum/biographies/jpeary.shtml.

Julien, Isaac. Introduction to *The Goddess* (1930), Eye Film Institute, Amsterdam (27 September 2012).

Julien, Isaac. Mellon Visiting Artist Lecture at the School of the Arts, World Leaders Forum, Columbia University, New York. November 17, 2011, www.youtube.com/watch?v=Hhks5oyH-mY.

Julien, Isaac. *Riot*. New York: The Museum of Modern Art, 2013.

Kudláček, Martina. Interview with Isaac Julien, *Bomb* 101 (Fall 2007), bombmagazine.org/article/2954/isaac-julien.

"Maria de Alvear." Other Minds: Revolutionary New Music, www.otherminds.org/shtml/deAlvear.shtml.

Markaele, Andrew. "Not Global, Trans-Local: Interview with Isaac Julien." Catalogue for *Isaac Julien: Ten Thousand Waves*. London: Victoria Miro Gallery, 2010.

"Matt Henson, Who Reached Pole with Peary in 1909, Dies at 88; He Was the Only American With Explorer." *New York Times* (10 March 1955).

Matthew Henson Biographies, Peary-McMillan Arctic Museum at Bowdoin College, www.bowdoin.edu/arctic-museum/biographies/henson.shtml.

Miller, Monica L. "Taking the Temperature of True North." *The Scholar and Feminist Online* 7.1 (Fall 2008), sfonline.barnard.edu/ice/mmiller_01.htm.

Mulvey, Laura. "Ten Thousand Waves." In Julien, *Riot*, 200–11.

Nash, Mark. "Electric Shadows" (Dian Ying 電影)." In *Isaac Julien: Ten Thousand Waves*.

Pai, Hsiao-Hung. "Another Morecambe Bay is waiting to happen." *The Guardian* (27 March 2006).

Peary, Robert E. *The North Pole: Its Discovery under the Auspices of the Peary Arctic Club*. New York: Frederick A. Stokes Company, 1910.

Robinson, Bradley. *Dark Companion: The Story of Matthew Henson*. Greenwich, CT: Fawcett, [1947] 1967.

Tang, Patricia. *Masters of the Sabar: Wolof Griot Percussionists of Senegal*. Philadelphia, PA: Temple University Press, 2007.

Turim, Maureen, and Michael Walsh. "Sound Events: Innovation in Projection and Installation." In *Oxford Handbook of New Audiovisual Aesthetics*, edited by John Richardson, Claudia Gorbman, and Carol Vernallis, 543–62. Oxford: Oxford University Press, 2013.

Vergés, Françoise. "Scapes." In *Isaac Julien*, edited by Christine van Assche. Paris: Centre Pompidou, 2005.

Afterword

The world only spins forward

Paul Attinello

When earlier gatherings of musicologists began to pose questions around lesbian, gay, queer, gender, and sexual issues, we had a number of preconceptions—but, because shared musicological discussion of sexuality was relatively new and there were few published texts, they were not necessarily the *same* preconceptions. The rapid development and expansion of musicological discourse around gender in the late 1980s and early 1990s was a product of the energetic articulation of very different stances, insights, hopes, and demands. This can be seen in writings that stretch and transform their own ideas in the midst of working out their implications, a process visible in the original *Queering the Pitch*.[1]

This suggests a plausible distinction between gender studies that are implicitly constituted as heterosexual, and those that are (triumphantly, anxiously, or even ironically) constituted as queer: although the essentialism of second-wave feminism did open out into the relative flexibility of its third wave, a queerer landscape of differences, fusions, created and amplified essences, movable and erasable boundaries and ambiguities could never result in a single realm of discourse—or, in fact, in a single realm of consciousness. Queer investigations, even those that try to establish new boundaries or foci, tend to open out into smoother rather than more striated spaces—rhizomatic rather than rooted—and our (possibly exceptional) capacity for rebellion, resistance, adaptation, and transformation is always embedded in those spaces, always a part of our work.

The world only spins forward: a line from the final speech of the play *Angels in America*,[2] which simultaneously focused and fragmented gay identities in the face of the existential challenge of the AIDS epidemic. "Spinning forward" does not, of course, guarantee liberation—discursive, creative, personal, or political—nor is it merely a call to arms for any specific cultural transformation. It is instead a more basic, but also more absolute, statement—that, once certain questions have been asked, once certain distinctions have been made, they can never be unasked or undistinguished; and that the proliferating mass of culture can never close, at least not completely, over the splits and fissures and new growths that have opened up in their wake.

The world only spins forward: especially among conversations as complex and multiple as those of alternative sexualities—even as we begin to be able to imagine a cultural stage where our alternativeness becomes flexible enough, relaxed enough, that we can experiment with new identities, even as we move through old ones. And conversations around music are inflected by that forward spin—not only because artists so frequently attempt to move into new and as yet undefined spaces, but also because, even among the perpetual backwash of familiar anxieties such as "we haven't gone far enough" or "we've made an error in going too far," the conversations themselves continue to open up further, with or without intentional action.

• • •

Across a time of political chaos and violence—the current rate of unpredictable change in the world is such that we, as authors and editors of this book, have an unavoidably heightened sense of history continuing to move forward, with an awareness of possibilities that might at any point throw our insights onto its rubbish heap—I write and teach, talk to colleagues and friends, see students and psychoanalysis patients...

Such experiences, hardly unique to me, may be at different points linear, agglomerative, fused, prophetic, or memorial: but when so many different stresses are pulling at (social, political, psychological, existential) systems, if we use our intelligence and training to attempt to be simultaneously aware of the large structures that move into and out of conflict, we may try to find levels of meta-awareness, meta-interpretation, meta-comprehension.

The world only spins forward. I know that my own awareness has shifted many times over the years, starting with disappointed indignation in the later 1980s and 1990s when I realized that musicology as it was then constituted was literally unable to absorb the complex views of culture I had discovered in so many books during the previous decade. Then there was the electric excitement of various experimental interpretations of gender, followed too quickly by exasperation at the conservative reaction (the one that is named "the music itself"). Now it feels as though we operate on a plateau of awareness that our field may *always* stumble around its own perceptual and ideological limitations—but, at least, those limitations are no longer so firmly embedded in our conceptual and social structures that they cannot be constantly undermined and deflected.

So we reach a point where much is said—and let me emphasize that: *much is said*. Which is not at all a complaint, but also not a triviality—a world saturated with communications as has never yet existed, a vastly denser hypermodern overlap of fact, opinion, interpretation, even lying, such that certainty is unavailable—but also such that we are forced to experience in endlessly proliferating detail the awareness that unambiguous certainty in cultural and psychological terms has *always* been an impossibility... and we realize, unwillingly (and perhaps with an understandably childish irritation), that we must resign ourselves constantly to *grow up*: not only in relation to music and our queer lives and meanings, but in relation to everything.

That is, after all, another meaning for "spinning forward." One of my colleagues has always been irritated by that final speech in *Angels in America*, feeling that it is too explanatory, too much like the proverb at the end of a fable—but there are insights that seem too simple or too didactic to bear repeating, and yet are powerfully true: what happens, what we create and enact and discuss, is not lost; even new disasters or collapses occur in a context of larger awareness, larger multiplicity.

The ambiguities of this collection point toward a cultural point of transition: clustering awareness, resentment, vision—so often in identity theory we have wished for a time when all our actions and intentions will be respected or allowed; but that is probably impossible, as humans carry their projections and limitations with them at all times. So, are we permitted impatiently to leap forward, to acknowledge endless, ambiguous difference? Intersectionality is unquestionably valid, and useful, but is largely an awareness of what is: we are reminded of the complex overlap of systems of genders, sexualities, races, classes, cultures, abilities... Unfortunately, intersectionality doesn't give us a new way to manage this differentiation: it clarifies how simple formulations of domination or oppression are inadequate, but it doesn't manage to change our relationship to what we are studying, which remains stubbornly chaotic and yet demanding. Each element of identity simultaneously insists on its endlessly proliferating uniqueness, while also insisting that its competitors respect it absolutely, without hindrance or change...

Ambiguity enters the conversation as a more relational aspect than intersectionality, which tends to distinguish—ambiguity does not distinguish, it illuminates blurred borders and overlapping images, and holds to the fact that they are blurred—that only a false theorizing would be able to, or want to, clear everything up.

A recurrent requirement in Jungian analysis is to *hold the tension*: if we know that relationships between conscious and unconscious, between personal and cultural, between individual and collective are not easily resolved into positive and negative elements, then it is important to stand back from attempting false resolutions—and instead to pause, to pay attention, to stay with. We may think that "tension" here need not include (or, at least, need not include much of) the tensions of anxiety, of fear, of panic: if identity politics have often been about freedom or safety or celebration, those can be the brighter faces of old traces of shame, disgust, and apprehension—but we may as well acknowledge that we will never entirely leave those behind, that ambiguity and freedom are not the same as perfect safety. Many creative artists understand and use this, but our theories are often discomfited by it: and our musical analyses sometimes try to force the world to give us the safer world that our theories seem to want.

Admittedly, the desire to remain constantly aware at a meta-theoretical, meta-cultural, meta-relational level creates its own problems and hesitancies. Working with creative artists can remind us how irritating they find academics and theorists—how can we dare to elucidate, explicate, and at worst judge? And unavoidably I stand in relation to all this as Another White Guy: is the impulse to understand a wide range of artists and writings as a whole, in the largest possible context, merely a reflection of an exasperatingly immovable privilege? My justifications are partly emotional: the terror and sadness of an increasingly damaged world, the point of view of age, the (unanswerable) wish that we could discover a place, a theory, where we could all be comfortable in our skins—it would be wonderful to speak into that space, to create what we want or need.

•••

On the other hand, queerness, difference, and ambiguity all still occur at levels beyond our own immanent physical experiences. We can't leave the physical entirely behind (and why would we want to, as therein lie the original pleasures that brought us to these questions). But in this physical and social world, how can we allow a truly free flow between the interstitial and the essential? Because the "from" or the "against" or the "to" always imply a "here" or "there," a "this" or "that": an is-ness that is hard to escape for more than a brief instant.

It's impossible to avoid the implications of our endlessly queer focus on difference as well as identity: they are, after all, both sources of pain, of pleasure, of security and of unhappiness. Queer identities are different from other identity structures in terms of social psychology: unlike other identities, *we are always* (yes, almost always, but the "almost" is at a high level of probability) *born into the homes of the oppressors*. So our differences are where we locate both pleasure and pain—but can we explore these differences in ways that don't cast us into an inescapable intellectual dungeon, a kinky club night where we are never allowed to take off the mask and shackles and walk easily in the open air?

At a conceptual level, as Lee points out, "difference seems to alternately oppress and emancipate" [p. 3]. But behind our conceptual frameworks are earlier emotions, more primitive states, levels of queer experience that cannot entirely be managed at a conceptual level: if the pain of the adolescent disoriented by the binary gender framework of the parent/oppressor is never entirely erased, it will tend to reach for the relief of fluidity, then the relief of stability, then back, and then—what can the ultimate goal of our theory be?

There is certainly an element, from the more positive side of my Old White Man-ness, of simply wanting to make life easier for these younger scholars— of wanting them to find aspects of gender theory, identity politics, intellectual understanding, and cultural insight that actually make them happier in the world, happier in their skin. That probably sounds unimpressive, pathetically uncritical in an intellectual context: but it's true, I would wish that they—even in a world of amplifying oppression and violence—and nowhere near enough academic jobs—might have some queer place to stand where they can take abundant pleasure in their queerness.

There are other difficulties, of course. One of the goals (and sometimes one of the illusions) of academic analysis and understanding is awareness—which has roots in various intellectual and existential traditions. In fields of identity politics, such awareness is often an awareness of specific offenses against ourselves and those with whom we identify.

Unfortunately, this can become an endless habit of looking for wounds, which—especially in this vaster discursive world, one so connected that we are endlessly reminded of immense variations in experience—is both endlessly, and never, satisfied: we can always find disparities and pain, but it seems probable that we will always be able to do so. So, after decades of gender politics, can we refer to a larger point of view, one which includes our wounds and identities and concepts and differences—and ambiguities—and work out our meanings from that?

• • •

Returning to that title: remember its dramatic context. Prior is damaged, harmed by illnesses whose separate details are not interesting, because they occur in the *contextual* illness of AIDS: the body is itself the frame of collapse, so specificity would be useless pedantry. He stands outside, in winter, in front of a stone angel—an angel of hopes that we would be rescued, or that we could rescue ourselves, from the suffering of queerness. Behind Prior are his friends, who quarrel amiably over politics and history: he briefly silences them to speak into a larger future.

Admittedly, Prior's assertion can be seen as inflated, grandiose, informed by a status that reeks of privilege. But what if it also suggests a privilege that we all retain as living beings—the power to see our lives and our work from a larger viewpoint, to hold onto an awareness that *things have been done*? That, although we may still quarrel and analyze and counter-analyze, we may take comfort in the spinning-forward of our world of queer experience.

The world only spins forward. Ambiguities are themselves full of life. Essentialisms are filled with strength, with power. Transitions borrow and widen experiential connections. Yes, dead bodies in a Florida nightclub, concentration camps for gay men, battles between feminism and trans rights, rage and fear and danger and oppression: but the spinning forward helps make all of these inevitably more fluid—as well as more cracked and crazed, perhaps.

But such discursive spaces are also, always, filled with possibility: with the sense that something more open, more alive, seeks to exist…

Notes

1 Brett, Philip, Elizabeth Wood and Gary Thomas, editors. *Queering the Pitch: The New Gay and Lesbian Musicology.* New York: Routledge, 1994.
2 Kushner, Tony. *Angels in America: A Gay Fantasia on National Themes, Part Two: Perestroika.* New York: Theatre Communications Group, 1994.

Index

Printed in Great Britain
by Amazon

76748812R00120